SWIMMING IN TREES

a story of soul

For Jackie + Gerry
with love from
" The " Mom +
" the " DAD

[signature]

SWIMMING

IN TREES

a story of soul

MARIA STOKES KATZENBACH

DIVINA
A DIVISION OF MACMURRAY & BECK
DENVER

Acknowledgments are due and are gratefully made to the following:
The quotation from "Thinking Rock" appearing on page vii is by Kenneth Patchen,
from *The Collected Poems of Kenneth Patchen*. Copyright © 1957 by New Directions
Publishing Corp. Reprinted by permission of New Directions Publishing Corp.
The quotation from *Notes from Underground* appearing on page vii is by
Fyodor Dostoyevsky. Copyright © 1994 Random House, Inc. Reprinted by
permission of Random House, Inc.

Printed and bound in the United States of America

1   2   3   4   5   6   7   8   9   10

Library of Congress Cataloging-in-Publication Data
Katzenbach, Maria.
Swimming in trees : a story of soul / Maria Stokes Katzenbach.
p.   cm.
ISBN 0-9659521-3-4 (pbk.)
1. Katzenbach, Maria.   2. Women authors, American—20th century.
3. Women—Religious life.   4. Spiritual life.
I. Title.
PS3561.A778Z47   1998
813′.54—dc21
[B]   98-36017
CIP

Swimming in Trees cover design by Laurie Dolphin.
The text was set in Granjon by Chris Davis, Mulberry Tree Enterprises.

Publisher's Note: This is an imaginative reconstruction of the inner
reality of the author. Any similarity between the characters, actions, or
events depicted herein and actual people, actions or events, living or
dead, is entirely coincidental.

for my parents
who weather the tempests
of all their children's psyches
with unbounded love
and courage

Both the author of the notes and the Notes *themselves are, of course, fictional. Nevertheless, such persons as the writer of such notes not only may but must exist in our society, taking into consideration the circumstances under which our society has generally been formed. I wished to bring before the face of the public, a bit more conspicuously than usual, one of the characters of a time recently passed. He is one representative of a generation that is still living out its life.*

—*Fyodor Dostoyevsky,*
Notes from Underground

On this day while I am alive. . . .

And murder shines his bloody claws
On every clean and good thing,
I truly believe
That the beautiful will come again. . . .

That nothing can stay its coming. . . .
O look; it dances!
It touches your faces. . . .
Again and again, the beautiful . . .
Always and always
The life of life and death
Dances O
It so wonderfully cleanly dances.

—*Kenneth Patchen*
"Thinking Rock"

Origins

I don't know how long I have been standing beside this frozen pond. In the pond is a dead tree, its barren branch protruding like a charred arm from the ice. My eyes cramp in the frigid air as I stare at the tree. The branch points away from me to a horizon eager to swallow the sun. It is a cold cairn marking a dead end: my life.

It is not that the tree evokes memory; I have never forgotten a moment of what happened. It is the mystery calling to me, demanding that I enter into it.

I study the way the tree is pointing west. West was the direction of the murderer's escape. I laugh out loud, and my laughter spirals out into the cold air like the smoke that unfurled from the murderer's mouth. I came to Colorado to distance myself forever from the cottage in the woods in the Hudson Valley, where I had little company other than trees and a murderer. I thought I was escaping her, but we both have traveled in the same direction. She will follow me forever, until I deliver the message she came to give me and tell our story. I ask myself, as I have countless times since it happened, How do I tell the story of Her murder?

The answer came in a local bookstore, where, not long ago, I found myself holding a book I had no memory of selecting. The book was the true story of a West African man undergoing the terrifying, and potentially fatal, rites of initiation into his destiny. I can think of nothing more remote from my life story than his.

I opened the book, glanced through a few pages, and then my heart was racing and my mind exploding as revelation crashes into mystery. The writer describes a danger of the initiation process in which actual death is the certain result. One must avoid certain trees, he writes, when they are in a toxic, lethal phase of their yearly cycle, for if an initiate uses such a tree as the path to the soul realm, the initiate will be killed. There is a name for this phase in the life of a tree when it has the power to kill, and the writer has put the name in italics to emphasize that it is a word in a remote West African native dialect.

But it is no foreign word to me. The name for the tree that can kill in West Africa is identical with the name of the murderer who came rushing to me from trees one afternoon in America, when I was twenty-eight years old and happened to look out my window and wonder out loud what my destiny was.

Part One

Destiny

I reconstruct, here, from the ashes of life.

The murderer entered one afternoon in late autumn. As on most days, with a discipline that I still find admirable though it produced nothing but ashes, I was banging away at my IBM Selectric, the apex of technology in 1981, the year my story begins. The IBM Selectric was a sacred object at that time in my life, endowed with the power to produce pages and pages of sellable prose. But that afternoon, as my fingers flew over the keys in their untamed way, the sound of the clacking of the keys resembled shamanic drumming. The gray machine sat on my desk as if it had been placed there centuries ago, a sarcophagus in the form of a hippopotamus from the tomb of a nameless queen. Instead of commercial prose describing this world, my profusion of typing mistakes engendered strange syllables and unintelligible words that could have passed for an ancient chant—say, the mumblings of the priests over the dead body of this same nameless queen as they conducted her into her tomb, the hippo-Selectric carried before them, totemic guide to protect her on her journey into the realm of the dead.

My mind drifted away from whatever it was I was writing, and I looked out at the trees surrounding the cottage in the woods where I was living at the time. The light was gilded with the last breath of harvest, like the butternut and acorn squashes at the local farmers' market, a rich hue climaxing before the inner gold fades into the mantle of winter. Daydreaming inside the honey light, I found myself taken back to a sun-filled afternoon in my girlhood. I saw the sunlight streaming down on the hands of my brother, holding magnets before me. He had teased me, saying he was a magician with the power to make these three stupid circles of metal stick to each other. I needed no demonstration to prove his magical powers. He was older than I, and being older is the sum of amazement and power to a child. It was my brother who needed to believe himself magical as he held out those three magnets in a tower, holding them from the bottom in the palm of his hand. With a natural feel for the drama of these things, he slowly placed his thumb and index finger on the rim of the topmost magnet. "Now, look closely, Meem," he said, calling me by my family name. "See? See how I'm just holding the top one with my fingers?"

I nodded. "I see."

"But don't you want to make absolutely sure that I am really doing real magic?" I stared, very intensely, at his face. "Meem. You're supposed to look at my fingers."

"I thought eyes told you what was true."

"That's lawyers, like Dad. *I'm* a magician."

I obeyed and studied his fingers, noticing only the way the sunlight moved over them. "Okay. Now what?"

"Magic time!" His green eyes lit up with the sure knowledge that I would believe him. "I am now going to let go from the bottom and none of the magnets are going to fall. Watch." He then said the ritual word, "Abracadabra!" And let go of the tower of magnets from below. The tower dangled, not a seam, not a slit, in perfect wholeness.

"Let me try," I begged.

"You know," my brother said, "you can't just do magic when you want to. You have to wait till you're ready."

"But how will I know when I'm ready?"

"You won't," he said. "I will."

I waited lifetimes for my brother to give me some sign that I was ready for magic. My being was caught, breathless, in the pause, until I could not bear it any longer. I waited until I saw him go next door to play

8

catch with a neighbor and then crept into his room. Unfinished model airplanes were all around me, like birds undone to their bones, and a peculiar smell of glue mixed with boy made me acutely aware that I was trespassing in strange territory. I waded through an ocean of sports equipment toward the table beside his bed, convinced that the magnets must be close by when he slept, as responsible for the course of his dreams as they were for mine. I found them in the drawer. I stared at them, wanting my hand to move out to them and seize them. But my hand would not move. No amount of will and desire could force me to take the magnets myself. I dragged my soul through the following days and nights, teetering on the slim sinew of hope that he would reward my faith in him, afraid he had forgotten his promise.

He tossed the magnets into my lap one morning at breakfast, without ceremony. I looked up to see him wink at me. He knew without my having to say a word. My relief that my invisible passion was somehow visible to him was a greater magic linked to the magic of the magnets in my lap. We were joined, my brother and I, by mysterious, unseeable, unspeakable forces, as the magnets were. As I manipulated the magnets and sensed the air wobbling like water, resisting like stone, packed together like earth, I believed it was our love that endowed these circles with elemental powers of transformation.

Swimming in the mutual sunlight of past and present, I gradually noticed that the light around my cottage in the woods was pulsing. It seemed as though the trees themselves were breathing, as though a strange, exterior breath were issuing from the last shreds of the honey light clinging umbilical to the branches. The more I stared at it, the more the light and the trees seemed possessed of a regular pulse, like my own. The breathing of the trees was both impossible and actual, something you expect to disappear the moment you name it. But saying to myself, "It seems the trees are breathing," did not diminish the peculiar sensation that I was surrounded by breath.

I then did what I always did when I didn't know what to do next: I lit a cigarette. It took only an instant to strike the match, inhale, and blow out the fire. But in that instant, as the thin trail of smoke rose from the match, a dark vein appeared inside the trees, coursing through the golden light like a Panther. My heart raced. I looked away from the movable black vein at the words on the page in my Selectric, as if looking at what my imagination had put onto the page would undo what was happening in the trees around me.

Actually, that's a lie. The truth is that I called the Panther out from the trees.

The Panther rushed inside. She wore a black leather jacket, un-zipped, studded with silver spikes, undone buckles jingling at a tapered waist and at her wrists. It seemed inseparable from her body, a second skin. Yet she wore it with self-consciousness, and it squeaked as if still trying to find the creases of its latest incarnation. This marathon woman, catching her breath inside my cottage, was a new shape the Panther had assumed, and it—she—was not yet accustomed to this particular re-quirement of skeleton. She wore a strange shirt, neither t-shirt nor but-ton-down. Below the jacket, her legs were encased in tight-fitting black jeans ending in black boots, which she stomped to get my attention. Her hair, stringy and falling all over her face, was jet black.

She was the Panther, that is all I can say even now with certainty, ex-cept that she had a message to deliver to me. And this was my first clear thought about her: that I was her destination, what she had been running to reach, because she had to tell her story to me. Not just anyone—me. So I said what anyone says who wants to hear a story, what the kings and queens in the ancient dramas say when they know they cannot escape the story the oracle has released into the human heart: "What happened?"

She looked up, brushing her hand through her black hair. She sucked in her breath, it caught in her mouth, and then it exploded.

"I killed Her," that voice said.

With those words came her name. "I killed Her" was planted in my mind as "Manda," an association so instant that I did not, at the moment, notice it.

Manda caught her breath. Her hair swung back and forth over her eyes. "That's right," she said. "She's dead. I'm alive. You can tell I'm the one who's alive because I'm the one who's breathing. Aren't you happy I finally showed up?"

I shook my head. "I don't know what you're talking about."

"Her. I'm talking about Her."

"What Her?"

Manda pressed her fingers to her forehead. "The Her I killed. The murder you asked for, Minimind."

"I didn't ask for a murder."

Manda sighed. She again passed her hands through her hair and, again, it fell over her eyes. "You think I would come all the way to this princess's excuse for communing with nature and tell you I've committed a murder if I wasn't at least halfway certain you'd be pleased someone had finally done your dirty work for you? You think I would come and tell a *stranger* I just killed Her?"

"No," I said, not sure quite what to say. "I think you'd tell me only if you thought I would be . . ."

"Nice," Manda said, slicing the word with her smile. Then added, "Actually, I was expecting more than nice."

"Thanks?" I said, incredulous. "I'm supposed to thank you for committing this murder?"

She paced back and forth, so like a caged beast that her sisterhood to some Panther somewhere seemed certain. "You got anything to drink? I'm thirsty. It sort of takes it out of you. Running as long as I have. Which, for your information, is approximately twenty-seven thousand years. Went down, down, down with Baubo. Sad, sad time."

I went to the kitchen, a tiny alcove to the left of my desk. I opened the refrigerator and found a diet cola. But I didn't drink diet cola anymore. I drank it when I was younger and wanted but one life: the dancer's. I looked over at where she was standing. Her skin had no shine but was a flat, matte white. Her voice was the organ with the most vitality; it had all the sinew, muscle, fiber, strain, pulse, stomp, and cackle her skin seemed to lack.

I handed her the diet cola. She cracked the flip top open with a calculated roughness and sipped the foam from the top. "Whenever I drink this shit," Manda said, examining the can, "I imagine I'm an aborigine and a white man has given me this drink and I go back to my tribe and inform them that this ghost-skinned guy with the exploding stick has come to destroy our whole tribe of dreamers. This diet sweetener crap," she said. "It's imagicide. Dreamkilling."

"So why drink it?" I said.

"To prove the white hunter wrong. It's medicine. Strong medicine."

Manda reached into the breast pocket of her leather jacket and produced a cigarette, which she lit with a lighter produced from some other pocket of her leather skin. Not a cheap disposable but an old-fashioned lighter which left a faintly sweet gas in the air after she closed the lid. She inhaled on the cigarette as she looked around my cottage, studying it as one would a hotel room where one had to stay for a long time.

The floor was wood, painted moss green. The effect (I liked to think) was of the floor continuing the grassy meadow around. There was but one room, with a small loft bedroom above. The exterior was white stucco with dark criss-cross wooden slats and a steep shingle roof.

"Very princess," Manda said. "Grimm. What a WASP with an education like you would choose for her retreat in the woods. But . . ." Manda smoked, squinting those eyes I still had not seen. "Too 'nice'," she said the word like a hiss, "for what we've got ahead of us."

"This . . . murder."

"Hey," she shrugged. "Your idea, not mine."

"I don't know why you keep saying that."

"The novel you're writing," Manda said, indicating the pages that had been coming off the Selectric. "It's a murder mystery."

"No. It's not."

"It is since you called me, Minimind." Manda sighed, dropped the cigarette on the floor of my cottage, and ground it with her heavy boot.

I mumbled to myself, "There's no murder in my story."

Manda shook her head back and forth. "Don't blame me for your plot. All I am is history."

Out of her mind. Or, rather, in her mind, way in, complete with her own poetry. I spoke gently, my voice pitched in the dulcet tones of the therapist to help me believe that I was the one in control, and Manda mad. "So. Tell me. Who's Baubo, and why is it sad?"

Manda sipped at the diet cola, shuddered, whether from the "medicine" or from my question I couldn't tell. Another cigarette appeared. She exhaled the smoke in laconic, hostile spirals. "I hate nice. I hate nice that is really snooping for pathology. Baubo, for your information, is not some secret code word in my elaborate psychotic system of murder logic. Baubo," Manda went on, tapping the ash onto my floor, "was an ancient goddess. Pig headed. When pigs are involved, you know it's very old. Old as Demeter, this way to Eleusis. Baubo was even older than that. She was here to belly dance and tell dirty jokes to women during childbirth so they would laugh away the pain."

"And she's dead?"

Manda flashed on me, her whole body rigid, alert, as it spun and turned to face me, those eyes hidden behind the veil of her black hair seeming on fire. "I told you not to do that!"

"What?"

"That acting-like-you-don't-know-what-I'm-talking-about crap!" She threw herself down on the couch and put her legs up on an ancestral chest I used as a table. "You have any idea how exhausting it is to run for twenty-seven thousand years?"

"I suppose I should, if I created you."

"Drop the monotheism," Manda said. "It will only get in the way. You did not create me. You created the murder. I got stuck in your murder mystery. You gotta start listening carefully if you wanna do this story right. And, let me say here for the record, you want to do it right."

"I am not writing a murder story," I said flatly.

Manda sighed. She rested her head on the back of my couch, her hair falling away. Her eyes were closed. "I was afraid you'd be resistant. Nice girls don't do murder, article of faith. The dogma of Nice takes another interesting woman down. They really do a number on you WASPs, don't they?"

"You're crazy," I said, more out of frustration than conviction.

"*I'm* crazy."

"Aren't you?"

Manda whooped. "Really, really, really stupid question to ask a crazy person," Manda said. "One of those questions that you can't answer, like the conundrum of the Cretan who says he's not a liar—is he lying? Or is he telling the truth? If he's lying, that means he is in fact a liar. Source of endless masochistic pleasure to philosophers. You are a far more likely candidate for some fancy psychotic footwork at this particular millimoment than me. You are the one actively engaged in conversation with me, a voice with boots on. Don't forget, Summacious: You invited me in, not the other way around."

"You're lying," I said. "I don't think you actually killed anyone. I think . . ."

"What you think, Minimind, doesn't matter anymore," Manda interrupted, her hoarse voice cracking. She was lighting another cigarette, and the fumes mixed their lingering sweetness with her smoke. "It's too late. You called, I came, we're here."

"In any case, I don't write murder stories."

Manda jumped up off the couch. Her black hair swirled as she turned to look at me. Her face was purplish in the twilight, her eyes hidden. "I have been running for twenty-seven thousand years to find you. And I am not going back there into those trees and start running another twenty-seven thousand years because you are scared—that's right, scared. You just don't want to write this story. But you called me—Manda—out from the trees. And I answered; don't forget that—I answered your call, and even though I admit this cottage is way, way too fairy tale for me—you do know those Grimm boys ripped everything off from these old women whose names, nobody knows? But this is how it is. I am your murderer. And there's not anything you or I can do about it now. It's too late and this is America and in America, murder is the medium."

We looked straight ahead, I from my vantage point behind my Selectric (which had recorded nothing about her so far), Manda standing in the middle of the room, where she had been dropping ashes since her arrival. We were both staring out at the trees. The last of the golden light was sucked up into them, hoarded inside the black bark against the coming winter solstice. The darkness advanced, confident.

With darkness would come the cold, and my cottage was inadequately heated with slipshod, expensive electric heat. If I wasn't to freeze that night, I needed to light a fire in my fireplace. But to reach the fireplace, I had to cross the room, and I sensed that there was an unspoken, invisible barrier between Manda and me which I must not cross. I needed a fire and food, things a body on this side requires, while Manda needed only smoke to subsist.

I arose from my place behind the desk, came around the side. As I entered the area between Manda and the trees out the window, Manda left. She disappeared as a shadow does when a sudden change of angle from a moving body eclipses the reflection. So my body, as it moved through her space, eclipsed her voice. Silence. No echo of her voice, no cackling, snarling trace. It was a relief, yes, to have that demanding, explosive voice evaporate into the dark, as if she had been sucked back into the trees. I turned all my attention to my own body, feeling more than a small reassurance to discover that she was not permanent.

Since I had moved to the Hudson Valley, I had learned the art of fire making and took both pleasure and pride in building one. I had secret methods with newspaper kindling, my own highly elaborate stacking and arranging system, and the true fire maker's feel for what logs should go where. It was one of the few, if not the only, practical art that I had mastered, and when I made a fire I always had a sense, even if fleeting, of my capacity for survival. In the present context, visited by a murderer issued from trees, proof that I could survive was pressing. The fire gently going, I warmed some homemade lentil soup and poured myself a glass of cheap red wine. I took my dinner to the fire, turning a log before I settled down. As the warmth of the fire mingled with the warmth of red wine, I felt something stir inside me.

Her name—Manda. She never spoke it out loud to me. That first night, sitting before the fire, I went over every detail of her arrival. I could find no introduction in it. Did I (do I?) know Manda from another "sad, sad time"? I could not answer this question and others—What call did I make, and why was it answered by a murderer? Which way to Eleusis? Where, Baubo? I would be asking myself all of this for many years to follow.

I stirred the logs in the fire before me. Sparks flew as some obstinate lichen caught fire, moss crackling. Manda had killed "Her": This was the beginning of the story, the message the Panther had been running twenty-seven thousand years to tell me. I had no idea who She was. Yet I felt Her absence to be a keen surgery, absolute. Sitting beside the orange glow of the fire, I sensed Her being as one feels a memory. I could not remember where or when but only the thing said, the perfume inhaled, the season detectable by the quality of air on one's body, the arousal by the moon so clearly before one's eye. What horizon cradled that moon, what one's skin knew or was about to discover—none of these had found their names yet. The poem remains, but not the circumstances which gave rise to the poem. "She" was all these things—a lost fragment of a lyric of a song I once knew, a perfume arising from some niche inside the cosmos where season and gland had produced Her one scent, and a power emanating from Her, as devoid of personality as the moon, without precise biography.

I did not know Her name. But I knew I had loved Her.

The feeling was so strong that She was dead, and my grief so tied to the loss of Her, that I wanted to tell someone about it. More, I felt the injustice of Her murder and wanted to proclaim it. I wanted my little cottage in the woods to become an amphitheater, and the bad news from the Messenger to be heard by all the audience, and for them to tremble at the horror of it.

Fragments of words ran through my mind, words which might have become a poem, a chant: *What season of the skin do I remember make way for graves, where the seed was, the body lies inside no moon crack the skin make way*—these words and others ran together like a poem runs along the currents of language before emerging from the linguistic chaos as a poem, a chanting trancelike current of words in which the most clearly recognizable ones burst forth into consciousness:

Moon! Seed! Murder!

I had to tell the authorities.

I looked up from the fire. Outside the large sliding glass doors of my cottage was nothing but dark. Not the quasi-dark of the perpetual penumbra of industry. The dark was preindustrial, no city lights to reflect off the atmosphere, no streetlights to poke holes in it, no industrial castles to ward it off. Old dark, fairy-tale dark, Hades dark. It was that darkness I would have to enter if I were to report Her murder.

A knife came into my mind. When I held knives, they had always spontaneously attacked me, buckling at the ripples in a peeled carrot, sliding on the slick sheaves of moist onion, slicing my fingertips. But all I could think, as I looked at the immeasurable dark between my house and the car, was that I should have a knife. In case. The Panther was out there. Not a gun, as if I already knew that posing as a white hunter would not do me any good against the Panther's "dreamkilling" medicine, the diet cola. But a knife, likely to be dropped in the moment, enemy of my own hands—only such a weapon seemed capable of slicing that darkness

18

between me and the car into tiny pieces. And when those tiny pieces of dark fell away from the blade after performing surgery on air, my fear would fall away too. The fear that Manda was telling the truth: that Her murder was my idea.

Armed with a knife I knew to be useless, I entered the dark to go tell the authorities She was dead, slashing at nothing with nothing.

I negotiated the dirt road in my car without headlights, guided only by the light of a half moon coming over the open fields. Against the lip of the moon, I could just make out the dark shape of the horse stables between my cottage and the main highway. The stables were huge, hulking, crooked buildings that housed over a hundred horses, trained and rented out for fox hunts. Many a dawn I had heard the hooves of the horses galloping by, and the horn blast through the last tendrils of a dream to announce the sighting of a fox.

One evening a few weeks before, when the trees were at their peak, the oxblood maples and the lurid oranges confounding sunset with vein and leaf, I had seen a red fox, camouflaged by the confluence of sky fire and tree fire, poised at the side of this same driveway. The fox's tiny etched face, the small eyes, turned on me and held me in their gaze as trees, sky, fox fur all blended into each other in that eruption of the blood of the earth which is autumn before we enter into the white snowscape of bone. As I drove in the dark, the memory of the fox protruded from the neutral, silvery moonscape of the night like a wound which had sealed itself struck open, freshly bleeding again. The ruddy image, so dissonant against the cool silvers of the night, seemed like the murder hidden inside the pale, bloodless skin of Manda, the violence which already was but whose story remained camouflaged by her black and silver costume.

I continued on my journey, compelled by grief for Her.

An abandoned stone house set back from the highway rose up inside my eyes. Then I curved past the cemetery. Looming above me on my left, perched precariously on a steep hillside, rose the dark-stoned Gothic-style "home," as it was called, no one wanting to use the word "asylum." I decided then that none of these battered, morbid buildings would appear in the pages of my murder mystery.

As I came into Rhinebeck itself, these lurid visions quieted down into quaint. Nice. What Manda had protested I was. I passed the fussy Victorian facades that greeted me as I rounded the top of the hill. The Beekman Arms, with its classic lines and black-and-white paint, appeared on my left. The black wooden sign with the handsome gold lettering, Beekman Arms 1701, Oldest Inn in America, stood before me as the gateway to ease and comfort away from Manda. I considered a glass of red wine at "The Beek" but then thought better of appearing at the police station with wine on my breath. So I turned down Main Street, past the carved wooden Indian in front of the corner smoke shop, past the hippie store turned to expensive imported clothing; past the art gallery, adjacent to the jewelry store run by a lawyer who had quit the law after ten years prosecuting drug lords in the city. On my right, the "novelty" store—which carried all the craft projects by all the elderly church women and was a veritable mini-empire of heart-shaped multimedia—sported a new hand-painted sign. Then Kilmer's, the local grocery run by good, solid Dutch for generations directly across the street from Eisenstaedt's, the deli run by good, solid Germans for just as many generations—this was my Main Street, impeccable, innocent, with only a hint of corruption. It was a "picturesque" town that fit neatly into a tourism brochure, exactly the stage set I wanted for my fiction: a place where murder was unimaginable.

"You saw a woman," the police chief said, not yet interested. (Supply for yourself the fluorescence, the Styrofoam cups with coffee and the uneven rims where bored deputies had picked off whole civilizations of

shards, the Naugahyde chairs with the squeaky center springs, the crack
running zigzag through the seat, stitched and restitched.)

"Running through the trees," I said, as if this were a revelation, a
clue (as it was, of course, but I didn't know that yet).

"Yeah, go on."

"Well, she was running. Running hard. Out of breath. Like she was
escaping or something." The Chief was a patient man. "And then she
stopped and she came to my door. She was thirsty and would I give her
something to drink. So I gave her a diet cola and she said something
about how she always imagined she was an aborigine when she drank
diet colas and that a white hunter had given it to her because he wanted
to kill her tribe of dreamers and she'd killed someone and —"

"Stop. Could you go back. . . ."

"She said that whenever she drank diet cola —"

"Not that part. The other part."

"She had killed someone."

"Can you describe her?"

Her.

Oh, her, Manda. "Short. Black hair, about this length," I said, hitting
the middle of my neck. "Thick, very thick. She was wearing a new black
leather jacket."

"How do you know it was new?"

"It squeaked when she moved."

"Yeah, go on."

"Black jeans, big boots. Lots of silver on the jacket. Studs. She
looked like a Panther."

"What were her words exactly?"

Drop the monotheism, murder is the medium, this is America.

"I killed Her." The Chief stared at me. "I killed Her and her name
was Manda."

"Whose name? The victim's?"

"No. The murderer."

"The woman in the trees."

"Yes."

The Chief was one of those large men who sighs with his entire body. "And then what?"

"She talked."

"About this murder?"

"She had her own reality system," I said.

"And?"

"She left. Then I came here."

The Chief here interrupted to make a call on the CB. He sent out a patrol to my house to search the grounds. I had visions of flashlights shouting through the trees shimmying to the intrusive music of the lights, sniffy dogs peeing to mark their territory, and Manda perched in a tree, stretched out along a fat limb, with her Panther tail swishing back and forth.

"And that's it?"

I looked at the Chief's face. Where had I seen his face before?

Manda leapt from the tree and —

I had recently seen a movie starring Ellen Burstyn and Melina Mercuri, the full title of which escapes me. It had the word "passion" in it. Mercuri played a famous Greek actress cast to play Medea, and Ellen Burstyn played a corporate wife who was in jail for actually having killed her children. Dramatic Medea and real-life Medea. The scenes of Burstyn carrying a huge kitchen knife and chasing her screaming children through the rented apartment filled with its American gadgets had set my stomach into turmoil. The instant the credits started rolling I raced out of the theatre across the street for cigarettes, the great stupefiers of sensation.

In the smoke shop, leaning against the high wooden counter worn by over a hundred years of flannel shirt sleeves scraping against it as they handed over their nickels and dimes for a smoke and a paper, the Chief had been chewing the fat with Mr. Bert, as he was called, short for some long, euphonic Italian name. Who has time in America for euphony?

"Yeah, yeah, I'm not gonna do anything to Freddie, pathetic you can't fix. Besides, just between you and me, Mr. B, Daryl, he comes in the other morning looking like the proverbial cat with the canary, I'm telling you, and it turns out his wife, she got one of these phone calls, from Freddie, yeah, that's how I found out, and Daryl's wife, Pat, she goes down on him for the first . . ."

At that point, I was seen, and the conversation ceased abruptly. The Chief nodded to me and smiled. He had marvelous broad, full lips, and his was the kind of face you wanted for Shakespeare. Sophocles. Restoration tragedies. It was a face on which you wanted to affix poetry. Not handsome, but just as beautiful conjures on the masculine something beyond nature, and handsome on the feminine, the Chief's face went beyond—just, beyond. That face opened like an anemone when he smiled at me. Opened and revealed vivid color, as if the life of him were suddenly flush. When the Chief smiled that smile at me after I had watched a corporate wife chasing down her children with a huge kitchen knife, I thought he was sent to me to act as a personal bodyguard against all the would-be Medeas out there. This man, the Chief, wore the sacred mask of poetry and had the power to ward off the hippocampic demons of the cinematic night.

As I sat across from that same face in the police station, scrambling through my brain for an answer, Freddie Van Heusen, who everyone in town knew was making obscene phone calls to women over fifty giving them instructions in oral sex, blinded me to Manda. I did not see the Panther leap from the tree and escape the flashlights because I was wondering what, exactly, Freddie Van Heusen said that had the power to inspire an older woman to go down on her husband after how many sexually flat years of marriage?

"I think Freddie Van Heusen might know something about it," I said.

The Chief was taken aback. "What makes you think that?"

"He called me," I said.

The police chief rubbed his eyes. "Was this phone call he made to you of an obscene type?" said the Chief.

"Umm, well, yes," I said.

"When?"

"This afternoon," I said.

"When this Manda was there?"

"Yes."

"And it was Freddie making one of his . . . Christ," the Chief sighed. Then he looked at me, thinking, his eyes studying me. "How did you know it was Freddie? He usually disguises his voice."

"I overheard you talking to Mr. Bert about him last Wednesday night in the smoke shop," I said.

The Chief did one of those nods which ends with an open mouth suspended in midair.

I reconstruct, here, from the ashes of the work of fiction Manda interrupted. The morning after my imagined scene in the police station, the first of many dialogues between Manda and me began as my novel surrendered to Manda's tale of murder. It was a silent exchange as an indistinct, semi-Manda hovered nearby, passing me information about her "fictional" life. I listened as the Selectric sarcophagus seemed to conduct her tale on its own accord, the keys drumming to the rhythm of Manda's voice The Murder Mystery. I expected Manda—the Panther in the cottage—would fade entirely as she acquired substance inside my fiction.

My logic was a creative writer's logic, grounded in experience. Characters often "appear" to writers, and seem real, and even dictate the story as Manda did in her silent way, delivering a childhood to me which fit a future murderer. She emerged in The Murder Mystery as a recognizable type in our society, the gifted individual who takes a wrong turn in childhood, and where there might have been another Picasso or Rilke, a storm-trooper Panther bursts out of the fragile shell of genius. I had every reason to believe that Manda was no more than a familiar phenomenon of the creative process, never suspecting I would burn The Murder Mystery before I finished it, turning all that was fictional about Manda to ashes to save my soul from the Panther.

From *The Murder Mystery:*

26

Manda grew up in a large brick apartment house on Chicago's South Side with a mother, a small, preoccupied woman, absorbed in a world of her own, muffled from within; a father who worked the night shift, drinking all day, raging in the living room as he threw Pabst Blue Ribbon beer cans at his wife's plants, railing against what he called "the fucking grass inside the house"; and a sister dying of a something inside her lungs that would never find a single diagnosis. The plants were her mother's only link to her home, a house in the prairie, outside the stench and the bustle of Chicago, where she had been raised by her grandmother. And so when her husband poured gasoline over them and burned them in the alleyway at the back of the house, with Manda watching, he was killing not house plants but generations of women, the sweet, gentle linking of woman to woman on the prairie.

Manda sneaked out to retrieve the ashes when her father left for his shift at the steel factory at four. She put as much as she could into the pockets of her pants and then carried the rest in a hammock of her shirt. She closed the hammock against the perpetual wind, the soft weight of the ashes bumping against her just forming breasts. The sensation was strangely pleasant and comforting to her. She brought them into the room she shared with her wheezing little sister and looked around for something special to put the ashes in to give to her tiny, quiet mother who never said anything to her but, "How is your sister breathing today?" and "How did she breathe last night?"

Their bedroom was a porch off the kitchen, at the back of the apartment building. The screen windows had been covered with layers and layers of thin dry-cleaning bags, the writing every which way all around them, overlapping, upside down, indecipherable, confused. Above Manda's bed the words overlapped to read "Dring eaners," a condensation from the King Dry Cleaners where Moms worked and had been filching the plastic for years to protect her ailing daughter against the wind and keep her as far away from their father as she could in their small apartment.

As she was looking for something to hold the ashes of her mother's heritage, Manda checked on her sister, who opened her eyes.

"Present for Moms," Manda said.

"What'd you do this time?"

"Something right," Manda said, as if her sister were as dumb as she was sick (which she was, of course). "Something good, even."

"Yeah, what?"

"You wouldn't understand."

Manda was scrounging around under her bed. She found a bowl with flecks of cereal clinging to it. She gave it a sniff, scratched off the cereal, and poured the ashes into it. They flitted up like tiny spores into the air. Her sister began to cough as Manda unloaded the ashes from her pockets.

"Manda?" Moms called from somewhere in the apartment. "Manda? Is your sister all right?"

"She's fine."

Her sister started hacking violently.

"Stop it," Manda said. "I know you're faking."

"I can't," she wheezed. "I am not faking."

Manda forgot about the rest of the ashes in her pockets. She dusted off where the ashes had spilled and pressed them down with her palms to hold them in. Her sister hacked.

"Shut up and I'll tell you a story," Manda said.

"Manda!" Moms called.

Her sister heaved.

Manda said, "A story about . . . " Manda looked at the plastic alphabet around them, their cocoon against the cold winds off the lake. *King Dry Cleaners*. Wrinkled, buckling in places, she formed a word from the nested letters: "Dring." "About Drings. Promise."

Her sister's breath caught in her and her eyes popped open. Moms came rushing into the room, tying her bathrobe around her tiny waist, naked underneath. Manda caught her mother's smell as she passed, a smell that was not the usual perfume Manda would steal a quick pulse of when her mother went to the dry cleaners.

"Here, Mama, I got your plants that Daddy—"

Moms rushed out of the room. Manda looked at her sister, whose eyelids were fluttering. Her heart jumped up. She heard a voice she had never heard before coming from her mother's bedroom. The next thing

Manda knew, a strange man with dark hair came rushing into the bedroom and gathered her sister in his arms. He was naked above the waist, and his pants were unzipped, and she could see he was wearing no underwear. He disappeared, her mother racing after him, and she was alone.

She was alone for a long time. Manda searched the alphabet around her. Dring. Eaners. The wind made the words around her flutter. In the magical land of Dring there were no factories, for everything everyone needed grew inside the Drings and all you had to do was peel them and there it was—food, words, love, a Dring held inside it all these and more, and they were everywhere, and all different colors and shapes and sizes, and everything was perfect in the Land of Dring until the Eaners came, which the Eaners always did. Always the Eaners would come and instead of gently peeling off the skin of the Drings for food and words and love, and then carefully putting the skin of the Dring back and closing up the wound and watching the Dring change colors and as it changed colors (which Drings always did when they were peeled, and it was both sad and beautiful, it was just the way it was, she would say to her sister) if you didn't say the magic words over the Dring right that minute, then the Dring would lose its color forever and would have nothing inside it but black wind, the terrible black wind, except that's what the Eaners wanted, they wanted the whole world to be filled with Drings with black wind inside them and all hard and scaly on the outside, and they came and they poked their horrible things, no, I won't tell you the name of their horrible things, you have to stop asking me, you're too young to know, they were just horrible poking things and they pierced the Drings with them and never said any magic words at all, in fact, the Eaners just yelled, yelled and pierced, and all the Drings lost their rainbow colors and filled up with the horrible black wind and then the Eaners, they collected the Drings filled with black wind and they took them back to their land and they opened them up and poured the black wind into these huge machines bigger than this whole apartment building, there were tons and tons and tons of these machines and they were these living machines and they needed the black wind for food, that's it, the black wind was food for the Eaners' horrible machines

which weren't actually machines at all, really, they just looked like machines, but what they really were was . . .

Manda looked at the layered hieroglyphs on the dry-cleaning plastic
for a name as she kept spinning the tale. King Dry Cleaners. Drings.
Eaners. The remaining letters made the word—

Clyks, they were the terrible Clyks and what they did . . . what they
did was they . . .

"Where's your sister? What happened?"

Manda swallowed. "Moms took her to the hospital."

They turned everything they touched into metal and it died, like
that, even people, if a Clyks touched a person, that person turned to metal
and that was that, they didn't have hearts or anything, they were just
metal inside and out, and nothing could ever get them back to being
human again unless they got back to the Land of Dring, because in the
Land of Dring there's all the food and words and love humans need and
they need so much, see, humans need so much food and words and love
that they have to have lots and lots of Drings around them to make it
okay for them to be human, which it wasn't if you were anywhere near a
Clyks, boy, you really didn't want to need any food or words or love if a
Clyks was around, so what happened was, see, the Eaners, they would
take these humans that the Clyks could turn to metal, because, see, if the
Clyks were fed enough black wind from the dead Drings—

"What's all over your face?"

"Nothing."

"I can see your face, you dumb shit. And I say it's covered with shit.
What's that?"

The Clyks, if they had enough black wind inside them it filled them
up and they started to move, and they could move very very very fast, before you knew it, they were touching you and you were turning to metal
inside and out and the Eaners, they would come then and they would
take you apart into pieces and make things out of the pieces of you—

"Where'd you get this stuff? Did you get this in the alley? Answer
me, you fucking little shit!"

—like all kinds of things, you never knew what, like they would
make you into a sink or a refrigerator or—

"Eat it. I said, eat!"

—or this metal machine that could eat up ashes and not choke except when they made it wrong and it couldn't help choking—

"Come here. I said, come here. You're being a bad, bad girl. Daddy's going to have to punish you for not eating your special dinner."

—or sometimes they would make you into this special kind of car that could speed away and go faster than anything in the whole world and then, then, you would turn invisible, because sometimes something would happen, see, and a Clyks would touch you and you would turn to metal but then, then you would become invisible, that's it, you would become invisible, and it was then you would try to sneak back to the Land of Dring, because you would only be invisible for a little while, you never knew how long it would last, because, see, this would happen but no one knew how, it was sort of like this wonderful mistake, and so you never knew if you'd make it across the border back to the Land of Dring before the Eaners and the Clyks caught you and turned you into metal for real, sometimes you only had maybe, oh, maybe like thirty-eight seconds, but if you got across the border, if you got across the border back into the Land of Dring, you became human again and you were safe.

Till the Eaners came again to pierce the Drings and it all started to happen all over again.

"But then, one day, one day this amazing thing happened that none of the very wise and smart people of Dring ever thought could happen. One day, just when it looked worse than ever, this person came in and he got rid of the terrible Clyks."

"How?"

"Well, actually, you almost died that day. That's how bad it was. Something had gone wrong with the Clyks and instead of black wind the Drings filled up with ashes, and—"

"Manda, the ashes aren't pretend. They're real."

"Whose story is this, mine or yours?"

"I know who it was. And he was real too. The ashes and Mick are real."

"It's not Mick. It's Mihalyi."

"I can only say Mick. He doesn't mind. He loves me."

"Thanks. Thanks a lot. You just ruined the story."

"Aren't you happy that Mick is real and Daddy's gone, now?"

"What do you know."

"A whole lot you don't," her sister said. She wheezed, and the dry-cleaner bags pulsed and flapped around them. "I know that Mick knows the magic words to say over the Drings to make them change their colors and hold something new inside. And you don't."

"Yeah, sure."

"So say them."

"I can't tell you. You're not old enough. It's a law. It's the only law in the whole Land of Dring. You can't learn the magic words until you're ten."

"I'll ask Mick. He'll tell me. He loves me the most."

"It's not Mick. It's Mihalyi. And he's the one who made the law, idiot. Don't you realize he's the King of the Land of Dring?"

I awoke one morning from a dream which stirred old questions in me to an early snow falling on the mounds of leaves, a sight that disrupted my sense of sequence and season—yet rhymed with the dream, which recurred throughout my life according to its own psychic schedule.

I came down the stairs from my bedroom loft to find my cottage empty, hushed by the muzzling snow. But I sensed Manda would come back, like the dream, according to my psyche's tempo. I felt that morning, as I had when she arrived on my doorstep, that she had chosen to tell her story to me and would not leave until she had finished her tale. The Messenger has but one purpose, to deliver the message, and I never doubted Manda would fulfill her role.

I made coffee and, standing in the kitchen, looked at my writing desk, covered with yellow newsprint, pads of paper of different colors and sizes, a broken mug filled with pencils and pens I rarely used. In the middle of the chaos, the Selectric squatted, more than ever like a guide for the departed queen. Her. Manda's victim. At the thought of Her, my body buckled and a wave of grief rushed through me. But no face would come to my mind, no name, no body—only the sadness at Her loss.

Instead, the image of the Chief's beautiful mouth filled my eyes. I wanted to send my epic poet police chief into the wilderness on a quest to relieve the anguish of Her anonymity and reveal who this woman was whose murder, though as blank as Her face, yet possessed the weight of the actual within me. But life had its designs for me, independent of my ambitions, and its own idea of what the story was going to be. I had to trust the Chief to begin the search without me and what words the hippo-Selectric would evoke, for I had promised my best friend that I would help her move that morning.

My friend was standing outside when I pulled up. The moving men, dressed in dark blue pants and shirts, obedient to the injunction of the snow to be silent, moved furniture swiftly up steep stairs into the second-story apartment. As I approached, I noticed how my friend's dark, curly hair caught the flakes all over the top, where they perched like lace. The effect was both ludicrous and saintly.

"Halo?" I said.

"Innocence. I'll take it no matter how it comes." No one in her family had ever divorced before her.

Boxes rose up through the stairwell on the mighty arms of the movers; a couch lurched upward, followed by a table suspended above a tall man like a roof, and then an easy chair, each article dusted with the censorious snow. My friend followed every article with her eyes as they disappeared into the stairwell.

"Rent is regression," she said. "Tell me this isn't happening."

"What part?" I said. "The part about how your husband stopped loving you or the part about snow falling on your piano?"

"Oh no, no, no, it can't snow on the piano," she said. She rushed to the moving men, who had interrupted the ceremony of floating furniture to consider the piano. It stood, obstinate, immobile, on the sidewalk sprouting snow. My friend swished the snow off the top and then took off her corduroy coat to protect the piano. I looked around, saw a pile of coats and blankets at the back of the truck.

"Get them, get them!"

She grabbed at a coat as it slithered down the sides of the piano, tying sleeves to sleeves to keep them on. "The piano can't stay here in the street," she said.

"We can't get it up there," a moving man said.

"But . . . it's my grandmother's piano," she said. The moving men shrugged. She looked at them all, standing in a line, her browny-green eyes like two ponds caught in snow. "I said, it's my grandmother's piano." The moving men stared. "From Poland. After they escaped the pogroms my great-aunt, my grandmother's sister, she went back and she found it, in the house, not a scratch. Not a scratch!"

"Yeah, well, it's too big to get up the stairs."

My friend shook her head, not in frustration with the moving men but with herself. She had a faith in articulation far greater than mine. She knew, she just knew, that if she told the men the story about the piano they would get it up the stairs. "This piano survived hell," she said patiently, the snow dusting her dark hair as the moving men stood wiping at the melt from their bald heads. "Not metaphorical," she said. "Real hell, historical hell," she said.

"High school is real hell," one of the younger moving men said.

"No, real hell is when your kid's in high school."

They laughed. My friend turned her plankton-colored eyes onto me, pleading for help. "It has to get upstairs. I need to know I can survive real hell," she said. Most people hoard their private symbols to themselves. But it was my friend's gift not only to see the meaning of her life as it unfolded but also to assume that if she shared it, others would immediately understand.

"We can't—can't—get it up—no way—not those stairs—those stairs are too steep—too much—not this—us," the moving men said in a halting chorus of protest. One of them added, by way of coda, "Lady, we're professionals."

She tried again. "If this piano could survive the Holocaust, it can get up those stairs."

The moving men shook their heads. "Gravity's gravity," one of them said.

"And history's history." My friend leaned over and tugged at the piano. It moved. "See? See? This is the power of history." She giggled. "Did I just say what I think I said?"

"It's wheels," one of the moving men said.

"Wheels are history," she said.

"Lady," he said, "wheels are the problem here."

"History's always been difficult for Americans," I offered.

The moving men were sharing looks about these two crazy women who talked this way.

My friend then said, "What we need is some fearless, inventive amateurs." And took off through the snow down the street. She worked part time at the Dutchess County Historical Society, an institution not at all as stuffy as it may sound. She was involved in a project to collect the stories of the elderly who had lived in the county since the turn of the century, and spent most of her days knocking on doors and asking old women to tell her anything they could remember about their lives. And they did. People spoke to her; either you have this gift or you don't, and those who do will tell you that they don't do anything deliberate or calculated. They are carriers of the ancient story fire inside them, and people gather around them as if they were mobile hearths and speak. People, usually women, would stop my friend on the street and share with her the richest loam of the latest gossip, adding, "You never know. It might turn out to be historically significant."

So when she took off down the street and began to knock on all the doors of all the houses, I knew, though the skeptical moving professionals did not, that people would come out of their houses and help her. At every door which opened, she said a variation of, "I have a piano which I should not have. It is a piano that is not supposed even to be. It survived when it shouldn't have. No one knows how. And I have to survive too; we all have to survive; who knows how any of us is going to survive, you know?"

The words worked like a summons to all the people inside the houses in the middle of town to join her uncertain hope for survival and place their faith in the piano. The amateurs came in a great migration out of their houses. Men in retirement who weren't good for anything but barking out directions and disagreeing with each other; an enormously fat woman who turned out to have the strength of an ox; a couple of men of indeterminate age with big bellies and completely flat buttocks which seemed to have been compressed into them, the belly protruding to compensate; and, quite by surprise, two magnificent, ruddy, strapping teenage boys, all inspired by the piano which had survived when it shouldn't have and, yes, they agreed, they had a strange feeling about whether or not we were all going to survive; did she have any idea what was going to happen?

One of the boys, Val, part of the grocer's family, with striking green eyes, stripped off an old plaid jacket and draped it over an exposed shoulder of the piano. Wearing only a t-shirt, heated up from within by some marvelous energy, he immediately assumed the role of the director of the obese, the lumpish, the compressed, and the other misshapen male elders anxious to survive. Epics need a hero, and life was more accommodating to the oldest form of story by supplying one than I would have been, were this all my fiction. Val rolled the piano up to the entryway. He divided the Chorus of Misshapen Men into two groups, each holding one end.

The Woman with the Strength of an Ox pushed back sleeves to reveal her enormous arms dripping with flesh. She squatted down. "Ready," she said.

"Everyone count with me," Val said.

"One, two, three," the Chorus of Misshapen Men shouted, and then one half of the piano rose while the other was held steady.

"Hold it!"

The Woman with the Strength of an Ox worked one side, Val of the Heat from Within the other, spinning off the wheels of the piano as the snow fell around them. The Misshapen Men held on as if for dear life. The professionals stood aside, waiting for the disillusionment of the amateurs when they found out that the piano just would not go up the stairs.

Val was pocketing the wheels in huge pockets which seemed to appear as called for. The Woman with the Strength of an Ox held on to hers, holding them up like ceremonial torches, as Val directed the wheelless piano onto a blanket which also seemed to appear, as he had, when required. Grunting, groaning, the Chorus of Misshapen Men lowered the piano which was not supposed to have survived but did onto the blanket. Val, his friend, and the Woman with the Strength of an Ox went around to the side of the piano farthest away from the door. Val explained the necessary movements, explained the reasons for the positions; the hero often has the best grasp of the forms necessary. When the Misshapen Men pulled the piano up, they had to remember that the bulk of the weight was going to fall on their side, Val explained. He turned to his friend, to the Woman with the Strength of an Ox. They nodded. They were ready.

"Move."

My friend's eyes never let the piano out of her sight. She followed it as the piano glided up the stairs. Her corduroy jacket lined with quilted satin slid off, falling away to the side as Val and the Woman with the Strength of an Ox seemed to defy gravity and redeem history, pushing the piano up the stairs.

"Why are they doing this for me?"

"They're doing it for the piano."

"What is it with this piano?" my friend said. "It keeps on being rescued."

"It refuses to let itself be abandoned."

She ran after it.

Upstairs, all the men were raising their arms, of every shape and size and degree of extension, in celebration as the wheels were screwed on by the Woman with the Strength of an Ox on one side, my friend on the other. The piano was then set down at rest against the wall in the living room, and another cheer went up. There followed a request for a song.

My friend looked at me. "This is what happened to my great-aunt. When they found the piano. They asked her for a song." She sat down at the piano, tried out a few chords, hit a few wrong notes, and then, as her fingers pried into memory and the chord yielded up the tune, the Chorus of Misshapen Men began to hum and sing. As the cranky retired sang, the lumps hummed, and the Woman with the Strength of an Ox sang in full baritone every single verse, one after the other, their faces lighting up, their cheeks flushed from the strain and the cold, Val just listened. The Woman with the Strength of an Ox made a face at him as she sang, nodding encouragement. She moved beside him and me and, linking her arms in ours, swayed with us back and forth while she sang every verse and we hummed along, halting but exalted.

When it was over, a great hoot of joy rose up.

The boss of the moving men then appeared, carrying boxes. He looked at the amateurs, then at the piano. "Told you the wheels were the problem," he said.

"Lack of faith," said the Woman with the Strength of an Ox. "Lack of faith was the problem."

They began to dwindle out, their voices already beginning to tell the story in scraps. "I didn't think it could be done," they said. "Impossible, it was impossible," they concurred. "There's no way that piano was going to get up those stairs," they intoned. "But . . ." they said. "But . . ." "But that's not your ordinary piano." "Right. It survived."

My friend was thanking the Woman with the Strength of an Ox. Nothing, it was nothing. Anytime, anytime. She needed anything, anything.

Val was untying his jacket from one of the piano feet. "So, Val," my friend said, "listen. Now that you've moved my grandmother's piano, you'll get to Hollywood."

"Yeah?" Val said.

"Absolutely."

"I do have a kind of a plan," he said.

"It'll work," my friend said. "The piano is going to return you the favor and get you out of this town and up the stairs to stardom. This is how life works."

Some people get transcendent pianos to help them fulfill their destiny. What I got was a murderer, waiting for me in the cottage in the woods.

A small package had arrived. It was from a local astrologer whom I had consulted a few weeks before. The consultation had been disturbing, but Manda's arrival had reconfigured disturbance (forever). I entered the cottage, a queasy feeling on me as I began to recall the uncomfortable interview with the astrologer. I put some hot water on for coffee, and just as I was trying to decide whether to listen to the tape or not, Manda's voice crashed in on me.

"King Pain," she said. "King Pain is what he was. And no search."

"No ... "

"No flashlights, no Chief, no goddamned search!" Manda screamed at me. She paced, fumed. Gone was the indistinct hovering Manda who had been silently transmitting her life story to me. Before me was the Panther, that storm trooper from the realm of trees, railing at me for scenes I was only considering putting into The Murder Mystery. "How come you told that mouth for Restoration tragedies about some guy named Freddie calling you while I was here?"

"I didn't write it down," I said, in my defense. I pointed to the pages of yellow newsprint accumulating beside the hippo-Selectric. "All I wrote about was the Drings."

"You may be writing about the Drings," she said, "but you're thinking about Freddie."

I reached for the manuscript of The Murder Mystery beside the Selectric. "Look for yourself," I offered. "All that's in here is about Moms, and your father, your sister, the Drings, Mihalyi—"

"I told you—he was King Pain. Get your goddamned names straight. Names matter, Summacious. Mess with the names, you mess it up. And, trust me, you do not, I repeat, not, want to do this murder mystery wrong."

"Okay, okay," I said, as I poured the water through the coffee filter. I watched the filter stain from the grounds as the cone filled up. The water spilled over the top. I cursed. I hated it when the grounds would not allow the water to go through. I scraped at the bottom, but I scraped too hard, and the grounds burst through.

"If *you*," Manda swiped with her voice at me, "would sit down and get to work instead of running around with your friend trying to levitate pianos and sneaking off in the middle of the night to tell some chief of police with a mouth he can't see when he looks in the mirror that Freddie's involved, I could trust you with the rest of my story."

"I made a promise to my friend. And she is in a lot of pain—"

"What does anybody on your side know about pain?" Manda said, disgusted.

I finished making a new cup of coffee, and let the silence rise up between us.

I said, "You know, I really wasn't thinking about Freddie. I was listening to you. Which is not, for the record, always that easy. And I would like to know what the Drings and King Pain have to do with killing—"

"Are you going to put Freddie into the story? And this mouth?"

I said, "You tell me, Manda," thinking this complete submission to her authority would get her to trust me again.

"Looking for your destiny in the stars instead of right here." Manda pointed to herself. "Your poor father. Thousands and thousands of dollars wasted on your education in a Tower. Can't even see the obvious."

"You're my destiny?"

She blew her black hair with exasperation. "Didn't you have the dream yet? The one you've been having ever since the afternoon you were—what? Four? Five? And discovered what happens to magnets when you turn them around. That dream, Minimind. You should have had it by now."

While the dream was utterly familiar to me, I had never been able to recall when it had first happened or what experience had inspired it. The moment Manda said that the cross-wise magnets were the dream's source, I knew she was right. The day my brother tossed magic into my lap, I had dreamed the dream in which I had been told my destiny.

In the dream, I am a young woman in a room inside a house in the woods (as I was, at the time of this story, a young woman in a room inside a house in the woods). I have been given the task to count my breaths. I sit at an ornate wooden table (as I was sitting at an ornate . . .) with parchment and pen before me (paper and hippopotamus). I am marking the parchment with dutiful strokes as I count my breath: I I I I, I stroke, and then the diagonal cross-line for the five. But here the dream begins to quaver: Do those strokes mean I have breathed four times? Or five? And what is a breath? I begin to panic; I do not know the system for counting; I am not sure what a breath is.

A strange man in a homespun robe appears. His robe matches the panels of the room, all the color of stripped wood, as if I am inside a tree and he is the part of the tree which can move and speak. He tells me that I must continue to count and to breathe. Even though I'm unsure, ignorant, afraid; for if I don't attend to my breathing, even in my doubt, I will not fulfill my destiny.

What is my destiny?

To continue doing what I am doing, of course.

Why am I doing this?

To fulfill your destiny.

The dream had followed me all my life, mysterious, frustrating. I held it inside me as a koan I was here to solve.

"Hey. Mutemouth. Didn't I do the breathing right?"

I nodded, feeling shifts within me as monotheism began to crack apart. "Yes," I said quietly. "You did the breathing right."

"You know, you really shouldn't rely on amateurs for this kind of thing." She nodded her head in the direction of the astrologer's tape. "You gotta watch out, you start messing with real hell and history or looking for your destiny in the stars. You miss that it's all right here. Right *here*," Manda finished, vigorously beating her own chest.

I had been referred to Gwen, the Astrologer, by the wife of the former drug-lord prosecutor turned jewelry store owner, a large woman whose geometric features, black glistening almond-shaped eyes, knee-length hair, and belief in nursing their son until he was four years old qualified her as a Mayan high priestess. The Astrologer seemed to have descended from the same tropical tribe, displaced through eons to the Hudson Valley. She was a voluptuous woman herself, with graying shoulder-length hair cut in a geometric style and thick bangs that accentuated her broad cheekbones, enormous crescent-shaped blue eyes, and generous lips. She too had the heft and curve of jungle and drum.

When she opened the door to greet me, she whispered, "Hello," in a tremulation passing for a voice. Her breasts were as abundant as her voice was vacant, and the dissonance between her solid, sensuous body and her voice was as disquieting as the snow on the leaves. Her lips moving anxiously, her eyes skittering like water bugs across the surface of my face, the Astrologer seemed so agitated and helpless that I instantly regretted my impulse toward destiny.

"I'm sorry," she said. "I just . . . this is so awkward . . . but of course it makes sense that you would arrive at exactly this moment, with your sense of drama; you're a Scorpio, Scorpios love drama, sex, death. . . . I just received a very upsetting . . . a very strange phone call. . . ."

"Don't worry about it," I said. The Astrologer looked at me, her blue eyes blinking. "The chief of police is already taking care of it."

"Scorpios are supposed to be psychic," she said. Her voice trailed off into skepticism or fear; it was difficult to tell which one.

"He wasn't threatening, was he?"

"Oh," the Astrologer said, "it wasn't from a man. I don't think." She tossed her hair, which swirled softly as it settled on her shoulders. "I really couldn't tell," she said. She sighed; the mountains of her breasts gave birth to a new world. "It's just that I live alone. . . . It's not what he said, it's just . . . it made me feel so . . . so vulnerable. . . . But you're a Scorpio, and Scorpios are fearless, so you probably don't understand. . . . I don't mean that as an insult; it's just the way you are. It's my damn Pisces moon," she said. "It always gets me into trouble with my feelings. I don't know if it was a woman or . . . the voice was so . . . the words, they felt so . . . so old. . . ." She shook her head, as if to call herself back from a trance.

She suggested herbal tea to calm her nerves, asking if I would like some too. I disliked herbal tea intensely. But I accepted. Our tea brewed, liquid trees in our mugs; we sat down in a light-filled living room with plants on slim bent-wire stands smiling happily in the sunlight. She fidgeted with the pilules of her acrylic sweater, a startling electric shade of blue. She looked up at me, her blue eyes intensified by the hue of the sweater. "Someone I knew was in trouble, no, not trouble. Danger," she said. "In my dream. She was on the bridge . . . and . . . there was this serpent. . . . " She shook her head to dislodge the dream from it. She looked away, out the window, and drifted away.

"Gwen?"

She slowly turned her head toward my voice. "I'm sorry. You must think I'm so pathetic." Gwen's lips fluttered, and I was sure she was going to burst into tears. She said, "I was going to call her—the woman who was in so much danger—in my dream—when this strange phone call happened, and I don't know if she's all right. You must think I'm crazy, but I haven't talked to this woman . . . in my dream . . . who was fighting for a very long time, and the way the dream ended . . . You must think me the weakest . . . it's just what happened, after . . . I must stop!" Gwen forced herself to smile at me. She took a folder from a nearby table and said, "This will distract me. It's your chart, and it's very complicated. But before we do . . . I was going to ask . . . Would you mind if I looked at your palm for a moment?"

"You read palms too?"

"Not exactly. It's just that sometimes those marks help me understand something in a chart that doesn't make sense." I held out my hand. She studied it and then said, "I thought so." And gave my hand back to me. "Thank you."

She then told me about my chart, leaving unspoken the rest of her dream and the revelation in the lines of my hand.

The tape that had arrived had a note around it, fastened with a rubber band. As I picked up the tape and removed the note, I glanced over at Manda. She was sitting on the couch, staring off into the trees. I opened the note and read:

> I wanted to tell you that I did actually make the phone call, after you left. But I couldn't reach her. The woman in my dream. The people who should know where she is, don't. I am thinking of going to the police to report her officially missing, but before I do, I was just wondering if you could tell me what you know about these phone calls. I apologize for how I am acting, but I can't help it and with that Cancer moon of yours, I'm sure you understand.

"Manda?" I said very softly.

"You make me very nervous with that 'nice' you're doing at me," Manda said.

As gently as I could, and trying to sound merely curious so as not to reveal the hint of terror in me at what I was imagining possible, I said, "Are my dreams the only ones you know? Or do you know other people's dreams too?"

Manda didn't speak for a long time. She kept her face turned from me. In her silence, I began to let myself believe that the question was absurd, and that Manda was just building up to another harangue about my stupidity to top all the others so far. But when she did speak, she said, "Another surprise point in your favor, Summacious. You're learning faster than I thought you would." Manda then leaned forward, and paused. "Tell you what. I'll cut a deal. You tell me more about this Freddie, I'll tell you the ending of Gwen's dream."

"But I don't know anything about Freddie except what you already know," I protested. "He calls older women and says obscene things that don't seem obscene, somehow. Gwen called them 'old.' The words he used."

"Old," Manda repeated. "Anything else?"

I ran through my mind everything I had overheard about Freddie Van Heusen. "That's all I know."

"Not enough, Summacious. You gotta find out more about Freddie before I tell you what happened to the woman on the bridge."

"Did you kill her?"

Manda stood up, abruptly. She turned around and faced me. Snarly. "You think I'm going to fall into that trap, Minimind?"

"Trap? What—?"

"Do you really think that pathetic amateur astrologer who doesn't even have the bucks to get the chart done by the Big Computer of the Stars, that mistral of a woman with the dried-up voice, could dream me? I am very selective about whom I choose for asylum," Manda finished.

"Why did you choose me?"

"You called. I don't answer everyone's call, you know."

"Did Gwen call you too?"

"Maybe."

"And did you answer her call?"

"What matters, Erasermind, is that I answered your call. I am the one with the map you need."

"How are you my destiny?"

Manda exploded. "God, I hate you WASPs! I hate how you need *proof.* And you never get enough proof, no matter how hard I try. You have no idea what it takes out of me to pay a visit on your side, and what do you pathetic WASPs do? You keep on asking me how I got here instead of accepting the gift I bring you. I take back what I said about you being my asylum. You are a lousy host. How much more proof do you need? You had the dream about your destiny, Gwen had the dream her sister was in mortal danger, and then I showed up and told you I'd killed Her—"

At that moment there was a knock on my back door. My friend was standing outside. She had come with her son, Benjamin, who was five. I had completely forgotten that I had promised her Benjamin could see me today, the day of the floating piano of history and the real hell of divorce. I looked—but Manda was gone. I opened the back door.

"Benjamin has something to tell you," my friend said.

The sight of Benjamin's face washed away all my frustration with Manda instantly. Benjamin had huge green eyes like his mother, curly thick hair, and a round, elfin face. He was wearing a leftover part of a Halloween costume, a soft felt band around his head with two golden horns, and a sweatshirt that read, "Utility." He looked at me and smiled. Ever since I had met Benjamin, when he was just two, he'd had the effect of snatching me away from myself and into his world, a world in which everything around him was worthy of his attention. In the spring just past, I had spent a day with Benjamin collecting slugs. It had been raining for thirteen consecutive weekends, and, though the lilacs were more fragrant and bounteous than anyone could remember, most complained at the sky's conspiring to ruin their leisure time. Not Benjamin. Benjamin looked at the rain, Saturday after Saturday, and told his mother, "The sky has to rain a lot before it can make rainbows. All it can do is grow slugs, for now. Actually," Benjamin had continued, "the sky has to grow the slugs before it can grow the rainbows."

I squatted down to Benjamin's eye level. "Hello."

"Hi." Benjamin looked at the twigs, then at me. "I was worried you didn't have enough to keep you warm," he said. He held out the twigs.

"Did you collect these yourself?"

"They're the old lilac bush," Benjamin said. "The one in the back. Of our . . . " He struggled, looked at his mother.

"Home," she said. "It's still your home, honey."

Benjamin licked his lips. "We had to . . ." He paused again. "See, what happened was . . . the time had come. For the lilac bush."

I took the frail branches of the ancient lilac bush and thanked him. Benjamin stared at the twigs in my hand for a while. Then he reached over and looked inside the small basket his mother was carrying. I could see pieces of dirty toys, a few cola-can flip tops, half a yo-yo, and other unidentifiable objects only Benjamin could tell you the stories for. Benjamin looked at me, and then he anxiously called his mother's face down so he could whisper. She nodded and said to him, "Meem will understand."

"You tell her."

My friend smiled at me. "Benjamin was going to give you the basket too. But I think he sort of needs to keep what's in the basket. Right, Benjamin?"

I looked at Benjamin and said, "What's inside the basket, it keeps you warm, like the twigs will keep me warm. This way neither one of us will be cold."

Benjamin's smile was like a giant canoe.

"Well," my friend said, sighing. "We have to go, don't we? We've got a lot of unpacking to do, Pumpkin."

"I'm not a pumpkin, Mom."

"Monkey."

"Monkey either."

My friend smiled. "Okay. What are you?"

Benjamin's eyebrows went up and down, and the felt band with the golden horns wiggled. "I'm in disguise," he said.

"Well, come on, Mr. In-Disguise. We've got to get your new bedroom ready."

Benjamin looked at me. "Are you going to use those tonight?" he said, indicating the twigs.

"I don't know," I said. "Should I? Or are they for some special fire?"

"Special fire," Benjamin said.

As they were leaving, my friend turned to me and said, in a low voice, "He's worried about you, Meem. He thinks somebody you love must have died. Actually, he thinks the reason it rained so much last spring was that you needed the sky to cry for you."

After they left, I stood looking after them for I don't know how long, holding them in my mind's eye long after they had departed. Then I heard Manda saying behind my shoulder, "The kid knows what's going on here. How come you don't?"

"I do," I said. "It's just that I can't stand to hear it," I finally admitted, my whole being wrapped in grief. "I just can't stand to hear how She died. My bones can't take it."

I felt Manda hovering as a warp of air near me, a mime of the physical contact she was incapable of. I swallowed, feeling all that was in my belly which I had been fighting off, the unbearable sadness of Her death which I had tried, but failed, to hurl away from me into the mouth of an authority who had the official power to catch Manda and put her away—it swelled and consumed me. When she spoke, it was right next to me, and almost kind. Manda cleared her throat and said, in the same quiet, intimate tone, "Mihalyi gave me the magic words for the Drings. Mihalyi told them to me and . . ."

They were not like any words Manda had ever heard or found in the plastic sheets around her and her sister. They were a different music, like the music Mihalyi would sometimes play for Moms on his viola, and Moms would do this other amazing thing, she would smile, and almost dance, and Manda would feel this thing between them, soft and comforting, kind of like the way the ashes had gently pulsed against her breast, like she was swinging in this invisible hammock between Moms and Mihalyi, who would sometimes sing when he played and those words would tumble out of him. They were perfect words. Words you understood differently from words you knew the meaning of. They were words that turned into colors inside you, and feelings, and made it all right to be human. They even made her tongue feel different when Mihalyi would slowly teach them to her, one by one, and they would roll around her tongue and make it dance while her tiny mother sashayed and all the tongues of woman shimmied with understanding.

"They didn't work," Manda said, her voice utterly flat.

"They didn't . . ."

"That's right, Summacious. They were Honeytime words. Baubo words. Dringing. They were the old song. But the song changed. And they didn't work anymore."

I said, "Because he—Mihalyi—like your father—"

Manda stomped, shaking the floor beneath me. "No! He didn't. Mihalyi never touched me. All this is about is the song. *The words of the song didn't work anymore.* That is all you know and all you need to know."

I felt tears rising to my eyes. "The words of the song didn't work," I repeated, and the sadness Benjamin could feel inside me dislodged itself from my belly.

Manda nodded, speaking in her rasping whisper. "That's right, Summacious. She's dead and the words of the song don't work anymore and the King of the Land of Dring has turned into King Pain. It's the saddest story on earth. No one can bear knowing it's not Honeytime anymore, and there's no Dringing since She died," Manda said.

"Maybe you are my destiny, and maybe I thought I wanted to find it," I said. "But I didn't expect . . ."

"Of course not," Manda said. "You expected cheery capitalism. Destiny as profit. Scrambling for footing on the evolutionary ladder.

Moving up. But you, Summacious, *you* are the magnet turned the wrong way. Your destiny's so *not* happy it's almost communism in disguise," Manda said. "Destiny doesn't take you up. It takes you down, down."

"I wish you'd never showed up. I wish I'd never called you out from the trees. I wish you were still running," I said.

Manda's voice was hushed, melodic with quickening gentleness. "I had to tell someone on your side."

"Tell what?"

"That She's dead."

"Why? And don't tell me I can't ask you why. I have to." Manda nodded. "Okay. Okay. Just this once. Why you have to know is because Her story is the only story that matters."

My stomach churned with wine and smoke and emptiness and despair. "But you haven't even told me who She is!"

Manda said. "Her."

"Her Her Her Her Her," I repeated, hitting my fist in time to each outburst. "Who is Her?"

Manda chewed on her lip. "You know Her," she said.

"Baubo. This pig-faced goddess. That's who you killed. Twenty-seven thousand years ago."

Manda paced, pantherlike. "Look," she finally said. "Baubo was there. Went down with Her. That's all I can tell you. You have to get the rest yourself."

"Why?"

"Destiny doesn't have reasons," Manda said. "Just consequences."

Her

Spent, I went to take a shower.

A shower was not a simple action in my world at that time. The rusted-out shower stall that my traveling landlords refused to replace was not a place where I could wash away anything, let alone my sadness at Her death. I needed cleansing, purging, and my own distance from Manda and her anguished persistence that she was my destiny.

Some form of placental mysticism was in order, waters through which I could pass and emerge on the other side possessed of the courage Manda was correct in saying I lacked. A shower was all I had for such sacred Dew, so I gathered up my things and took off in my car, northward along River Road, heading for the Kingston-Rhinecliff Bridge to the Kingston Y.

The Kingston Y, on the other side of the Hudson River, was as unlikely a sanctuary for sacred Dew as one could conceive. It would never be on a New Age global tour of sacred places, having none of the sex appeal of a Mayan temple or the droopy, mist-swaddled humorlessness of Stonehenge, or the Tantricism of the electromagnetic disturbances reported to occur in the Four Corners area. The Kingston Y has no outward affinity with any indigenous peoples and does not, according to official history, belong to a preindustrial time when magic, not murder, was the medium. No extant chants or rituals to be found there. Just gossip and exchanges among the women about good manicurists, what type of flu is going around, and who's been called up for jury duty. But the Kingston Y was all I had for Dew at the time Manda found me in my cottage in the woods. If this story has any lesson, beyond the amazement of ashes transformed into Dew, it may be not to take the global tour to realize your destiny but to work with what's in your immediate surround, no matter how inadequate or unlikely a vehicle it may seem.

"Inadequate" is virtual flattery when it comes to describing the Kingston Y. Built at the turn of the century on a rocky outcropping, its homeliness was exposed for all to see. One wanted something to hide this monster from sight, but there was a stubborn glory in its proud situation on the hill, a defiant indifference to what people might think about it. Uneven bricks the color of burnt barbecue sauce surrounded windows painted acid yellow. These same bricks mounted upward till they came up against a gutter system of gargantuan proportions, outmoded as Newtonian physics, with four enormous funnels painted the same eyesore yellow. These gutters gave the building the air of some four-legged robotic tarantula.

As further proof of its indifference to public opinion about the beautiful, a wing had been added of poured concrete which had been decorated with a polka-dot tile design and resembled a picnic placemat. Enormous sliding doors in aluminum frames extended on the right side as one approached, and on the left, poured concrete walls fell down to an asphalt parking area. A ruder building I have never known.

Yet inside, up the stairs, through the hallway, past Betty, tough, scrawny-necked gatekeeper, guardian of the baskets, dispenser of locker keys, one entered the senior women's locker room. Inside one could find, on any given day, an Irish grandmother with a rose tattoo above her flaming red pubis who would tell you, if you asked, "It's for my man. Marks his grave"; or a flock of mothers in various stages of pregnancy moving their bellies in one great migratory mass from locker room to pool, where they bounced with gravid elegance through water, their voices rising and falling in secret confidences. There one found the stray woman of forgettable features, forgettable body, who you were never sure was a different woman or the same from one day to the next. Only if you were to sneak a look at her breasts would you have your clue to her identity. For once you had spent some time in the senior women's locker room of the Kingston Y, you realized (if you were honest) that a woman's most distinguishing feature is her breasts. It took less than a minute to know that the ideal breast which you had despaired of not having belongs to a rare few. It took longer for you not only to digest the magnitude of the lie but to grasp that it had denied you your most singular claim to yourself, your particular droop, perch, sway, point, mound, slope, the personality of aureole, experience of nipple, mosaic of vein, hieroglyph of mole, freckle, beauty spot. You could not help but wonder whether the same variations occurred in nether parts, and a surreptitious peek at the Irish grandmother's tattoo and what lay below it was enough to convince any woman that she was as distinct between her legs as she was in her mind and to hint at the possibility that there was to the contours of her desire a shape as unique as each petal of each flower hidden between a circus of thigh in the senior women's locker room of the Kingston Y.

Of all these bodies in various stages of dress and undress, identity and anonymity, mated, singular, aged and agelessness, there was one who reigned supreme. She was short, her skin the color of roses and copper folding in waves of flesh, a tidal event rolling from her breasts which covered her entire chest, her nipples at the very bottom like bell clangers, her belly abundant, her thighs cornucopias, and above all this, always naked, a small head with tufts of hot red hair perched doll-like, delicate, with a pair of enormous eyes as quick to sadness and joy as a mime. Her name was Rulla.

It was Benjamin's mother who had first taken me to the Y. Rulla was the first person we saw when we entered the senior women's locker room. She was sitting on a bench beside the Irish grandmother, who was sporting pink lace lingerie that day. Rulla was studying the rose tattoo as the grandmother, svelte, curved, tough, muscled, and not to be lied to, was explaining, " . . . shot, damn fool. Trying to be a hero, thank you very much. Had no business, with six kids, getting involved with that godforsaken mad bunch, those crazy IRA, you know what I'm saying? Shot. For no good reason. I'm not saying I'm not for freedom, mind. But a child whose father's going to go be stupid enough to think he can be a hero and get his great-grand-self killed won't ever have time to be worrying about freedom. He'll be too hungry to be thinking about anything but his stomach, you know what I'm sayin'? Got this put on the day I buried him. Swore I'd never be with another man, and I put roses on his grave back home and a rose on his grave here where he used to like to bury himself, you get my meaning."

Rulla nodded. Then, in a thick accent, she said, "I like very much this . . ." She indicated the Irish grandmother's underwear. "This is what you wear for yourself? No. This is no dead man's flower," she said, pointing to the rose.

"I'm in America now," she said. "New life, eh?" She winked.

Rulla then looked up to see my friend and me. She smiled at us and nodded. "I am Rulla," she said. "You come here to this place, it is very good for women."

The senior women's locker room was the center of a vast network of corridors stretching off and up and down in a labyrinth as disorienting and deceptive as the original of Daedalus. It took us weeks before we knew our way around, and even then, when we had the main pathways laid down in our minds, we would often find ourselves on the wrong side of our destination, in a room we had not known existed. Once we opened a door onto sudden air.

Hidden within this devious maze of grayish-white, antiseptic routes doubling back around themselves as they spiraled past the whirlpool room which spun away from the spiraling staircase and seemed to float in its own orbit with its own gravity, then past the swimming pool in all its underground aqua glory, up some more stairs, taking a left at a fork in the hall, one reached at the end of this labyrinth, exhausted and confused as Ariadne without her thread, the dark, secret heart of the women's steam room, the eternal spring of what I had for Dew.

We had come upon it one day by accident owing to an event which took place in the women's weight room. The weight room was hidden in the upper reaches of the Y, and many went only as far as the entry, climbing steep stairs to it and then, at the threshold, turning around and going down the stairs, then back up, then down. You must stretch your mind back to envision this weight room. No treadmills with computerized panels. No all-flex machines. Not even Nautilus had arrived at the Kingston Y weight room. But what they did have was something far more remarkable than all these machines put together.

It was an artifact from the era of our childhood, an anthropological treasure from an era in which women did not go to the office in tailored suits only to hit their coiffed heads against the glass ceiling. Then women but dreamed that they went to the office, where they sat in their assigned cubicle wearing a Maidenform bra. My friend and I had grown up in front of our black-and-white television sets watching *Queen for a Day* for cues as to what we needed to do to become rulers of our anatomical destiny. The advertisements which ran during *Queen for a Day* held as much information about the standards of queenliness as the show, probably more; for in between the sagas of the contestants we would hear about such dire fates as vacuums that did not work, stains on carpets impossible to remove, the effervescent miracle of Polident for those cursed with removable teeth. But of all these alarming prophecies for the '50s housewife, the worst was "the heartbreak of psoriasis," a fate which each of us, though my friend was growing up in the Jewish suburbs of Long Island and I was in Washington, D.C., firmly ensconced in Kennedy's Camelot, dreaded.

Psoriasis. One did not have to know what it was to know that this word described something unbearably sad. Psoriasis sounded like grief itself, a word of lament, with the sibilants and the long, crying vowels between, an ancient Greek word of soft, echoing rhymes with "sorrow" and "sister," "sorority," "sadness," and "misery" gathered up into it. These hidden rhymes embedded in psoriasis carried the fullest expression of feminine anguish known to all women everywhere, a condition of their very skin which bespoke miseries untold. Psoriasis, this terrible fate of the skin of women everywhere—heartbreak indeed. The promise of a magic cream that would wipe away all the scars and agonies of the psoriasis to which our skin was heiress, the eons of mourning for our vulnerable epithelial selves eclipsed by a future of the joy of skin cured of heartbreak— miracle, redemption of suffering, savior of womankind.

Oh, but the magic cream that would end the heartbreak of psoriasis was not all that the great pharmaceutical god of feminine products had to

offer. There was among his armamentarium of remedies against all female corporeal sufferings a machine so marvelous, so wondrous, that one
could hardly believe it existed. A woman who had access to this machine
was guaranteed not to spread at the hips. The widening of her pelvis
which was the consequence of giving birth need not be inevitable anymore. The settling fat around her hips which was an artifact of the ne-
cessity of the mother to survive disaster, global ruin, famine beyond the
cave, could be reduced if a woman—an enlightened woman—an industrial woman—would spend a few minutes a day on this magic machine.
After all, women no longer had to worry about survival since their migration from the cave to the suburb.

My friend and I, in our respective ethnic neighborhoods, avidly
studying *Queen for a Day* for clues to our future, had both watched in
amazement as a woman stepped onto this magic machine to demonstrate
its wonders. She placed a wide canvas belt snugly around her hips, swad-
dling them in its ample width. We watched as she carefully determined
the optimum stimulation she could stand and turned the hip-reducing
machine on. The canvas belt vibrated, the woman's postpartum hips jiggled, and, with a smile on her face and her voice shaking from the machine, she informed the host, "I-i-i-it e-e-eve-e-een fe-e-e-els g-g-g-
good!"

At the top of the stairs, just beyond the threshold of the Kingston Y
weight room, were three of these very machines. When we first came
upon them, we stood in awe. We could not believe they actually existed
in the world outside '50s television. Yet if any place would hold these
treasures of the housewife queens, it would be the Kingston Y. They were
aqua-colored, with chrome paneling molded like wings, reminding one
of old Cadillacs. The belts were clearly the originals, for they were frayed
and stretched from what my friend and I quickly realized was frequent
use.

"My god," my friend said. "They're real!"

We touched them lightly, like the uninitiated tampering with the
props of holiness. These machines had awed us when we were girls anxious about the arrival of hips and children and the widening they implied,
with burning questions (as we passed the yellow-and-black signs mark-

ing Bomb Shelter) about survival and whether maybe there was not a possible return to the cave coming, and coming soon. There was something numinous and taboo about the machines. We could not, for weeks, bring ourselves to use them.

Then, one day, believing ourselves at the cutting edge of a feminine evolution as we worked out on the new portable gym the Y had installed, we caught sight of a woman approaching the hip-reducing machine. My friend made faces at me, jerked her head in the direction of the machines. I turned to see a very generous hipped elderly woman in pink sweatpants looking around her. I immediately turned my head back around, able to make out the pink figure in the corner of my vision. My friend started to talk to me, signaling to make conversation to let the woman think we were not paying attention to her.

The pink woman hesitated and then, perhaps deciding that we were preoccupied, or perhaps to initiate the young kids on the block into the hidden wonders of the Y, she stepped onto the platform and slipped the canvas belt around her multitudinous hips. There followed an agonizingly long period of adjustment as the woman struggled to make the overstretched canvas belt stay up. She finally managed to position herself at the edge of the platform, thus creating enough tension for the canvas belt to fit snugly. There was a moment, an intake of breath, a quick glance at us, and then the pink woman, her back toward us, turned it on.

The vibration of the canvas belt set every cell of fat around the woman's hips hidden under pink into motion. The quality of jiggle was astounding. The pink woman's hips were a carnival of pulse, quiver, and shake. Her face was turned away from us, and so we were at liberty to stare at the way the hips sent trembling tremors down her thighs. The canvas belt threatened to fall away from the sheer force of all that pink flesh set into motion, and the woman caught at the sides of the machine, holding on, as if she would levitate as effortlessly as the piano. As she grabbed the sides of the machine, we heard a distinct moan coming from her.

My friend's mouth fell open as we watched the woman begin to rock—barely detectable beneath that camouflage of quivering pink—and then, suddenly, sooner than expected, we watched as the woman's entire body imploded in orgasm. Her knees clasped together, and, against all the powers of electricity and engineering, this old, overweight woman in pink, as she came, held herself utterly still for a few seconds while the machine rocked on the floor. The canvas belt fell off her hips in the still force of her ecstasy, the power of her pleasure triumphing over the mechanical forces of reduction of the bones which spread, inevitably, with childbirth.

Then, with a delicate sense of ceremony, she turned off the machine, stepped out of the canvas belt, and, grabbing a nearby stair railing to keep her balance, she walked slowly and with great dignity down the stairs and away.

I had the feeling that suddenly, anything was possible. If women could have orgasms in advertisements on '50s television, well, the world which we had thought closed opened up as wide and yielding as those pulsating pelvises big American companies were paying a lot of air-time money to show us.

"Meem?" my friend said, using my family nickname. "We grew up watching married women having orgasms on television and thinking our mothers never did."

"This is a historical problem. A serious historical problem," I said.

I then caught my friend's eyes. They were sparkling. "You're not," I said.

"Of course I am," she said. "I'm over thirty."

"I don't think you can measure ecstasy," I said.

"That's what all those sponsors on TV probably thought too."

She ran over to the machine. She peeked down the stairs, catching the last lingering image of the old woman's paradisiacal pink, and then studied the machine. We were the only people in the weight room, and we knew from experience that few entered, but, nervous that we would be discovered, I posted myself at the top of the stairs while my friend fussed with the machine.

"It's Goldilocks," she said. "It's the Goldilocks dilemma of the right size."

"I thought you were never supposed to admit that size matters," I said.

"Actually," she said, "you're supposed to say it's big, no matter what size it is. That's the American way of ecstasy. And this," my friend said as she held out the canvas belt on the first of the three machines, "is big." It was the same one that had just yielded for the woman in pink an experience that had definitely made her feel like a queen this day. My friend stepped onto the platform and hoisted the belt up around her hips. But she ran two miles a day, and though she had a child, the belt fell away from her hips no matter how far out on the edge of the platform she stood. Cursing, she then tried the second machine, leaning back to see if that would work. But she fell off the platform. No platform, no vibration. It was the third machine which proved to be "just right."

My friend took a deep breath. She put her hand on the power switch and, closing her eyes, she was about to let her rip when her eyes popped open. "I thought I heard someone. On the stairs."

"Me too," I said. I looked down the empty, silent stairwell.

"Well?"

"I can't tell. Maybe."

My friend stepped off the platform. "Maybe I should just, you know, test it to see if it works before . . ."

"Good idea."

She flicked the switch. Zip. She jiggled it, but nothing happened.

We went back to the locker room to change into our bathing suits. It was the hour when the secretaries flocked like birds to the long mirror, their makeup in plastic cases lined up on the counter. They leaned forward, stretching their mouths in that curious way women do when they are applying mascara. Others teased and flounced and sprayed their hair. My friend and I passed behind them on our way to the lockers. My friend stopped to look at this ritual before the mirror. It would later show up as a painting; now it was a gathering to her eyes.

As I turned to call for her, I felt someone bump into me. Her perfume came into my nostrils, and I felt the touch of her arm on mine. But when I turned to see who it was, there was nothing but air. And the perfume, lingering. I looked around to see a tall, red-headed woman, her back to me, heading for the door. Tucked under one arm, she held her plastic basket with her Y clothes. By now my friend had finished gathering to her eyes what she would make into art and was standing beside me, following mine. We watched as the red-headed woman opened the door and slipped through.

"Another long-armed woman," my friend said.

It was part of the elaborate lexicon of our friendship that there were two types of women: long-armed and short. Long-armed women could negotiate the locker-room door while holding their Y basket without having to resort to using their hips. My friend and I were both short-armed women who had to hold the door with hips and the basket with two hands. Long-armed women were, in our view, capable of holding whatever they wanted. Short-armed women like us could never hold enough.

Before I quite knew what I was doing, I was racing out the door after her, or maybe it was just after her perfume. As I opened the door, I saw her ahead of me, down the long corridor under construction. I felt her perfume move over me as I followed, my friend behind me, calling, "Meem! Meem? Wait!"

Ahead of me, the redhead walked through the door, which opened onto sudden air.

I followed, my friend racing to catch up to me.

We stood on the other side of the construction door, the sign Women's Steam Room directly before us. My friend opened the door; steam enfolded us. The beautiful long-armed woman with her faint but familiar perfume was nowhere to be found. We entered the mist, closed the door behind us, and lay in the dark.

The steam room was kind to my friend and me. It had a way of taking into itself all the grief we brought to it. The injustices of being short-armed women were passed back and forth inside the penumbral mist—what we had reached for and dropped, who we had held on to and lost, the longing to embrace more, the fear of what we would lose if we did. We brought our stories of all we had been able to hold of life and love we had dropped along the way to this tiny wet hut where the walls cried our tears. The long-armed redhead seemed to have known that my friend and I needed to discover dimensions of ecstasy one can only measure in the dark, where no one could see us, not even ourselves.

After a while, our minds adrift in the mist, my friend spoke. "My husband hasn't touched me since Benjamin was born," she said softly. If she cried, I didn't hear it. The steam room masked her tears with its own. After another interval of silence, she said, "That's a long time, not to be touched."

"Long time," I said.

That overcast late November day when the waters of the Hudson were swollen with the glacial slabs of ice, as slow, ponderous, and intractable as my grief about Her, I found the steam room empty as we had the first day. I entered and stripped. I turned the steam on high and lay down in my corner to surrender myself to unconsciousness—unconsciousness, I should write, beyond the reach of Manda, an unconsciousness without biography or story, the darkest recess where the dew of the cosmos is made. To surrender to unconsciousness in the steam room was to reach beyond our idea of the unconscious into a region as strange as the wrong side of the moon, a region of Before.

I had lain there a while, long enough to drink from the hose provided and settle myself down again and to feel a calming, clearing effect; long enough, certainly, for arguments with my destiny to evaporate and my bones to melt away into pleasure, not terror, the alchemy of this sad, dewy trace of women working its magic on my body, which had been ravaged by Manda's voice, when the door opened. In the dark, I knew I was but a shadow inside a shadow. Protocol said I should identify myself with my voice. From the cadences of "oooh" and "aahs," I could tell that two women had entered, and, like almost all the other patrons of the Y, they were elderly.

One of them said, "I like it like this."

"Is it dangerous?"

Yes, I thought. It's very dangerous. The walls cry for you, ecstasy is measured by invisible instruments, and bones become milk.

"Oh, no, it's restful. Let's leave the lights off just this once."

I didn't even know there were lights. I was not surprised when the two older women started talking, for I knew how, with my friend, the lulling hissing of the steam and the dark engendered in us conversations we would have nowhere else. The women sat themselves near the door and the drinking hose, and in the shadows I could make out the outlines of flowered bathing suits over ample bodies, the same proportions as Queen Pink, and something strange on the head of one of them which it took me a moment to identify as an old-fashioned bathing cap with the snapping chinstrap dangling off to one side. I was about to say something when one of them said, "I'm going to give Daryl a big surprise tonight when he gets off duty."

"You make him one of your meat loafs?"

"I went to Woodstock, Muriel," the voice said. Her voice sounded like chocolate-chip cookie dough tastes.

"Hippies," Muriel said in a voice like cardboard. "What'd you go all the way to Woodstock for?"

I could hear my heart pounding, and I knew I needed to get out soon. "Silk underwear."

Muriel, to my surprise, gave out a hoot. "Pat Edwards," Muriel said, "I swear you've gone completely out of your mind since you got that phone call from Freddie Van Heusen. What's a woman your age doing buying silk underwear in Woodstock?"

"I am pleasing my man and myself," said Pat Edwards of the sweet dough voice.

"Oh, hell," said Muriel. "What you want to do something stupid like that for?"

I knew what she was planning to do once she put that silk underwear on. Lying there risking a heart attack rather than reveal myself, I listened as Pat Edwards described for her friend Muriel, whose other parts had been turned into cardboard as well, the preconscious, primordial steam of Before rising up around us, her trip to the underwear store in Woodstock. "She stocks large sizes, Muriel, how about that?"

"Large enough?" said Muriel, a woman who had clearly given up on the possibility of silk against her skin long ago.

"Plenty large enough," Pat Edwards said. "And there's private dressing rooms with mirrors in them."

"Oh, Lord." Muriel wiped the steam from her face and snapped at her bathing cap.

"The woman who runs it," Pat Edwards was saying, "she's so nice, Muriel, really. She told me that she was so happy I came in."

"You spend a lot of money?"

"Well, I spent much more than I planned to, but that's not what it was."

Muriel had perfected the art of the "harrumph."

Pat Edwards, with the fervor of any recent convert, was not to be discouraged. "She said to me that it made her so happy to see a woman my age enjoying my body and taking care of it. She even told me that there's a goddess, she named the lingerie store after this goddess, I can't pronounce it, it begins with a V, that's all I remember—" (Muriel here snorted, condemning all words referring to women which began with V) "—who was big, a big goddess. She said that historically, goddesses are big."

Muriel made a variation on her harrumph, communicating utter skepticism about all things goddesslike.

"But there are," Pat Edwards insisted. "There are lots and lots of goddesses, and they're most of them really big, big as you and me."

I had maybe—maybe—a minute before my heart exploded.

"She said all kinds of interesting things," Pat Edwards went on. "Why, did you know, Muriel, there was a goddess, she had a pig face and she used to dance and make women laugh during childbirth. Isn't that just such a wonderful thought, Muriel? Wouldn't you have liked to laugh?"

"Don't trust my heart in this heat much longer," Muriel said. She lifted her bulk from the lower bench where she had been sitting. She opened the door, letting in the light. I held myself (naked) perfectly still. "You getting out?"

"Just another few minutes for me," Pat said.

I lay there in the dark with Pat Edwards and Baubo. It was as if Manda's voice and story had been released from my sweat into the Dew where Baubo had landed on Pat Edwards's skin. Inside the steam room, the story slipped out of my hands.

Pat Edwards finally arose. She bent down and sipped at the drinking hose, and then she opened the door. "You want me to leave it open or closed?"

If it is possible to blush when one's entire body is pink from steam and heat, I blushed. "Open," I coughed.

Pat Edwards said, "I think next time I'll try it naked too. After all, we're all women here, aren't we?"

"Or goddesses," I said. "Like Baubo."

"I was trying to remember her name—Baubo!" Pat Edwards laughed a rich, marvelous laugh, which I could hear reverberating off the tile walls as she walked away, my authority over the story dissolving in the Dew.

It was almost dark when I emerged from the Y. Where there had been colorlessness and the scraggly tangles of barren winter nests, there was now the smooth, undulating outline of the mountains against the winter-set sky. The day's cloud cover had been pierced, and a cobalt strand divided the voluptuous curves of the Berkshires and Catskills from the sky. I reached the bridge as the moon was rising. The frigid crusts of ice lay in irregular shapes on the surface of the river, while the pristine stars shone above, impervious and indifferent to the hazards of human history. But the night sky I saw on the inside of my eyes was thick as soot, starless, and belonged to neither the world of humanity nor nature. As I crossed over the bridge, I saw the night above Gwen's sister in her dream, as she stood on the railing of the bridge, battling the serpent. And I knew what the night inside her dream was: the body of the Panther purring in a sleek gloat of triumph, knowing the dream's outcome before the dreamer awoke.

My mind adrift in steam and goddesses and dream, I almost crashed into the back of a car stalled in the middle of the bridge. I jerked to a stop. Images of disaster flooded my mind: the disaster of the car, the disasters which might befall me, a single woman alone, in the middle of the highest bridge over the Hudson, stepping out into the cold, the disaster of Gwen's dream. Hating myself for my cowardice, I backed my car up a foot or so (there was no one behind me) and poked myself into the on-coming lane. No cars were coming the other direction, and so I drove around. As I pulled out, I saw there were two cars remaining. The first one had no lights.

The lightless car in front was empty. The car behind it had two peo-ple in the front seat, a man and a woman. The woman was looking at the empty car, perched almost exactly at the highest midway point of the bridge. She was shaking her head and shrugging her shoulders. It was impossible to tell whether she was remarking on the mystery of the empty car or whether she was its owner, shrugging at the man's sugges-tions for help. I passed by, telling myself that the sensible thing to do would be to notify the gas station up ahead at the intersection with Route 9G.

But it seemed that my mind was on a different mission. It was teem-ing with life-out-of-sequence as the Fertile Crescent ca. 6000 B.C. and Chicago ca. 1950 and a Panther, twenty-seven thousand years old, all con-verged on Rhinebeck, New York, in the 1980s. As I drove straight ahead, my mind leapt into the future. Baubo was not there, ahead in time, but abandoned behind me, on the other side of the river. No ugly belly dancer who reminded women, when they were in the humiliating squat of birth, grunting piggy grunts, of the ridiculous inside the beautiful as she shim-mied and teased, parody and celebration embodied in a dancing feminine clown. When their bodies are most distorted by the process of bringing life out of the surround of woman into the Great Surround of the world, Baubo would not be present to restore to women the memory of when their bodies had been the willowy amphora of Aphrodite. And when Baubo is no longer, the wooden benches in the women's steam room of the Kingston Y would return into the earth from which they were hewn. The canvas belts, the secret instruments of the ecstasy of Queen Pink, would shred into fibers for ants to make nests, crows to mate, and ter-mites to germinate their way through, leaving no trace.

What all this had to do with destiny and murder, I did not know. All I know now is that once I left the steam room the same evening Pat Edwards was preparing herself to become Baubo, time and place bent in on themselves; dreams belonging to another woman appeared inside my own eyes as The Murder Mystery breached the boundaries of reality as I had been instructed in it. The same stars hung over the Fertile Crescent then, Rhinebeck now, and the Panther had the power to hide them behind her murderous form inside an astrologer's dream which I was able to see as though I were the dreamer, Manda the dream.

As I left the stranded car behind me on the highest point of the bridge and descended to the other side and the railings too lowered themselves, I glimpsed the crusts of ice along the riverbanks sparkling in the moonlight. And suddenly I knew another fact about another woman's dream: The moon could be hidden by the pantherine sky, but not destroyed. When the moon is a blank in the sky, it is not gone, but lies shattered in pieces on the river just as my own heart and mind were shattering into multiple realities. I told myself, though Baubo will die, there will always be a moon which is west to someone somewhere, east to another, and not even the Panther, inside a dream, inside a cottage, inside history, can erase it.

These thoughts were a peculiar solace to my spirit, all I had for comfort that night when I apprehended that I would not be able to hold reality intact much longer. It was breaking up, and in the gaps between dream, history, and the present, I would find the Panther and her victims, Baubo and the elusive Her, if I were brave—or foolish—enough to enter those gaps in the cosmos to look for them.

I did not know, that night crossing the bridge after Baubo joined me in the steam room, that I no longer had a choice in the matter. I did not know I was going to slip away from this reality through the widening gaps and join the Panther in the dark vein where for twenty-seven thousand years murder has continued, uninterrupted, and will continue for another twenty-seven thousand years. But I knew that I would not find Her unless I did. Would my love for Her be strong enough to carry me to Her without dying myself in my quest through the gaps between multiplying realities beginning to appear to my eyes outside the walls of my solitary cottage, inviting me into their realms, exempt from time and place, with no promise of return? To survive, I would have to become the moon myself, adept at lunacy. And I was terrified to risk my sanity to undertake a quest for no living, dancing Her, but for the Panther's dead victim. Finding a goddess resurrected in a steam room was rupture enough of my precarious sanity. But deliberately to enter into the same cosmic vein as that resurrection to track down a corpse—surely that was lunacy personified according to anyone's lexicon?

Just ahead of me, the turnoff to River Road appeared, a hole in the woods leading to a dark tunnel. Directly before me, Route 9 and Route 9G intersected, and there was a huge car dealership. I could see its lights from as far away as this turn off to River Road. Even the dark winding road lit only by the moon which might lure me farther into madness was better than those glaring lights ahead. I checked my rearview mirror, preparing to slow down to make the turn, when I saw the car behind me, the man's car, approaching.

The woman was no longer with him. He was alone, and moving very fast. He pulled out and passed me, zooming by. Was this the speed of escape or the urgent speed of rescue? Was the woman back there in a freezing car, with no heat, waiting? Or . . . was Gwen's dream happening?

I pulled over onto the broad knoll and stopped.

Those lights. Those hideous transgressors against the natural dark, those enormous buzzing eyes, which never close, shining upon the chrome hoods, undoing cyclical life, holding night in hock to day—I hated them with a wild, inexplicable vehemence. The wonder of a goddess alive in the steam room, the wonder of a boy who could feel my sadness better than I, and my persistent, grievous love for Her coalesced. It seemed as though Baubo and Benjamin both knew Her too, and were aligning themselves inside to force me to turn away from the lights, back to the woman on the bridge inside the darkness of disaster and dream.

The car was empty.

My mind hurtled itself out of my body, breaking like fireworks over the bridge. I saw myself turning around in the middle of the bridge to chase the man in the car down in classic television car-chase style, committing in real life an act of subliminal advertising. He in the Ford, I in my Honda, would chase each other under the glare of the Ford dealership. I could almost hear the smooth, oily basso profundo of the voice-over saying, in reference to my Japanese model following the American model, "Don't believe what they tell you. At Ford, we've always been ahead of the imports." At this point, the camera would show the Ford pulling into the dealership. From the Ford would then emerge a male actor whose physique was a perfect match to the narrator's voice, while from the Honda would emerge . . . well . . . me, hair in post-steam room disarray, sweatpants in fugitive pink, no makeup, and I would watch as the man went around the other side door to let out a beautiful, coiffed, long-legged, long-armed woman with long . . . red . . .

The woman in the car. I had not been able to see her face, but I had seen her hair. Grief swept through my vacant breast as it had the first night Manda arrived. I had to tell someone. Someone in authority. The police. Then I remembered: Daryl was on duty this evening.

Only Pat Edwards and I knew what Daryl would find when he came home. It seemed cruel to postpone the discovery by the deputy chief of police of Rhinebeck that he had been married to a goddess-in-hiding all these years. Daryl was probably, at this very moment, wondering whether the night of oral amazement when Pat had gone down on him for the first time in their thirty-seven years together was an aberration, a weird mutation from their years of marriage, not to be repeated. Or whether the nights would nurture her illicit passion like nature nurtures a useful limb, and their marriage would evolve into something of rambunctious splendor. It is very likely that Daryl was preparing himself for the useless mutation theory rather than the useful rambunctious-splendor one, because Daryl, like any other American, had a limited idea of what useful was. He couldn't see the purpose (evolutionarily speaking) of pleasure. Though Daryl had never been told in so many words, he didn't need to be told that evolution of the species did not depend upon oral sex. Such delight was an anti-evolutionary event; the innocent pleasure of sucking on any part that seemed to offer the most sucking possibilities, unnecessary. Sex suck-play was one of those extras in life, like an electric can opener, which a man like Daryl found hard to justify.

In Daryl, these wonderings about the nature of evolution and the purpose of play were contained in the three words he said to himself as he looked at the clock, waiting for six o'clock to come so that he could get home and find out: "Better not hope."

If I didn't go to the authorities, Daryl could leave on time and get back to his Pat, who was going to prove his system of evolutionary ethics inadequate. As I turned the car on the bridge and raced after the Ford into the evil Land of Clyks, a vision formed in my mind like a shield. I saw Pat, Baubo incarnate, standing in her kitchen, dressed only in lilac silk and perfume. I filled my eyes with the sight of her, shadowy in the cheap fluorescent-tube light of her kitchen. It was a practical light, for Pat and Daryl Edwards were, above all, practical people. They had only two types of candles in their house: the emergency utility one, a stump of white wax, and the ones in their plastic covers in the drawer of the pie cupboard they'd inherited from Daryl's mother, purchased every year at the post-Christmas sale at the Kingston mall, waiting to be unsheathed at their annual Christmas dinner. Into their house I put, with my imagination, another candle, purchased in Woodstock the same day as the lilac silk and her revelation that she possessed goddess dimensions. She would light the candle; it would release the fragrance of gardenia. The scent would be everything Pat Edwards hoped it would be, a scent neither she nor Daryl had ever experienced before. For Daryl and Pat, you see, had the same idea of hope; it was that thing which was both sweet and strange at the same time. Their marriage was a good one, durable against all the elements that corrode hope every day. I saw her carrying the gardenia-scented candle from the kitchen and up the stairs to the bedroom. She would put the candle down on the bedside table and stare at it for a while, pleased with its mutable reflections around the room. She would then go to the window to draw the curtains. For Pat wanted the room honey toned, and she (and I) wanted it that way for reasons neither she nor I could explain. It was not that the honeyed light was exciting; almost the opposite—it was comforting. She would turn from the window to see the bedroom bathed in pale amber, the flame flickering, and swell in the glow of a Dring, waiting for Daryl to come home.

The sound of a car . . . Daryl . . . no, not Daryl. The chimerical vision disappeared as the sound of a car interrupted my fantasy of a fictitious deputy police chief discovering a new theory of evolution when he returned home to find his wife turned into a goddess. The transformation of a bedroom into Manda's Dring inside the home of a couple whose lives

I was conjuring out of a few words of an interrupted conversation in the smoke shop about Freddie Van Heusen's obscene phone calls broke apart like the moon on the river. And as obscenity in one reality could emerge into a song of feminine ecstasy, old as Baubo, young as Aphrodite, I was slipping into the noumenal world against my will as the sound of a car inside my vision, carrying the goddess's unlikely, innocent consort, became Manda's Clyks. All I was envisioning about the purpose of delight in another evolutionary channel was eclipsed.

I saw the flashing lights in my rearview mirror. I pulled over and slammed my hand against the dash. As my imagination frantically created a scene of a woman preparing herself for sexual ecstasy, as if such a vision had the power not only to alter the story of human evolution but also to carry me safely into the darkness to find Her on the other side of a shard of moon floating on water, I had completely forgotten that this area of the road was a speed trap. It must have been the end of the month, when revenues were low, for them to be out at this time of night. As I stopped, I looked ahead at the intersection. The light changed to green, and the man in the Ford rushed ahead.

A policeman approached.

Just don't be Daryl. Let me still pretend Daryl is opening the front door and grumbling to himself about the cold as he dutifully and habitually hooks his jacket over the hallway hook. And then, as he straightens the wisps of his thinning hair after he removes his acrylic knit cap, the strands poking upright on his head in comic prefigurations of his imminent arousal, he reminds himself of his evolutionary position: Better not hope. But before he says those words, he turns around to see his wife standing naked but for a shiny lilac thing draped over her enormous body. And Daryl is too bedazzled by the goddess before him to limit what he can hope for from his unremarkable life. Let me bring my vision to fruition, please, I said to myself, having no idea to what god or goddess I was making supplication.

My supplication was answered by that Mouth for Restoration Tragedies, filling up the window, leaving nothing in my view but its beautiful shape. "License and registration, please." I handed them over as sweat trickled down over my ribs. Those lips said, "It's cold. I'll be back,"

74

and the Chief took the official pieces of my identity with him to his squad car. I watched in my rearview mirror as he wrote out my speeding ticket. *She's dead.* The words brought me back to the hollowness of the grief I had felt the first night when I had told him, and with the grief came Benjamin's worry that I needed things to keep me warm. I was afraid that the beautiful mouth would return and those lips would find a hysterical female, crying about a woman who was dead whose name and identity she did not know but whose loss was beyond endurance, asking him to help her find Her.

I swallowed air, trying to control myself. It seemed to help. Then into my nostrils came his scent, the purely masculine scent of his whiskers carrying the imprint of his musk in their tiny glands. He leaned farther down this time, to hand me the ticket. The speeding ticket appeared before me, and if there is any emblem of authority in this world, it is a speeding ticket. I could not help but chuckle at this talisman of the actual before me, and the chuckle made me forget about his mouth. I looked out the window. His eyes were enormous and black; full brows arched over them. Everything on his face was exaggerated, larger than it needed to be, as if he had been given a face intended to convey emotions from the amphitheater's center all the way to the farthest reaches of the farthest row. It was a face that did not require a close-up but, instead, was suited to a time when there were no instruments to move in upon the human to reveal the subtle range of emotion.

My heart was pounding, my desire to pass on the message from the Panther to this face that belonged to another time and place beginning to win out over all fear, when he said, "You know, you really shouldn't smoke."

"It's a hazard of my profession," I said.

"What's that?"

Evolutionary theorist? Dream invader? Disciple in the noumenal arts of multiplying realities? Active hallucinator of the authority looking at me? Death detective?

"Writer," I said. "I'm working on a murder mystery."

"Funny. You don't look like the murder-mystery type."

"You don't look like a policeman."

"Yeah, a lot of people, they tell me that. It's the Greek in me. My mother's side," he said. "Look. You can't be driving this fast on black ice."

"There was a woman . . ."

"A woman . . . ?"

"Alone. On the bridge."

He nodded. "I'll go check. You remember what I said about the black ice. It's fatal more times than not. I don't want to be meeting you next time in an accident."

The following morning, I sat down at the Selectric sarcophagus and lit up a cigarette, as usual. The draft of The Murder Mystery was piling up, acquiring a satisfying heft and size. The sight of all that canary-yellow newsprint was reassuring the morning after the events on the bridge. I reminded myself that I was in the throes of creative inspiration and shouldn't be surprised to be imagining that things were happening in the Rhinebeck around me which were happening in the Rhinebeck in my novel.

The Rhinebeck in the novel was the immaculate Main Street of the first night, when I saw myself going to the authorities and telling a fictive police chief about a murder. Fictive, I repeated to myself, fictive police chief. There were no goddesses in The Murder Mystery, and certainly no Baubo, and—I reminded myself—no Freddie Van Heusen making obscene phone calls. Therefore: no mouth open for Restoration tragedy. I thumbed through the manuscript, reorienting myself to the Rhinebeck I had created. I was skimming through my passable prose when I came upon a chase scene through the woods. I read more carefully. "Daryl" was chasing the "Panther" through the woods, some woman who was wearing a black leather jacket. I read on until I reached the point in the scene when the "Panther" gave up running, exhausted, and collapsed at the base of a tree. Daryl caught up with her. A brief dialogue followed:

"Hunting season," Daryl managed to say between breaths. "Dangerous, leather, dark color like that." The woman sitting at the base of the tree brushed her hands through her hair, which fell back over her eyes. Daryl went on, "Lost a kid just last week. Hunter thought he was a deer. Don't want a repeat."

The woman took out a pack of cigarettes and lit one up. Daryl studied her as she smoked, taking her appearance in, her heavy boots, tight jeans, peculiar white shirt, the leather coat. He couldn't make out her face, obscured by her dark hair, but he could see that her cheeks were eerily pale, especially for someone who had been running as hard as she had. Daryl was struck by how she did not cough. Most people, he thought, can't smoke after running without coughing. She said, "That's why you're chasing me? Warn me about the hunters?"

"Was," Daryl said. "Figured you were one of these crazy cross-country joggers, these marathon types."

The woman chuckled. "I am, in a way. Been running for a long time."

"In those shoes?"

She made no answer. She dropped the cigarette butt on the ground, studying her own foot encased in the boot. Daryl moved in closer while she was absorbed. She was rubbing the last of the loosened tobacco into the dirt when she said, "Close enough now?" Daryl froze. She stood up slowly, gliding her spine along the tree for support. "Think maybe you're still a little too far away," she said as she extended both her hands out in front of her. "You look like the kind of man whose mother taught him to be polite."

"She did," Daryl said, taking a step closer. "But you've been watching too many movies. I don't carry cuffs." She dropped her hands.

"I'm so tired," she said. "You can't imagine how long I've been running."

"What you running from?"

"To," she said quickly. "To you."

"Me?"

"Aren't you the authority who can lock me up?"

"Have to have more of a reason than you wanting a rest."

"Murder enough reason?"

I sat back, lighting a cigarette. I let the scene fall down through me, like the ashes it would eventually become, slowly absorbing Manda's surrender to the authorities. I must have known that she had let herself be caught, since I had written the scene. But it seemed new information to me. This scene, like all the others in The Murder Mystery, had been "dictated" to me by Manda as I transcribed her silently transmitted images and words through my fingers, clacking on the keys of the Selectric as fast as I could to keep up with her tumbling, implosive voice. I had been telling myself that the rapidity of this transcription of the murder plot from Manda to me, the author, was no more than the heightened intensity of creative process when the artist is lost in an altered state in which everything flows effortlessly—inspiration.

But as I sat there, reading unfamiliar prose I had written while in this altered state, I grew uneasy. I looked back at the scene in which Manda held out her arms to Daryl, confessing the crime to him almost as swiftly as she had confessed it to me. I could not escape the sensation that I had not been inspired by Manda but had inspired her—breathed her in to me. And in the same way that I did not know the system for counting my breaths, or what a breath was, in my dream about destiny, I had been writing The Murder Mystery without knowing what I was doing, what the plot was, breathing Manda in without knowing what a "Manda breath" was.

I looked through more pages of the manuscript. I made a mess of the sequencing as I frantically searched for whatever it was I was looking for. Finally, the pages strewn all over the desk, I put my head in my hands as I had seen Manda do many times, surrendering to the trap in which Manda had managed to snare me.

There is another authority.

I looked up at the sound of a voice, expecting to see Manda. The cottage was empty. I waited for Manda to appear, knowing her well enough by now to guess that she would enjoy chortling over her victory. I could almost hear her saying, "You got a hell of a situation there, Summacious. Daryl isn't the kind of a guy who is going to feel comfortable with a self-confessed murderer running around. He's going to get the story out of me, and you know what? It isn't going to be that difficult, either. As I trust you have already come to appreciate about me, I like telling stories. My sister, she couldn't get enough of my story about the Land of the Drings. I'm an epic type, old style, those hypnotic sagas that go on for days and days and days."

Use the other authority.

I let out my breath in a long, slow stream, my heart pounding. I began sorting out the pages of The Murder Mystery, trying not to notice that my hands were shaking. I grouped sections together with paper clips and piled them up neatly beside the Selectric. I paused as I held up the section I had written about the Land of the Drings, about to place it on top of the scene I had just read through. I had the uneasy sensation of my hands obeying instructions I was not giving them, as if answering the imagined voice of Manda. *Yes, Daryl probably would like to hear your story about The Land of the Drings. . . .*

Considering how much Daryl likes old stories, with goddesses.

Again I looked up, more quickly this time. But the words had not come from Manda. I looked at my hands as they laid the pages about Manda's imaginary land on top of the pile. As soon as they were placed there, they ceased shaking. I watched my own hands take up another piece of paper, turn on the switch of the Selectric, and glide the paper in. Into my mind came the vision of Manda, in jail, settling in to tell more of the story about the Drings to Daryl—

Not Daryl. He is only the deputy to the Chief.

My heart pounded, and I again exhaled slowly to calm myself. The visions from the previous evening rushed in, of "Daryl" making love with a steam-room goddess whose conversation with cardboard I had overheard. The bridge rose up too, and with it the vision of that mouth which both was and was not real. I shook my head to fight off these inversions of fiction with life, terrified of what they presaged for my psyche. But instead of shaking the memory away, I felt hands holding my head gently, trying to soothe me, bringing me to stillness slowly, kindly. The mouth that I had seen through my car window came into my eyes.

The Chief's mouth is the authority you are seeking.

I slowly exhaled again as I felt hands holding me, expanding into the sensation of a body supporting me like a great lap, an embrace as enormous and all-encompassing to me as a mother must seem to an infant. The mouth opened inside my eyes as from behind me, the invisible seduction of an anonymous embrace went on until I was utterly calm, aware only of my breath coming and going, and the harmony of the rocking with my breath, and the stillness of the floating mouth before me pulsating in the same rhythm, its lips taking on the aspect of a rose.

Walk into the Chief's mouth. It is the entry to my maze.

It was a hushed voice, an echo of Gwen's vacant mistral, weak and tremulous.

Freddie opened it for you so that you could find me. I am—

"Morning, Summacious."

I jerked out of my trance state, almost toppling backward as I felt the great lap instantly leave me. Where the roseate mouth of the Chief had been, there was Manda, as she was most mornings, sitting diagonally across from my desk on the couch, smoke spiraling upward, black hair covering her face. I stared at Manda, dazed, afraid to speak. I had the sudden bizarre conviction that if I opened my mouth, the voice I had just heard would escape and Manda, that voice with boots on, would stomp it out, grinding it into the ashes of her perpetual pack.

"What, no greetings for your one and only murderer this morning?"

I shook my head slowly back and forth.

"Summacious, you coming down with the flu? Do we have a hormonal blip to deal with?"

Another slow shake of the head, followed by my belly rippling, as it does in the dry heaves of panic. I concentrated on my breathing, thinking of nothing else but in, out, inhale, exhale, one, two, in, out. . . .

"Getting wobbly, isn't it, Mutemouth? Not sure which Rhinebeck you're living in."

Inhale, exhale, in . . .

Manda tipped the chair onto its back legs and sent another spiral of smoke upward. "I have to admit. I've been puzzled by how long it's taken you to get it. I thought someone with your imagination would get there a lot faster." Manda sighed dramatically. "But whoever tunes your fantasy instrument could use some tips from the pro." She grinned.

I took a deep breath and exhaled, and then another, until I felt safe enough to speak. "Get where?" I asked, the words of that gentle vacancy subsided inside me.

"To the map, Bimbette. The map you have to chart of the Rhinebeck behind this one. And that one," Manda said, gesturing to the canary-yellow manuscript.

I said, "I thought it was in between, not behind."

Manda let out a long, low whistle. "Impressive, Summacious. I see you've been doing your make-up homework. Here comes a bonus question for my star pupil," Manda said, teasing me with a shake of her hair over her ears. "What am I *not*?"

"Nice," I said.

"That's cheating."

I gently put my hand down on the top of the manuscript, with the curious sensation that I was holding it still. "You are inside these yellow pages, Manda, locked up in a jail cell waiting to go on trial for murder. And what is about to happen is . . ." Was that perfume?

"The suspense, Summacious. I can hardly take it."

I breathed in a sweet, familiar scent and said, in a calm tone of voice, "Your mother is going to visit you."

Manda paused, tossing her hair about as she seemed to register surprise at my words. I had never before told Manda what a scene in The Murder Mystery was going to be. Slowly she ground out her cigarette stub with the heel of her boot. "Summacious, I regret to inform you that you got the bonus question wrong." I kept my hand on top of the manuscript as she started in on me. "The Manda in that stupid Murder Mystery of yours is about as real as the Rhinebeck you've put in there, that virginal Main Street without any of the awkward details like an *asylum,* for instance, to mess up your precious objective correlative for innocence. There're different kinds of innocent, Summacious, and different kinds of fiction, and they aren't either one of them clean. And what you've got there under your hand is worse than clean. It's sterile."

My eyes darted over to where Manda was now standing, staring at me with those eyes I couldn't see but whose gaze yet penetrated my being. I sat, clenching my jaw. We were locked inside that word, "sterile," staring at each other. I said, "I think—"

"I told you a few millennia ago, what you think doesn't—"

"You are scared," I said over and through that voice.

"Scared?" Manda screeched. "Me? A murderer with twenty-seven thousand years of professional experience?"

"Yes."

Manda chortled. "This is fun, Summacious. You thinking up something that I am scared of, when you and I both know it's your—"

"Mother," I shouted, bulldozing my voice through hers. "Who is on her way, right now, to see you in prison."

Manda and I were both breathing hard. My hands shaking, I stared at the blank sheet of canary-yellow paper in the Selectric.

"Summacious, if I am in prison, you are."

"That's right, Manda," I said, holding my voice steady. "I am in prison. I figured out your trick this morning. You have imprisoned the author by surrendering yourself to the authorities."

Manda grinned. "Told you I was a professional."

"I have to hand it to you," I said, "you got me."

"Aren't you going to at least try to get me out of prison, Summacious?" I detected the hint of a whine of disappointment. "Twenty-seven thousand years of reruns can get sort of boring. I was hoping, when I chose you for my asylum, I might get lucky. Figured you might wobble enough to make things more interesting. I haven't had the thrill of escape for a while now."

"Didn't you hear me, Manda?" I said. "Moms is coming to visit you."

"Since when does my mother know I'm in jail, Summacious?"

"Since right now."

"What did I do to you to deserve this kind of treatment?" Manda said.

"You killed Her."

Again, I reconstruct from the ashes of fiction.

Moms was a minuscule woman, her features and gestures as delicate as the stitches in the seams of Pat Edwards's lilac silk. Among Manda's earliest memories was creeping out of her bed after she had gone to sleep while watching her mother's weekly hair trim. Every Sunday night the ritual would begin when Moms opened the cabinet doors under the sink and took the colander out. First, the ritual ablutions, washing the colander with Palmolive soap, scrubbing it vigorously till its entire aluminum surface had suffered another night of being scratched and scarred. The rinsing: long, luxurious, with Moms holding the colander before her, perfectly still, her hands under the water, her eyes closed, as secret, silent prayers were chanted. The drying: only her mother's mother's white linen dish towel with the initials embroidered on it in decorative embosses impossible to decipher, a code for her grandmother's name, which was never pronounced in the house.

Moms would then perform the most thrilling part of the ritual: the removal of her blouse. Standing before the colander, the fluorescent light from above the sink illuminating the holes, Moms would unbutton her blouse only as far as the waistband of her skirt, leaving the blouse tucked in. She removed her arms and let the blouse drop, its sides spreading like wings. It never slid out of its hold in the waistband, but fell about her

hips like a sacred sash. As she watched Moms, her careful, small, graceful motions were a clue to Manda as to why Mihalyi visited, what the
smell coming from Moms and Mihalyi involved. Her mother had been
supposed to be a ballerina, but she said she could only dance on grass.

Moms would reach out both hands for the colander, pluck it from the
counter, and, holding the colander before her, blow gently over it. There
were nights when Manda thought she could hear a faint, quavering whistle as Moms's breath passed through the holes. She would then place her
fingers in prescribed positions known only to her and raise the colander
over her head. She moved thus, colander perched above but not yet
landed, to the oval mirror. Then, the terrible agony of watching her
mother adjust the colander would take place, going on it sometimes
seemed to Manda for hours, before Moms removed her fingers. Moving
with great care so as not to disturb the perfectly placed helmet with its
musical star-holes, Moms would reach for the scissors which hung from
their exclusive nail. Manda held her breath as Moms's tiny body stretched
out its tiny arm and her tiny fingers grabbed the scissors. Don't catch,
don't snag, don't stick, don't drop, Manda would silently invoke her own
scissors prayer from where she stood watching.

When the scissors were safely in her mother's hand, Manda let out her
breath. Moms would pause, scissors held, studying her face. Then, with a
dexterity which always astonished Manda and filled her with something
akin to hope, as if proof of hidden grace in her mother was proof that
grace lay within her too, and maybe love would come to her as it had come
to Moms, her mother would snip all around the colander. The infinitesimal pieces of hair would fall over Moms's face and shoulders like spiky
dust, for she never cut off more than a fraction of a fraction of an inch; her
every gesture in life was miniature; her nose would wrinkle, tickled to
sneeze. But sneeze she never did. Never. This sign of control and decorum, combined with the genius of the blouse at the waistband, the surgical fluency of the scissors, forced into Manda's tight, cynical heart a shaft
of hope as small as the fallen hairs, and, as she would watch Moms replace
the scissors on their nail, remove the colander and return it to its ceremonial place underneath the kitchen sink, dust her nose and cheeks off, lift
the blouse from its perch at her waist, slide her arms in, rebutton it, and

never, ever have to tuck it in again, and then and only then shut the kitchen closet door to keep the ritual instruments safe, Manda would feel her body willing to surrender itself to the unconsciousness of night and whatever dreams would arise, grateful to her mother for proving, yet again, that not even the constant raging muttering of her father could interrupt Moms's ritual grooming of herself for her lover.

Moms brought the colander with her in a bowling-ball case to the jail cell where they were holding Manda for murder. Manda knew immediately what it was. Moms said nothing. Manda said nothing. They both stared. After a while, Moms quietly unzipped the bowling-ball case and revealed the colander. She removed the colander and placed it on the table. Manda watched Moms open her purse (black imitation cowhide, large gold clasp). Moms put her hand in and then stopped. "There is something I should tell you," Moms said.

Manda nodded, waiting.

"When they phoned and told me," Moms said, struggling, "I did something. "Moms said, "I signed up to go to the moon."

"The moon?"

"When they told me. What . . . happened," Moms said, her hand still inside her purse. "You can sign up to be in the first lunar colony," Moms was explaining. "It doesn't cost anything. I'm on the waiting list, but I feel strangely optimistic."

I heard Manda chuckling. I stopped typing and looked over at Manda sitting on the couch, smoking. "It's funny," Manda said. "My mother comes to see me in prison, where I'm being held for murder, and she's 'strangely optimistic.'"

I sipped at my coffee. It was cold, rancid.

Manda flicked an ash. "She won't visit me again. This is it."

"I say your mother comes again."

Manda was shaking her head. "What's bothering my mother at this moment isn't whether I'm guilty of murder. That's what is bothering you and me in this prison we're in together." Manda tossed her hair. "*My mother is worried about getting the colander to the moon.*"

"She is going to leave it with you," I said, thinking out loud. "And that way, she has to come back for it. When her number on the waiting list for the moon comes up."

Manda dropped her face down, holding on to her forehead, her hair spilling through her fingers. I looked back at the manuscript, then at Manda, her head bowed, the hair covering her face as it always did. She mumbled something I could not make out. "What—"

Manda shot her head up, her hair flying, her eyes a tantalizing flash. "Nothing, do you hear me? Nothing will make Moms leave the colander with me. Least of all your imagination. How many times do I have to tell you, Summacious? The song doesn't work that way anymore."

"Whose song, Manda? Yours or mine?"

"Ours," Manda said. "Our prison song."

"Our prison—but my song. My novel. My words. My story, my way. Moms is coming back." Manda jumped up from the couch. I said, "That's why her name is Moms, with an 's,' a plural. Because she makes more than one appearance."

Manda shook her fists in the air and spun on her thick heel. "Stop this, Summacious. Stop acting like you are the one in charge of the spelling for my family history. And while I'm at it, stop trying to get me to feel the feelings you want to feel, inside that piece of sterile garbage called The Murder Mystery. It's a dud, Summacious, and this little trick with an 's' is not going to make anyone's mother return," Manda snarled at me. "I am going to say this only one more time. You want to do this right. The consequences if you do this wrong are a kind of sterile not even you can conceive, Summacious. You make Moms zip up that colander and take it with her to the moon, and she doesn't come back."

As she spoke, the veil of her hair swung back and forth over her face. The words popped out of me before I knew what I was going to say. "Let her see your face in prison."

Manda stomped the butt of her cigarette in the ash circle, where she was standing, in that region where she was most palpable. She grabbed at a clump of hair, but, like the perpetual pack, there was always more hair hiding her eyes. "What? She's going to cut my hair with the colander like she does? Like some sort of initiation rite? Like if I do this weird thing then I'm a member of her Loon-Moon Grasses-to-Ashes Tribe?"

"Yes," I said, my heart now racing. "Yes. She's going to pull a pair of scissors, *the* scissors, out of her purse and cut your hair with them."

"Cut my hair."

"It's classic," I said. "Classic initiation rite."

"In a jail cell."

"Yes."

"With scissors."

"The scissors. They're in the purse. She's got her fingers on them right now and is about to pull them out."

"Moms got 'the' scissors past security."

"They're special scissors."

She snorted. "They have to be magic to get past security."

"They are magic," I said. "They belong to Mihalyi. That's why they had the power to get rid of your father. Because they belonged to the King of the Drings."

Manda sat on the couch, a medicinal diet cola materializing in her hand. "I told you already," Manda said. "The words didn't work. Words, scissors, same magic required. Zip." Manda stretched her legs out and drank her "medicine."

I was staring at the diet cola when I heard myself saying, in a soft voice not entirely my own, "There has been an accident." A rip in the seams, an invisible labyrinth appearing, an entry to an invisible maze formed by the mouth of a man born from a transparent womb of breath.

"Accident." Manda's voice was flat.

"It may have been fatal."

Manda lit up a cigarette in slow motion. She turned her face toward the trees as she smoked, the quiet and stillness of her being more alarming to me than her usual menacing stomp, explosive whirl. "Are you sure you know what you're doing, Summacious?"

"Last night, Baubo showed up in the steam room of the Y. And then . . ." Careful. Remember what the Chief told you; the ice is fatal more times than not. "One of the authorities," I said, slowly, "made love to her."

"What do you mean, *one* of the authorities?"

"The Chief," I said. "The Chief authority."

The diet cola evaporated.

Manda moved her tongue around on the inside of her cheek, a nervous gesture I had not seen her make before. My heart was racing inside me, and my throat was dry. I wanted water more than I could stand. But I was afraid to leave the seat where I had felt those anonymous arms rocking me, telling me to use the authority I was using now. I needed to be in the vicinity of those arms if I were to keep my courage—if courage it was—to begin changing the direction of Manda's murderous inspiration.

Manda was parading around the middle of the room, inside the circle her cigarette ashes made. "What is this, Summacious—resistance I expected, but not the sentimental bullshit variety. I suppose there were candles and the light made everything soft-focus? Vaseline on the lens, Eraserbrain, does not real Honeytime make."

The scent of the perfume was so faint that I could not be sure if it was my memory of it, from a few moments before, or another visitation. But as I breathed it in, I heard again the last words that perfume had spoken, and I said to Manda, "I'm not the one who made Honeytime, Manda."

Manda snorted. "At least we got that much straight, Summacious. I was worried you were thinking you were an authority on this subject."

"It was Freddie." Freddie Van Heusen whose name alone had the power to open the mouth of a chief, and keep it open, all this time, until I can figure out how to enter through its restorative lips.

Manda stomped. "Freddie! This character's dangerous, Summacious, I warn you."

Instinct worked in me, not conscious thought or deliberate strategy, as I kept the memory of the perfume alive within me. What had the Chief said to me last night? *Black ice is fatal more times than not.* Panther ice, I thought, is a fatal coldness. He wrote me out a speeding ticket. *Go slowly, I don't want to meet you next time in an accident.* Slowly, I said to myself, proceed very slowly. Manda is scared, and that is not necessarily a good thing. A Panther, scared. Might attack all of a sudden. She is scared of Freddie. Of this mouth. Of Moms visiting her in prison. For the first time since the Panther had burst into my life, I felt the stirrings of power on my side of the dialogue. Uncertain power which I did not yet know how to wield; but I felt power in me, nonetheless. Slowly, carefully placing my words on the fatal ice of the Panther's frigid season, I said, "I'll tell you what you want to know about Freddie, if you will tell me . . ." I was surprised by what came into my mind. "How come Mihalyi is King Pain."

Manda squinted. She prowled. Finally she said, "What do you mean, Freddie made Honeytime, not you?"

My heart soared, and it was all I could do not to let fly a victory yelp. I had formed a sentence from Manda's world of words which she could not understand. I had created the first line for the lyrics of a song of my own made out of the Panther's breath. Things were wobbly, indeed, and it was not easy to stay upright on the black ice the Panther and I were stalking each other on. "They say Freddie's mentally off."

"This is not very impressive to someone with my background," Manda scoffed at me. "You have to do better than that, Summacious."

"No one is stopping his phone calls," I said.

"No one who?" Manda stood directly before me.

"No authority. The Chief is letting them go through."

"I thought you said these were obscene phone calls."

"And I thought you said there are two kinds of fiction, and two kinds of innocence, and neither is clean. Or did I imagine you said that, Manda?"

Manda dropped her head and ran her hands through her hair. She held her face in her hands, unable to hide her defeat. However, as defeated as I could see she was, the exaltation of victory in me from an instant before quieted. My god, I thought, what is happening to me? What is Manda? What is this mouth? Who—what—is the authority who is creating The Murder Mystery? What were those arms, that perfume?

It seemed a long time before Manda registered my presence. She said, "What makes anybody King Pain? He left." I stared at her. Manda, her eyes behind the veil of her hair, said, "A deal's a deal, Summacious. I am not the one who breaks promises. You told me about Freddie; I told you about King Pain."

"Mihalyi left you and Moms and your sister—"

"Did you write down that scene about Freddie and the Mouth—"

"Tell me —"

"Tell me," Manda yelled in her raspy, ash-grating voice, "the truth— is Freddie Van Heusen in The Murder Mystery?"

"Freddie and the Chief was just a fantasy," I said.

"Look at me and say the word 'fantasy' again, Bimbette." I dropped my head. "You are very close, Summacious, very close, to messing the whole thing up."

"Me messing it up, Manda? Or you?"

"You are not equipped for the kind of imagining you're heading into, Erasermind. You think any amateur on your side can do this just because they've had a real nice fantasy experience? What I do takes skill, and training, and a whole lot more imagination of a variety I do not see you showing me any sign you've got, yet."

"You're scared, Manda; you're scared because the Chief isn't stopping Freddie's calls, so Baubo, she got through. She got through to my side— alive. And your clever trick of locking me up when you locked yourself up isn't working out the way you thought it would."

Manda put her hands on her hips and shook her head at me. "The more you think you're getting it right, the more you're getting it all wrong. Every time Baubo shows up, Your Blankness, what happens next?" I couldn't think. "Oh, come on," Manda said, exasperated, "I worked hard on that story for my sister, real hard. I want the authorities to like it when I tell them the whole story, from beginning to end. I don't want them thinking I'm an amateur, like you. It's all right there, Summacious, in front of you, just under the scene with Moms; you need to refresh your memory." I stared at the yellow pages. "Go ahead, remove the scene with Moms, it'll help you get your bearings again. "

"She dances," I stammered, refusing to move the pages about Moms and the colander in prison.

"Why do you always make it so difficult for yourself, Erasermind, when I'm here to help you? All you have to do is move a few pages, and you'll find what you're looking for."

I gently slid back the pages about Moms, trying to peek at the others. My elbow slipped. I scrambled at the pages as they slid off the desk,

Manda chortling. I picked them up and was placing them back over the others when I caught a few words from Manda's epic saga about the Land of the Drings. I felt all the blood drain from me.

Manda nodded. "That's right: After Baubo dances, the Eaners come, and they poke holes in the Drings with their terrible monster Clyks. The Drings begin losing all their color. And the people, they get worried the Drings are dying, and they do the one thing nobody can do, Summacious. Nobody. Not even me. They look inside the Drings. And they all fall in."

Manda squashed her cigarette butt out on the ever deepening ashes of the Ash Circle, working it in with the heel of her boot, slowly, mocking me with the same gesture she had used in the scene in the woods when she turned herself over to Daryl. Then she looked at me and said, "It's a long, long way down. And nobody comes back, ever, not even nobody's mother."

It seemed odd to be repainting the metal railing in the dead of winter.

But there it was before me: four railings of a different color than the others, a hard, false silver coating over them, marking a space large enough for a body to fall through.

The weather had been weird. A few days of bizarre springlike temperatures which made the Christmas decorations all up and down Rhinebeck's Main Street seem especially irritating; then dropping down into the single digits. The sky had been gray and the snow locked into it by frigid air. Sometime the night before, the temperatures had risen into the forties. Today was the first day anyone would want to go out. Maybe it was the thaw, I told myself, as I slowed my car down and joined the midday traffic crossing the bridge. The extreme cold, followed by a few days of thaw, the melt of the bridge ice into those cracks, another seizure of cold—and the base of the railings would be riddled with cracks.

But I was seeing the beautiful long-armed woman, her willowy body against those weakened railings struggling against the man in the dark and then falling down, down, down. . . .

A woman was busy directing traffic, her huge torso covered with a fluorescent orange vest. She was waving me on. I pulled alongside her and said, "What happened?"

"Railings bust."

"How?"

"Lady, I'm not an engineer."

"Was there some accident?"

"There will be if you don't get a move on."

I sped off toward the Y. I raced through yellow lights, wound my way around the back way into the parking lot. It was ten minutes to one. I rushed past Betty, who gave me a strange look, and entered the senior women's locker room.

The women's locker room was crammed with women, as it always was at this hour of the day, when they held an aerobics class. The whole place seemed filled to the brim with secretaries. Around me the hum of women's voices rose and fell. I could see her, in my mind's eye, not so much her height and her hair as the stillness, the clarity of her movements that made her like the lotus in the eye of chaos. But I was seeing only chaos.

I had looked down all the aisles and checked discreetly under the curtains of the cubicles, trying not to draw too much attention. No Red-Headed Long-Armed Guide to the Source of Eternal Dew. I walked around to the aisle nearest the mirror, hoping to catch sight of her hair. The mirrors were crowded with dyed blonds putting on blue eye shadow. As I looked at them, lined up before the mirror, stretching their faces into the ugly light, they seemed like little birds on a perch, fussing with their feathers. I told myself not to panic. Maybe she was still in the shower, running late. Even if she had never run late before. I was on my way to the showers when I was stopped by Rulla, naked as usual, her round, soft body with the flesh falling over it in gentle folds like old, velvety sand pushed up by the same tidal shore for eons and eons, pinked from a recent soak or steam. Her brilliant red hair, not the gentle auburn of the missing Guide to the Source, wisped around her square face, the gray roots exposed.

"Where is your sister?" she said, in a thick accent.

It took me a moment. "You mean my friend."

Her lips matched her flushed skin. She smiled, showing bad teeth. "But she is your sister," she said, nodding gently. "Always you come to-

gether. Always you are laughing. Like sisters. I have a sister. So far away,"
she said. "So far." She looked me up and down, as if remarking on the
strangeness of my being clothed. "Is your sister all right?" she said, her
voice gliding in a rich glissando through the vowels.

"My sister's fine," I said.

"Why all this—" Limited by her English, she used the universal language of mime to imitate my harried look.

"You know that woman?" I said. "With the beautiful red hair?"

The naked queen of the locker room nodded. "So beautiful," she
said, and she took a deep breath, as if to inhale the beauty. "Just like my
sister, across the ocean. I have not seen her so long. Everyone sister here,"
Rulla said as she shuffled away on her broad feet.

Coincidence, I kept mouthing inside. Coincidence. She will return in
a day or so; it was only my cluttered, disaster-driven imagination.

I went to the Y every day for the next week. I didn't know her name;
there was no way to track her down; I simply had to wait until she either
returned or didn't. I had never seen anyone speak to her, or her speak to
anyone. I asked Betty.

"Her? The really beautiful one? Not like the rest of us pretenders.
Ask Rulla," Betty said. "I think Rulla knows her."

"I did. She didn't seem to know anything."

"What's she to you?"

*Her. Alive. Proof that Manda is a Cretan liar, like she said in the begin-
ning. And this murder she insists I asked for never happened at all.*

I drove slowly toward the bridge one brilliant afternoon, the temperatures soaring. At the crest of the rise, I threw my sweatshirt out of the
car and continued driving. When I reached the Rhinebeck side, I pulled
the car over where the Chief had blessed me with his mouth. I then began
walking back toward the bridge. The sweatshirt was my excuse; the
pylon my goal. The day was warm, but a wind whipped up from below
the bridge off the frigid waters of the Hudson, where the ice floes moved
like drowsy dinosaurs over the sparkling blue. My eyes watered, and by
the time I reached the center of the bridge, I desperately wanted the
sweatshirt. A car slowed down. I squatted down, picked up my sweatshirt, and waved the car by.

I waited until the car had disappeared into the dip at the far end of the bridge before I approached the recently repaired railings, their new metal paint a paler shade of silver, easily identifiable. I held on, tight, my mind filling up with the body of Ophelia laconically floating down the river, dead. Shakespeare witnessed enough for poetry, but not enough to save her, I thought. I made myself look over the railing, not sure what I wanted to find: poetry, or Her, or another blank to fill with my contaminated imagination.

The cement pylon was gargantuan, dropping down, down, down into the water below, a gigantic femur of industry. On the curved hump, like the protrusion of the femur where it joins the pelvic bone, was a stain, colorless, darkening the cement. Just as I was turning away, something else caught my eye. It was a red string, a thread, flapping in the wind at the elbow of the pylon.

I returned to my car and drove home. As the car wound its way south toward my cottage, following the curves of the river, I imagined the Red-Headed Guide to the Source floating, her hair splayed out on the top of the wedge of ice as she traveled south. The red thread on the pylon was attached to a blanket which unraveled as the ice took her away. It snapped, and the fragment of blanket that was left, a blood-colored rag, slid off, revealing that she was naked. The ice floe jammed at an outcropping, and her body fell off, but her hair was frozen to the ice, and her body undulated in the currents until it broke free. She slipped around the curve past the Esopus tributary, a pocket of black cool in summer where boys boasted and dove from rocks, past the bend in the river below Rhinecliff, cruising by the old Roosevelt estate, on south until she came to West Point, where the river curves around a large hill and the currents of the river collide in fierce, cross currents. Her body whirled around in the turbulent waters till it suddenly stopped, her hair snagged in a tree. There she remained, entangled in branches, a beautiful woman whose name I did not know, disintegrating, while above her, on the hill, young men practiced war with metal things for which they knew all the real names.

With the exception of The Beek, which had draped the tiniest of white lights around its trees and bushes, winding delicate spirals up the pristine columns, Rhinebeck was turning itself into a red-and-green nightmare of blinking plastic and deafening sound in preparation for the Christmas holiday. All up and down Main Street were enormous speakers, put up by Max, the former drug-lord prosecutor, now jewelry store owner. He called this parade of speakers his "civic duty" to share the skills he had learned as a light-show roadie during the '60s, when he did most of his wiring wired himself. The black boxes were spewing forth the ear-splitting, instantly identifiable sound of Alvin and the Chipmunks' "Jingle Bell Rock," which would have sent anyone scrambling for drugs.

On the corner of Main and Route 9, the wooden Indian outside Mr. Bert's smoke shop was bedecked in huge Christmas lights of all colors in a rainbow tour of cosmic consciousness, which seemed, at least to my friend and me, a statement. We were not sure what the statement was, but it crossed our minds that Mr. Bert had "changed" since he started hiring Freddie Van Heusen to work a few hours a week during the Christmas season. It was rumored that the abundantly rainbowed wooden statue was Freddie's idea. It certainly seemed excessive and eccentric enough to be Freddie's work. Across the street, on the opposite corner, the Army-Navy Supply Store had joined forces with a small real estate firm to put up an enormous plastic backlit Rudolph. There had been some debate in the *Rhinebeck Reformer* about whether Rudolph's red nose would confuse drivers if it were placed too near the traffic light. In deference to safety, Rudolph had been positioned with his rump facing Route 9, the red nose pointing directly at Freddie's wooden rainbow man.

The editorial page had been devoted entirely to the Rudolph dilemma. (No mention of the rainbow man.) On the back page, barely detectable among the holiday advertisements, was a small piece about the repairs to the railing of the Kingston-Rhinecliff Bridge. Repairs in the middle of winter, the author wrote, could be a sign of a "deteriorating infrastructure." There was no reference to an accident or a body. I had the uncanny feeling that my own infrastructure was no longer able to keep The Murder Mystery on newsprint separate from a murder mystery that obeyed none of the rules for time and space. It too was deteriorating. Into madness? Or into a mouth where I would find restoration in tragedy?

The solstice would be upon us in a few days. There is something about the dark starting to happen midafternoon, and knowing that the next day it will be darker, and the next, which makes one feel the darkness as it is being made. It was not yet four, and Rudolph was already glowing a shameless red as Alvin and his chipmunk chorus rent the air with their frantic wails. Freddie's wooden rainbow man twinkled gently.

"Tragic," a woman said as my friend and I walked by.

My friend stopped and pointed to a woman's sweater in a store window covered with hand-knit ducks. "I think," she said, "*that* might be *the* tragedy."

"Ducks are domestic tragedy. Alvin," I said, as his electronically induced castrati sound seared my eardrums, "is epic."

Behind us the conversation that had spawned tragedy as our theme continued. "Poor Lorely," the woman was saying. "She wanted to keep it a secret. They say he's been in and out of at least five institutions by now. I think it's downright noble of Mr. Bert to give him work."

"It's Lorely who's crazy."

"You want to go in and try it on?" my friend said, pointing to the duck-encrusted sweater and rolling her enormous green eyes in the direction of the women talking on the street.

"Ducks?" I said. "Me?"

"They're not me," she said. "My domestic tragedy is more the *pink-sweatshirt type,*" she said, jerking her head toward the women.

Alvin was rattling my brain, and I was slow to make the connections. "Your tragedy is pink?"

"More like a lack of pink," she said, again jerking her head in the direction of the gossips. I turned and caught a glimpse of a large woman with glasses and crimped blue-gray hair. "As in, needing the Queen of Pink to show up."

"Queen Pink?" I whispered.

She nodded rapidly as, to my horror, Alvin and his cousins began their version of "The Twelve Days of Christmas."

Behind us, Queen Pink and the other woman continued talking. My friend leaned down and pretended to be interested in some hideous gold rope earrings while other shoppers passed by.

". . . splinter," we heard.

"Lorely?"

"Swear to god."

"Well, Freddie's harmless, even if his mother does think he came from a splinter."

"Now, am I the kind of person who would make something like that up?"

"Well, these phone calls, they haven't hurt anybody, not one bit. They say all he does is read from this Swedish sex manual."

"Well, now," the other woman went on. "I didn't think much of it either, not when I thought he was just, you know, what he was," she said. "But it makes me kind of nervous, now I know he's not."

Alvin and the Chipmunks had reached the soprano refrain, "Five golden rings," sounding like one of Charcot's paid professional hysterics who so impressed a young dissecter of worms seeking the secret of electricity in the cells, named Sigmund Freud, that he switched from electric worms in the laboratory to a theatre of fainting women. My friend raised her head toward the speakers to deliver a curse upon them, or a prayer for redemption; I don't know, for before she could say anything, Queen Pink had recognized her as, "You're that woman who collects the stories. From the old women. For the Dutchess County Historical Society."

My friend was accustomed to such ambushes on Main Street. "Yes, I am."

"You spoke with my mother. She lives on the old Hockett property, in Elizabethville. Ninety-eight. She was just so touched that someone wanted to know about her life. She said it was the best Christmas present ever."

My friend always (always) remembered. "That was your mother?" My friend gripped my arm.

Queen Pink bit her lip. She nodded, tears forming in her eyes. Then she threw herself on my friend and wrapped her (long) arms around her as Alvin burst forth in full falsetto for the final wrap-up from twelve drummers drumming. Queen Pink said, in a husky voice damp with grief, "Thank you. Thank you so much for making my mother's last Christmas her best."

"Your mother's last . . ."

"Five golden r-i-i-i-i-i-ings," Alvin screeched.

"She died, yes," Queen Pink said, sniffling. She released my friend from her impetuous embrace. "You're one of the last people who talked to her. You might even be the last. They found her in her bed. Died in her—"

"Pear tre-e-e-e-e-e-e-e-e!"

Queen Pink dabbed her eyes with tissue and gave my friend one last look of gratitude, and then she and her compatriot gossip moved on. My friend stood utterly still, staring after them. Alvin was, for a blessed moment, silent. "I was the last person to talk to Mother Queen Pink," she said.

I stared up at the silent speaker, willing it to remain mute.

"You know what she talked about?"

Quiet. Not a sound. Remain so.

"Freddie."

Again.

"What Freddie had told her over the phone. She wanted to know if I'd ever done it. Oral sex. She'd never heard of such a thing." I turned away from the speaker, expecting my friend to whoop with her usual laughter at things vital. But her eyes were glazed over, and she was shaking her head. "I told her that Freddie is nuts," she was saying, "and everyone knows it except his mother. Lorely's been circulating the rumor for years about him being mentally retarded when what he really is is schizophrenic, and everyone knows but Lorely. I told her Freddie is crazy and that whatever he said to her on the phone was completely made up. There was no such thing. Thinking, you know, thinking that if I told her yes, there is this thing called oral sex and in fact it's quite wonderful, then she'd die feeling like she'd lost out on wonderful. But you know what she said? Oh, Meem. It killed me, what she said. She said, 'My husband always told me I had the craziest ideas and I should pray a lot harder.'"

The electronic falsetto shot through the speakers again, sounding like the sky itself in hysterics. Alvin's living, natural counterpart had long since gathered up his foodstuffs and wrapped himself into his tail, retreating into his own furry skin to become like a seed, awaiting the advent of spring. But not Alvin and his electronic eunuch ensemble. The glare of Rudolph's excited red beacon, reassurance that the goods will be delivered, no matter what, radiated through the dark of winter like a perpetual-motion machine of consumerism run amok. While Freddie's wooden rainbow man stood still, keeping vigil, his lights like the gentle notes of a flute.

My friend glared at the speakers. Then she began walking, fast. I ran after her. "Are you okay?"

"Of course not. I'm the last person Mother Queen Pink talked to, and I told her the wrong thing, Meem. I told her the wrong thing! I'm as bad as that—" She pointed to the blasting speaker—"that travesty. That obscenity."

"Won't you guide my sleigh tonight. . . ."

"You didn't know you were the last person," I tried.

"But I was." She was waiting to cross the street, heading for Max's jewelry store. "I was, and I messed it up. I messed up what she felt about her entire life."

"Used to laugh and call him names . . ."

"You didn't know she would die—" She crossed between cars.

Traffic. Alvin. Traffic. Alvin.

"Histor-eeeeee."

My friend opened the door and marched in, me running behind. My eyes scanned the room for Max. Instead I saw the crescent blue moons of Gwen's eyes. Gwen often worked for Max during busy times, and as we entered, she was busy showing a striking necklace to an elderly woman wrapped in a handwoven shawl of purples and magentas. The woman had short-cropped white hair and long, elaborate earrings. She was leaning down to look at her reflection in a mirror, the necklace clasped around her black turtleneck sweater. Against the black sweater, the silver links, each about three inches long, followed a gently sloping, serpentine line. Dangling over her collarbone, in the blank space right above the woman's breasts, was an opal set in an ornate gold circle hung as if suspended above a huge piece of cobalt-blue and brilliant green petrified wood. The effect was like a planet in orbit above the earth.

Just as my friend was about to ask Gwen where Max was, the woman turned to look at her. Her eyes were a startling green. Phosphorescent. My friend was frozen by the woman's eyes. The colors of the stones and the petrified wood made her eyes sparkle their wondrous color. The woman said, "I need a second opinion, as you Americans say." Her richly accented voice filled the room.

All my friend's urgency was eclipsed by that voice. She stood beside the woman and stared at the necklace, stilled by glimmer and melody. My friend said, "The necklace makes your eyes even more amazing, which they don't need to be, they're already more amazing than amazing, but the necklace really does make them more."

The woman looked at Gwen, then at her reflection. "My eyes are the color of petrified wood," she said, shaking her head. "Strange, no?" She took a deep breath and said, "Don't tell me how much it costs or I am afraid the spell will be broken. How do you say? I will take it." Her voice lush, her accent dense.

"Would you like Christmas wrapping?" Gwen dutifully asked.

"Oh no," said the woman. "It is an early birthday present to myself."

Gwen asked my friend and me if we would like to see something.

At the same time that I said, "The rest of your dream," my friend said, "Max." My friend looked at me. "Meem, we don't have time for a dream." She turned to Gwen. "We're here to ask Max for asylum from that . . . that . . ."

The woman with the phosphorescent eyes and I both heard Gwen's intake of breath. Her breasts heaved. "That's what the rest of my dream was about," she said. "Asylum."

The woman with the phosphorescent eyes looked at Gwen. "There are two meanings, yes? To asylum. Which one is your dream?"

"I don't know," Gwen said. "I woke up too soon to find out."

The woman with the amazing eyes touched the necklace where it lay inside the box. "Women and asylum and dreams," she said, the words issuing out of her slowly, with the rich "m" sounds evocative of something historical, something worth mourning. She raised those eyes to me. Immediately, I saw Manda as she had been when she first arrived, after running twenty-seven thousand years, out of breath, to reach my small cottage in the woods with the sagging porch and the rusted-out shower stall. *I am very selective about whom I choose for asylum.*

At that moment, Max appeared from the back room. He had a thick crop of salt-and-pepper hair and was wearing black pants and a white shirt with a brilliant red satin vest. It glared with the same obnoxious confidence as Rudolph's nose. Max approached, a big capitalist smile on his face. I had been known to spend an easy hundred dollars on earrings by the same jeweler who made Phosphorescence's necklace. He was holding out his hand to shake mine when I heard my friend saying, "Are you responsible for Alvin?" She pointed outside.

Max stopped and looked at her.

"Is this what you call that horrible screaming?" Phosphorescence said. "Alvin?" When she spoke the chatting of other customers ceased. It was as if her voice and her presence were all the music needed. Gwen's breasts rose and fell, and another universe was born.

Max said, "Chamber of Commerce asked me to set up the speakers."

"Do you control them?" my friend demanded.

"Hey," Max said, as the castrati strains of Alvin's "Silent Night" poked into our ears. Max was an intelligent man. "They gave me the Alvin tapes. The Chamber of Commerce. You would prefer Perry Como?"

"I have made silent prayers for Perry Como," my friend said. "Andy Williams. Pat Boone."

"Is this serious?" Max said.

"It's more like tragic," my friend said.

"Women," Max said, for he was surrounded by them, shaking his head. "This is a women's thing, right?"

"Women seeking asylum," Phosphorescence said.

Max then saw his way through this. A path opened up before him, as if by magic, and he took it. "I feel that it is sort of my duty, a kind of act of repentance for all the injustices that men have inflicted on women for two thousand years, to do my small part to make women feel beautiful. My way of offering asylum, as it were." He'd been a very good lawyer, of that no one had ever had any question. But he had never before met up with a woman with phosphorescent eyes who stood at least four inches above him and who had just spent a great sum of money at his store and was all the music needed.

"Turn off Alvin," Phosphorescence said, in her accent the words becoming a demon.

"Excuse me?" Max said, politely.

"I just paid you . . ." Phosphorescence here reached into her bag and produced the slip. "Four hundred and thirty-six American dollars and twenty-eight American cents for a necklace. Do you think you could make this Alvin to shut up, as you Americans say? Life is too short," she said, "for this ugliness."

The women gathered around released a sound which was part cheer, part giggle, part awe.

"What if I don't have the power to turn Alvin off?" said Max, lawyer.

Phosphorescence leaned over—but the effect was as if she elongated—and bringing her face close to Max, she towered over him. In a throaty contralto she said, "We know—you know—who does."

He bowed melodramatically. The red satin lowered itself down, down. And then, cocking his head to the side in perfect nonchalant, cavalier style, holding up one finger to indicate, "Just a moment," he spun on his heel and disappeared into his back room. We, the women, exchanged looks, and though our faces were all as different from each other's as faces could be, the expression was the same: We were not sure of what we had just done, or exactly why we had done it, or what, precisely, had happened, whether it was wise or ridiculous. But at the abrupt cessation of that noise, that assault against the season of the earth, that shout of perpetual light, we all began to laugh with embarrassed victory, but victory nonetheless.

Phosphorescence said, "No, no, do not laugh. Do not be ashamed. Life *is* too short for this ugliness. This joke. This insult."

The strains of Bach's First Brandenberg Concerto swelled into the cold night air. I closed my eyes in gratitude and relief. When Max returned, we all broke out into polite applause—except Phosphorescence, who listened to the Bach with the intensity of someone who has just been seized by private memories, the mournful m's of women and dreams and asylum. She then turned, the purple wool spiraling around her lean body dressed in black, another living goddess who had vanquished the Eaner god in his Alvin manifestation, appearing for an instant before exiting into the near solstice dark.

My friend and I stepped out into a Main Street dappled with melody, the Christmas lights gently pulsating to the slow movement of the Bach. Ahead of us, Freddie's wooden rainbow man kept his twinkling vigil over the twilight, his face turned toward The Beekman Arms, "oldest inn in America." As we approached, I recalled the conversation with Queen Pink and the gossip about how Lorely, Freddie's mother, believed Freddie was made from a splinter. I remembered the way the mournful Phosphorescence had found her way out of her grief about women and dreams and asylum to laugh when my friend commented that her green eyes matched the petrified wood of the necklace. Freddie's wood, sprinkled with lights, and the petrified wood radiant with the colors of the elements—magenta for fire, cobalt for water, ruddy brown for earth, and that wondrous green of earth and eyes, encircled by silver, fused together in my mind.

I turned to look behind me, perhaps to glimpse the departing goddess to convince myself she existed. As I was looking for a sign of her, the music slurred and, for an instant, the lights on the other side of the street dimmed. Then the music resumed its rhythm, and the lights came on. Though it only lasted a moment, the laspse seemed an answer to my search for the warrior goddess, vanquisher of Alvin: She had sought asylum herself, in some other Rhinebeck than this one.

This other Rhinebeck borrowed its layout from mine and was located between the Rhinebeck directly before me, decked out for the holidays, and the fictive one inside The Murder Mystery. Like its sister towns in fiction and experience, this other Rhinebeck had an asylum, a bridge over perilous waters, and, I now realized, a Main Street too. Max's jewelry store, Freddie's wooden rainbow man and the smoke shop, where the mouth opened which that soft voice had instructed me to walk through to find Her, were all on the same side of the street. I stopped for a moment to scan the stores on the side where the power outage had happened. Parking lot . . . five and ten . . . Rudolph and the real estate office—no territories emerged of the Main Street of the other Rhinebeck I was trying to chart. I looked again on my side. I had all the restaurants; the other side, an ice-cream parlor. Next to it, I saw the store with the duck sweater, where we had overheard the conversation about Lorely and Freddie and schizophrenia.

"Meem? You okay?"

The women talking about Freddie as a "splinter" had been standing directly in front of a dry cleaner's. It was dark, closed for the evening, but the decorative lights illuminated enough for me to make out the ghostly shape of the plastic-encased suits. "Yeah, fine," I said, my voice husky. It is one thing to attempt to chart a town which is not there, but quite another to behold the map emerging from it. I was discovering a Rhinebeck that was older than all others, and no product of my imagination. Main Street was there, requiring another pair of eyes to see it, and I was growing them inside my own. The Main Street these eyes-within-my-eyes saw was divided into the two sides of my murder story, the one I was writing and the one I was living. On one side, Freddie Van Heusen's name had opened the Chief's mouth, which remained open, gateway to an invisible maze where I would find Her; and on the other, there was Manda and the plastic casements of Eaners and Clyks—but Freddie was on that side too.

What was Freddie Van Heusen doing on both sides of the Main Street of the Rhinebeck I could see only with the eyes-within-my-eyes? What made Freddie the caretaker of a wooden man on one side but a splinter in his mother's mad womb on the other?

A voice calling my name ended my first foray into mapping the Main Street of a Rhinebeck that did not exist. Gwen was waving frantically at my friend and me. Max had released her a few minutes early from her shift, perhaps shaken into a mysterious generosity by whatever it was that had just happened to him.

There's a way of knowing another woman without knowing her, an osmosis of knowing in which women are passed around in conversations with each other, until, though two women have never met in the flesh, they have participated in some way (like my eavesdropping in the steam room) in each other's story. There's a way of knowing that is gleaned from the dropped seeds of the endless, eternal conversation of women. My friend knew Gwen from such gleanings in conversation with Constance, Max's wife, the Mayan goddess of the never-ending breast milk who had referred me to Gwen when I was seeking my destiny in the stars, instead of in the steam room, on the bridge, and anywhere else that was not my cottage, where The Murder Mystery lay untouched.

As the renewing melody of Bach and Freddie's wooden rainbow man escorted us across Route 9 to The Beek, the giddiness of whatever we were to call what had just happened with Max—victory or display of feminine foolishness, we were not one of us sure—reawakened whatever force had made me say to Gwen that I wanted to "see" the rest of her dream. I am Manda's dream of asylum, I said to myself again, to test it now, within the cascading arpeggios of Bach, as if truth were dependent upon what music was playing and where. Asylum, asylum: a place aside, a delay before judgment, a holding cell before a murder trial, a sanctuary. It fit the map of the Rhinebeck where the Panther knew of a sister inside a dream on a bridge.

As the map emerged from around me , the pattern of the story I was living with Manda revealed itself to be a rhyming reversal of inner and outer. From the very beginning, the normal patterns of life had been turned inside out: The breathing had been outside me. In the most obvious inversion of the conventions of the murder mystery, I had the identity of the murderer, but not the victim. Though Manda was "stuck inside my murder story," whenever I went into the fiction, she broke out of it—interrupting my writing with that irresistible, rasping, ash-filled voice of hers. A walking, talking specter was alive; She was dead—and yet had spoken to me. Hadn't She? Hadn't that been Her voice, interrupted by the living icon of interruption, Manda? The invisible, anonymous victim elicited in me a feeling of intimate, intense grief. And I could not shake off the conviction that the red-headed woman in the Y who had first guided us to the steam room, Source of Eternal Dew, was another one of the sisters who is not a sister who seemed to populate this other Rhinebeck. I knew that perfume, that radiant red hair. And Benjamin knew I knew Her. Perhaps he was right when he had said the sky knew why I was sad and cried the tears I couldn't, like the walls of the steam room weeping for my friend when she told me her husband had not touched her since she gave birth.

Baubo, whom I had firmly believed to be a product of my character's mind, turned out to exist in historical reality—as well as in the life of a woman who had discovered she was a goddess herself because of a phone call from Freddie Van Heusen. And now, this latest point on the map of the other Rhinebeck. Sanctuary was on one side of Main Street, madness on the other. And Freddie Van Heusen—somehow—lived in both.

I looked at Gwen, walking beside my chatty friend, their breath rising in small clouds from their mouths. Gwen caught me looking at her. Her eyes, those blue crescents, were like enormous planetary bruises, so sad that I thought my heart would crack. Something had happened. Something bad. And I was certain it involved the woman on the bridge with the deteriorating infrastructure.

On winter nights as cold as this one, The Beek always had fires in the fireplaces. As we stepped into its busy, bustling warmth, the interior softly lit by the old-fashioned lights hung low and spare on the low beams, we were immediately taken away from our century into an earlier one. The Beek's promise of sanctuary held firm against the disrythmia of the latter twentieth century as the three of us made our way to one of the welcoming fires, where we were told we could wait for a table for dinner. A wingback, a Shaker, and a nondescript footstool were pulled up around the fire, and, ordering a carafe of red wine to warm our hearts and tongues, the three of us sat down with unashamed hunger for a century prior to the hallucinatory electronics we had just vanquished.

It was around such a fire as this one that women used to sit, spinning and carding wool, mending the broken seams of their children's clothes. The three of us sat down to the fire in The Beek and allowed a silence to fall between us. It was not a solemn silence, nor even, precisely, silence; it was a quieting and stillness in the circle between us, the fire glowing into it, as around us the sounds of eating and conversation rose and fell in untroubled spontaneity. We detoured around Gwen's dream for I don't know how long, like medieval musicians playing the impromptu part of a hocket.

We found ourselves talking about what had just happened to us in the jewelry store. We felt the celebration, the flush, the wonder at ourselves, but what were we celebrating? What was that—war? Folly? Women being foolish? Women being wise? Buffoonery of a particular style belonging only to our gender? A scene which could happen only in 1981, in America, with women over thirty? The smallest slice of history imaginable? Or was it something terribly important, a holy thing we dared not name for fear that its powers would be diminished in the naming? We tossed it all around and came to no conclusion; yet the goal had been accomplished: to speak of it, somehow, even if naming it were not possible. It was something real, even if we could not say precisely what.

Only then, well into our second glasses of red wine, the promise of the table within minutes, the fire turned and kicked and a new log put on it by a boy with flushed cheeks, did Gwen introduce the official subject by saying, "I don't know anymore what to believe. My dream was much more real than most of my days are. My days, they seem . . ." But here that mistral–Marilyn Monroe voice of heart-wrenching vapidity broke off.

In the silence—fraction of a second—my friend said, "How could I have lied about Freddie to the Mother of Queen Pink herself?"

"Freddie?" Gwen said as she saw her own dream, which was supposed to be center stage, lose the audition for the part.

My friend went on, "He's been making these obscene phone calls to these old women; I talked with one of them, God, Meem, the Mother of Queen Pink herself. Lorely is nuts, you know. Totally nuts," she said to Gwen. "She thinks Freddie was conceived from a splinter."

110

"They're not obscene," Gwen mumbled; only I heard her. She looked at my friend and said, louder, "Who is Queen Pink?"

"Hope."

"Hope?" said the voice eroded by the winds of history, or the breath of an unspoken dream, I did not yet know.

"Queen Pink is hope for us all that no matter how little our mothers ever knew or thought to get, it's still possible to get it."

Gwen choked on the wine and started to cough.

I rushed in, heroic, fumbling. "Some of the women he calls, they find out they're goddesses."

"Goddesses?" said Gwen.

"After Freddie called one woman," I said, "she went to Woodstock and bought herself silk underwear and found out from the woman who owns the underwear store that she's as big as goddesses historically were, and now she's sucking her husband off—"

My friend splurted red wine all over herself in a great spray of comedy, her natural element. She looked at her drenched front, and as she frantically wiped away at it, she was saying, "How do you know that? You don't know anything about Rhinebeck. I'm the historian. Not you."

"I heard it in the steam room," I said.

"Oh, well, if you heard it in the steam room . . . I have to go wipe this off," she said, leaving me alone with Gwen.

As soon as she was out of earshot, Gwen said, "Do you really want to know how my dream ended?"

Did I? Did I want to find out whether Manda was confined to my cottage in the woods or roamed inside the dreams of other women as she seemed to find her way into mine? "You don't have to tell me if you don't want to."

Gwen looked down at her lap, where her long, gracious fingers were twirling the stem of the wine glass back and forth, like a woman spinning thread. "I found her."

My heart, inexplicably, raced. "Your sister?"

Gwen raised her blue eyes from her lap and stared at me, dumb-struck. "What do you mean, my sister?"

"Your sister, on the bridge, who was in such trouble . . ."

"What makes you say she was my sister?" Gwen said again.

"You told . . . " I blanched, remembering. It was Manda who had said the woman in Gwen's dream was her sister.

Gwen had not taken her eyes off me. "The woman in my dream was my sister's *daughter,*" she emphasized. "My niece. Her mother was my sister. . . ." Gwen hesitated. "She killed herself about ten years ago. And her daughter . . ." But she shook her head, as she had at our first meeting, and said again, "Why did you say the woman on the bridge was my sister?"

"I . . ." Stalled, scrambling for an explanation, and looked at the fire glowing in the fireplace. A terrible impulse seized me, and I said, "The dream I remember you telling me . . ." The flames seemed to draw the lie out of me as I continued, "Was your sister, on the bridge, fighting . . . a serpent . . . a Panther, wasn't it?" I made myself look away from the fire to Gwen's face. "But you never told me who won the fight. Your sister or the Panther."

"She's dead," Gwen said.

"In the dream . . . ?"

Gwen was shaking her head slowly back and forth. She bit her lip and sipped her wine. The glass shook in her hands. "In the dream she was falling off the bridge. Down, way down. It felt fatal. And then . . . then, it was." Her crescent-shaped blue eyes went to the same place of mourning Phosphorescence had gone to, some interior region of her body, seeking asylum for a woman's dream. "My niece killed herself, just like my sister, her mother," she said. "But I can't help thinking of it as murder."

At that moment, the beautiful young boy, his cheeks still flushed pink, dropped an armful of logs into the basket beside the fire. Giving us a smile so radiant with perfect, pure life that one's cells forgot they shared the earth with Alvin, he excused himself for interrupting us and then stooped to tend the fire. My throat went dry, and my wine had no effect. It was not that he looked like my brother. It was that he carried inside him the same seeds of masculine grace as my brother, and they were just beginning to flower in him. "There, ladies," he said as he released flames from between the logs and the fire leapt out from within. "That should keep you warm." Another of his smiles, and a shank of dark hair fell over his eyes. The firelight obscured their color, but they glistened with the same bright vitality as Phosphorescence. Then he departed. I watched him disappear into the next room, the warmth of the fire he left behind him another cairn marking the route my soul was mapping with my eyes-within-eyes. I do not know long I looked at a beautiful young man who was not there until I heard a gasp beside me.

"Oh my god. She . . ."

"Gwen, are you all right?"

She swallowed and stared at me, though I do not believe she saw me. "She . . . my niece . . . you . . . How is it possible . . . my sister . . ." Gwen blinked again and said, "I can't go."

I reached out to touch her arm. "Gwen, I can't follow what you're saying."

"I can't possibly go to the funeral. Not now. My father will be there. And I can't . . . I can't look him in the face, not now."

"I'm afraid I still don't understand," I said gently.

"I think . . . I think you're right. She was my sister. My niece." Gwen searched my face. "Scorpios like you are have a way of knowing things. . . ."

"Gwen, wait, no, you're just imagining this," I said, my heart pounding. "I don't know what made me say the woman on the bridge in your dream was your sister. You never said that, really, and even if Scorpios have these abilities, I promise you, I don't. I'm sort of a dud, starwise, that *Babylonian* cosmology didn't take on me, really. I . . . I've been . . . writing, working really hard on this book, and my perspective is shot. Totally. I've been getting very mixed up. I see people who aren't here. . . ."

But Gwen was shaking her head the whole time I was talking, and I finally stopped babbling. "You remember how I told you that I'd had this strange call? Just when I was about to call the asylum?"

"What asylum?"

"She was at the home, you know, just south of here. I picked up the phone to call, I was so upset about the dream, and Freddie was on the other end of the phone. He was about to call me."

It was now my turn to stare at Gwen with bafflement. "But how . . ."

"He was a close friend to my . . . I don't know what I should call her."
Gwen's voice dropped into its own husks. "They were together. In that
place on the hill," she said. "The home that's really an asylum, even
though no one wants to say so."

"Freddie was there?"

Gwen's eyes looked up, and I heard my friend's distinct laugh. Gwen
jumped up. "I have to go." She put on her coat and pulled an old knit cap
over her head. The effect was to make her blue eyes jump out. She stood
there, and I could tell that she wanted to say something but was afraid.
"Would you come with me? To the funeral? It's in the morning." Gwen
dropped her face. "I can't face my father . . . now . . . alone. . . ."

My friend returned, accompanied by a short, round-faced woman.
My friend gathers people to her wherever she goes. Most of them turn out
to have gone to high school on Long Island with her. One had the feeling, hanging around with her, that this Long Island High School was the
only high school in America. Always there was a story, an amazing coincidence, a "Can you believe it?" The round-faced woman had been in my
friend's sophomore class and was now living across the river. My friend
introduced her as Nan but was then told that she was no longer Nan. She
was Marona. Marona had been invited to a party in nearby Rock City, a
big bash, and had invited us to join her. My friend, I knew, would go and
be disappointed with me if I didn't. Marona looked at Gwen and said,
"You can come too. It's one of those big, open parties."

Gwen shook her head. "I can't. I have to be somewhere in the morning, and since I don't have a car, it's going to take a long time to get there."
She appealed to me with her eyes.

"Oh, come along," my friend said. "Maybe you'll get some business."

"Oh," Gwen said, sighing. "Business." She looked at me. "Are you
going?"

"Meem, you have to come," my friend said to me, her mouth stumbling comically into the center of pain, as it always did.

"I'm not sure—"

"You have to celebrate the victory over Alvin." My friend looked at
Gwen, whose fate was to be an afterthought, a gesture of politeness. "You
too. You have to celebrate the death of Alvin too."

Gwen was staring at my friend, whose green eyes glinted in the fire-light. "Didn't I get the stain off?" My friend said, looking down at her blouse.

Gwen shook her head. "It's just . . . your eyes," Gwen said. "They remind me of my . . . sister's." Gwen cast a glance at me. "The one who died."

"Your sister died?" said my friend. "I'm sorry. I wouldn't have mentioned this party. I didn't know."

"Neither did I," Gwen said, and left.

"Meem?"

"It was a suicide," I said.

But it felt like a murder.

Rock City was a rude cluster of buildings that had sprung up around a now defunct quarry business. The houses were scattered around a flat bowl in between hills, and if one didn't know where to turn off Route 9W, one would never even know Rock City existed. It had the quality of an abandoned campsite, the tiny cottages tossed around a large building in the center, almost like a lodge, which was where the party was going when we arrived. When Marona said it was a bash, she was right: The house was jammed with people, the music was blasting, and it was clear that everyone had invited someone who didn't know anyone there.

The house belonged to a couple with three young children. He was a construction worker; she, Bettina, was a dancer. I knew her by sight; I had often watched her going up the stairs of the Starr Building (the same building that housed the movie theatre where I had seen Medea's passion), my heart longing to follow her to the top-floor dance studio. The topmost floor of the Starr Building was a curious place. Ever since a legendary bookstore had vacated the space, tenants had come and gone, each experiment failing. Bettina had invested money and sweat—her husband, Tug's, mostly—on converting the space into a dance studio. She was a gangly woman, bony with a chiseled, angular face, with unexpected round breasts perched above her ribs. They were the only soft part of her and seemed not to fit her wiry body. But I soon learned that she was nursing her youngest, aged two. Bettina welcomed us and invited us in as she grabbed at a wayward child and then called out to her husband, "Tug! Tug!" The child tugged on her arm, and Bettina rolled her eyes at us. It was clearly a favorite joke. A tall man with a face cratered by acne appeared. Bettina and Tug shared a peculiar rough-soft quality, as if they were from the same tribe of hill shepherds. He swooped the child up onto his shoulders as the child screamed with glee.

"There's food," Bettina said. "Come."

We had given up our table at The Beek, and so food was the order of the moment. My friend, the historian, wanted to know all about the house. Rock City was a missing chapter in the history of the county. She was always trying to get the county historical society to gather stories and make records of the life being lived in the present, for future archives, and as Bettina answered my friend's questions about the house, the people who lived in other houses around hers, how long she and Tug had been there, I knew my friend was in her professional mode. I wanted food, however, as if food could erase my swirling thoughts about Manda and murder and dreams and sisters and murderous suicides. I let my friend be swooped away by Bettina on a house tour while I went in search of nourishment against the Manda inside me. As they disappeared into the crowd, I caught Bettina saying, "A former meat-packing plant. We sleep in what used to be the refrigerator, which I thought might work as a sort of birth-control backup force, you know, if we made love in a walk-in refrigerator, maybe, for once, I wouldn't get pregnant. . . ."

I asked Tug, his boy perched way above me, the direction to food. The boy answered, "I see food. Over there." He pointed. He giddyapped on his father's shoulders, unable to contain his excitement. Tug winced.

"Hey—careful. Your dad's still not better, remember?"

"Go, horsie, go to food!"

Tug grabbed his son's legs and held them firmly.

"Damn piece of granite fell on me last year. It just hasn't been right since. But it turned out to be a good thing, getting off that reconstruction job for the Y. Gave me time to do the studio for Bettina."

"Giddyap, horsie," said his boy again, and they disappeared into the crowd, gently loping. Tug called out, "Food's to the left."

This meat-packing plant of a house was a labyrinth jammed with people. There were rooms spawning off other rooms, skylights and lofts in places you least expected them, walls suddenly appearing, then disappearing. I made my way, zigzagging through the din, jealous of this couple and their adventures in reconstruction. I felt at once consoled and aggrieved as I made my way through the home of a dancer and her husband who built the space for the dance, the classes in the studio, and the dance of the women in the Y, those underwater ballets of the gravid mothers, the tease of her feet shuffling in the whirlpool where Rulla held court, the shimmying of Queen Pink on the Cadillac orgasm machine. To dance again, I thought. It was rumored Bettina was giving belly-dancing classes. Not belly dancing, I told myself.

The house was bending and the labyrinth forming and unforming as I moved through it in my quest for food, the mobile architecture of dream buildings confusing me. It was a Hades, the soul realm of the floating spirits in as unlikely a location for soul as for Baubo. Are all the asylums in this other Rhinebeck inside Her maze? I walked around the corners and under the exposed beams where death had been kept in storage. Would I find Her here, dancing in the sacred spring with the magic that can heal the bones of fatal accidents and suicides in life that feel like murder in dreams?

I came around a corner, passed under a swinging hammock— empty—walked beside a ladder floating in midair, and felt a fern graze my head. I looked up to see a woman's face covered in feathers.

"Where's your costume?"

Seem to be doing this scene without one.

"Didn't the Dancer tell you to wear a costume? At least a mask."

The Dancer hasn't spoken to me yet.

"I'm an owl."

"And I'm a dove," another face said.

Owl Face Woman was mottled the colors of the earth in the season of the winter solstice. Dove Face Woman was like the snow locked into the sky. Both of them were rounded, plump, and their voices matched their faces. Owl Woman's voice was hooty, Dove Woman's brisk. "Do you like our masks? Aren't they beautiful? They're real feathers, you know. She's Owl. And I'm Dove."

You already told me. . . .

"We make you nervous, don't we?"

Very.

"Owls do make mortals uncomfortable. You know what it means when a human being sees an Owl?"

Ghost stories.

"Aren't you renting that cottage in the woods that looks just like a fairy-tale one?"

"There are all sorts of bird stories in Grimm," Owl Woman said, her feathers shivering around her dark eyes. "About human beings becoming birds, birds becoming human. There's one story about a little girl whose brother is brutally murdered, you know, and he becomes a bird, and sings a song, and in the song she discovers the true story of his murder."

And with that, they began to disappear. "Say hello to the Dancer for us," Dove Woman called as she faded away behind a wall which I could not recall having been there before they spoke to me.

Food, I said to myself. Food will stop the walls from moving and birds speaking to me about fairy tales and murders I want to forget. I was walking through the space where the bird women had been when I caught the scent of perfume. I knew that perfume. The redhead, the one who had led us to the steam room. I looked around me. Faces expanded, contracted, as I moved through the crowded labyrinth. A window appeared, the moon through it. I thought I saw Owl and Dove Woman standing in front of it. I went toward them, afraid yet irresistibly drawn. Their birdy voices chirruped and their feathers quivered as I approached. They seemed to be talking to someone, but I could not see who; a large indoor fica tree with a trunk of braided branches was beside them. I looked to the indoor tree and thought I saw the flash of red hair when I felt a hand on my arm, holding me.

"You are here with your sister?" Rulla said.

She was clothed, and so it took me a moment before I accepted that the thickly accented voice was, indeed, the same voice that went with Rulla's usually naked body. She was wearing a long muumuulike thing made out of what looked like leftover upholstery, in dark burgundy, thickened with floral fuzz, and so far as I could guess, and knowing Rulla's preference for nothing but skin, she was naked underneath. Her patchy, thin hair was hidden under a scarf, and she had painted her eyes in kohl, her lips bright, hot pink.

"She's here somewhere," I said, looking to Rulla and then away, back to the tree.

Rulla followed my gaze. "My beautiful sister. The Dancer." Rulla sighed. "Such a sad, sad time in my beautiful country."

"Rulla," I said, my eyes fixed on the figure near the tree, "I would very much like to be introduced to your sister."

"My sister is so far away. She is dancing for the shah, you know, the shah? My sister, she dances for him."

"I mean, your sister over there . . ."

"Yah, my sister, over there," Rulla said, wistful. She pulled my arm. "Come. We eat now. You are hungry, no?"

"Yes—but—"

"There is beautiful food. Come."

Rulla pulled me away. I turned to see . . . the moon, nothing but the moon in a window, inscrutable.

Rulla led me around another corner, and before us appeared a long table laden with food. The smells of the food filled the space where Her perfume had been, and hunger overwhelmed my already overwhelmed senses. Maybe if I just ate, I told myself, the walls would keep still, and the bird women would return, and they would lead me to Rulla's "sister," dancer for the shah, guide to Eternal Dew, who would at last get a name and a face and I would know that Manda was lying, that there never had been a murder, that She was here and alive.

Pointing to a stewpot on the table, Rulla said, "Lamb," rolling her eyes at me. She shimmied her shoulders, as I had seen her do in the whirlpool to tease and delight the wizened men. She turned her eyes upward, as if lamb were a gift from the gods. "Delicious," she said.

120

It then struck me that I had never before seen Rulla outside the Y. "What are you doing here?" I said, taking some of the lamb; it smelled wonderful.

"Bettina, she is my student." The note of pride was unmistakable in her voice. "Belly dancing. I teach in Bettina's studio. Only very special women I take. Only sisters." Rulla then shimmied again, this time more than just her shoulders. Her long muumuu wobbled as Rulla, humming some private tune that I could actually hear over the blasts of Crosby, Stills, and Nash, moved over the food, plucking, gathering. "I was very famous in my country," she said. "When I was younger, oh! You cannot imagine. I was dancer for the shah too," she said as she continued to pile her plate with food and more food, more than she could possibly eat. As I filled my plate, moving around the table, Rulla humming in joy at the memory of herself dancing for the shah, my foot stumbled against something. Rulla looked up. "My bag," she said. "Careful. Please."

She took another plate and placed it on top of the one she had loaded with food. She came next to me and gently lowered the double plate into a large shopping bag. "So much in America," she said. "So much extra. Extra, extra, extra," she said as she stood up and began sashaying her hips, beginning to hum again. "Oh, yes," she said, "you cannot imagine, you American, dancing like Rulla dance in her country, with her sister."

I was not the only one watching the short, fat, muumuu-upholstered old woman with the black-lined eyes begin to move around the room, humming louder now. A small crowd gathered around Rulla, and we could hear the tune she was humming more clearly than the blast of hippie nostalgia. Rulla, aware of her audience, began to clap in time to her secret tune, in a rhythm that was unfamiliar to us. She clapped it out carefully, loudly emphasizing the beat, as if instructing us, and the small crowd began to follow. Rulla smiled. The crowd was mostly women and one enormous man with white hair and a long white beard. The features of his face were as delicate as his body was not, and his eyes were twinkling as he watched Rulla. He was the first of the audience to get Rulla's rhythm right, and as she passed him, she nodded. She circled again, and again, three times, then stopped and stood before him, her squat body shaking one way, then another. She tickled invisible streams of hair with her fingers, set light into laughter, and her arms, as she raised them slowly up the sides, to the beat, spiraled like water snakes furling, rippling, unfurling, twisting, so smoothly, wondrously, I found myself lost. Her arms teased waves out of an invisible ocean as she slowly stepped away from the large white twinkling man, moving backward, into the space that had formed inside the circle of onlookers.

Then, on the beat, her arms stiffened above her and she jumped, shouting, "Hey-ah!"

"Hey-ah!" replied the twinkling man.

That doll-like mama hippo's rolling tides of copper and rose flesh began to move in ways that we could not believe possible. Facing the enormous twinkling man, Rulla lowered her hands slowly, moving them like wise velvet serpents, until they were resting on her hips. She then had the cheek, the bravura, the audacity to grab at that thick muumuu and pull it tight around those hippo hips of hers. It was not a boast but an invitation to the twinkling man to join her in the marvel of dance, in the wonder of bodies that mean what they move, an offering to him of the skin of the radiating cosmos, a beckoning to engage in the abundance of life with which she had been blessed. She began to move her hips forward and back in a motion which would have been obscene in anyone else. But in Rulla, it was not the motion of fucking, it was an oceanic swell, the tug of the crescent moon on the crescent hips of woman, the rhyme of the cosmos with the rhyme of a woman's bones, rhythm inside rhythm inside the dance. Her ample body moved like the earth must have moved in the mind's eyes of the ancients when they sang such a song as the one Rulla was now singing, full throated and off key. And it was beautiful, this was the song of Rulla's flesh, this song she sang with her entire being, and the man with the twinkling eyes, Santa Claus himself, heard it. He heard the song of Rulla's bones, the song of the earth for her lover the sky, and he could not restrain himself any longer. He'd been waiting for this dance for the two thousand years since Christianity had hurled his elfin self out of the earth and into the sky. Now that Alvin had been silenced, he could at last come down from the sky and join her.

He stepped into the circle with a delicacy to match the fineness of his features, a lightness of foot and hand that made all his weight like a buoy of joy. His eyes sparkled, and Rulla felt that spark coming toward her. She moved herself forward, gliding on the fluid bones of her sea-self as he made tiny pulsations, little bounces of his enormous body, joyful little sparks. He was delight, she was desire; he was flash, she swell; and the two of them circled each other in anticipation of the ecstasy of their meeting after so many eons of being apart, lovers returned through eternities of loneliness to find the ineluctable chemistry of his bright spurt and her silken rolls, as vital as it had been the first time, when he was a hunter with a bow and she a maiden who tended the pigs.

By now the crowd had doubled, and the sound of the music had all but faded from our minds as we clapped to keep time for Santa Claus and the anonymous Venus of Hacilar and Catal Huyuk as they approached each other inside this spontaneous circle in Rock City. As they moved closer and closer, the clapping got louder and faster, but the two of them were lost in each other's rhythms, the pulse and surge of each other, the reunion of the tidal with the gleam, ocean with spark. He made a tiny step, Rulla glided toward him; another bounce, a slide; a step side to side, a pelvic scoop, and another, till their bellies were within touch of each other. Santa Claus seemed to freeze up at the last moment, not sure; but Rulla knew what to do with the suddenly fearful man. She had known what to do for eons past counting. She had known what to do long before the sky ever guessed its role in creation. She grabbed his hips and, looking right into his face, she pulled his belly to hers. At the moment of contact, a great yelp went up from the crowd. Rulla held his belly to hers, and she arched herself backward, and then she began to shake. Beside me, I heard someone say, "My god, she's going to shake her bones!" It was Bettina, another child cradled on her hips.

"What's shaking her bones?"

"Watch. It's what only the best can do. It's almost impossible."

Rulla, her eyes closed, in a trance, moved away from Santa Claus, whose dance now faded away, the climax over. He watched as Rulla extended her arms, the elbows bent just a little, and began to shimmy. The crowd had stopped clapping; they stood completely still, as if hypnotized by the sight. The burgundy muumuu quivered all over, and then something miraculous happened, Rulla's entire body began to quiver all over, as if she were showing us the invisible secret dance of her nerves, as if those cheerful, twinkling pulsations of Santa Claus had entered her and filled her entire body and ignited her bones with the sky god's brilliance and she was about to dematerialize into pure energy. I saw right through the muumuu to her body, I could see every fold of coppery rose shaking, her broad bell-like breasts pulsing, every part of her was alive, as if on her flesh the cosmic pattern of life danced, set into motion by Eros, the meeting of man and woman, sky and earth, fire and water. I felt someone gripping my arm. It was my friend, her eyes glowing with rapture as we watched Rulla's body shaking from the bottom of her legs, passing up through those lunar hips like some cyclone of pure earth energy, upward to her breasts, her shoulders. And then her cheeks shook, and I heard Bettina gasp as the skin of Rulla's face fluttered like a moth's wings. She lifted her arms, and they too were shaking with the pulsing light of Him inside Her. She held them aloft, for one last moment, and then—stopped.

There wasn't a sound or a movement. It was as if she had pulled up from the earth its heart of fire and returned it to the sky god, cold in his lofty, vacant perch without her earthy hearth. Slowly, so slowly, she lowered her arms and came back to us from wherever she had been. She turned to meet the eyes of all gathered around her, not to receive their praise but to share in the mutual joy of what had just passed through her body. Her eyes rested on Santa Claus, and that woman, that Queen of the Y, that little round doll of rose skin, winked.

Santa Claus winked back.

A whoop went up from the crowd.

"Death to Alvin," my friend said.

"Long live the shaking of the bones," added Bettina.

"So sad," I heard another voice saying, and looked to see Owl Woman before me. "So sad that Baubo has to go down with Her."

124

It was late, the night cold. I dropped my friend off at her house in the middle of town and then made my way back to the cottage in the woods. The moon was the same inscrutable face it had been all night as I drove down Main Street. Ahead of me, the red light of the intersection with Route 9 was blinking, the hour being so late. Rudolph was dimmed. And there, in front of the smoke shop, was Freddie's wooden rainbow man, his lights twinkling randomly off and on.

I stopped my car at the intersection. Wooden rainbow man had been pointing directly toward The Beekman Arms earlier that evening, I was sure of it. But now he was pointing a different direction. I followed his blind gaze. His wooden face seemed to be pointing at a diagonal, away from The Beekman Arms, toward the Starr Building, across the intersection and to my right.

I sensed movement in my peripheral vision. I turned around and thought I saw someone in Mr. Bert's. A man? A mound of blond hair was moving behind the counter, back and forth. All I could make out was the head of hair, which quickly disappeared behind Mr. Bert's magazine rack, the one at the back with the hunting and outdoor magazines. Mr. Bert explained, to anyone who would ask (as, of course, Benjamin's mother had), that his politics didn't go by the usual names, but what they came down to was this: It was okay to carry gun magazines and candy in the same store, but not pornography and candy. He politely referred customers to the place that did, next to the gas station on the other side of town, adding that, so far as he knew, the owner didn't vote. And that, he had said, was how come it didn't bother him one bit what people might say about his hiring Freddie Van Heusen. He (politely) didn't give a damn about what other people did or said about what was right or wrong; it was his life he was living, not anyone else's.

A side door opened. Freddie was tall and well built, which I had not expected. His blond hair, I now saw, was a wig, perched precariously on top of his actual hair. He went to the wooden rainbow man and stood in front of him for a while, talking to the statue. Mine was the only car there at this hour, and I wished myself invisible when Freddie caught sight of me watching him. He grinned, and called out, "Can I help you?" in a voice which also surprised me. It was a rich baritone, and he spoke with authority. "Are you lost?" he asked, for I had not responded.

I shook my head from behind my closed window. Then, to prove I wasn't as lost as I, of course, was—lost beyond imagining lost—I made my way very slowly through the intersection, turning to the left, south, in the direction of the cottage in the woods. I was passing by Freddie as he began to play with the rainbow lights on his native tobacco god, for so the wooden rainbow man now seemed, divine, larger than human, beside this curious local Adonis sporting his blond curls, his broad shoulders, half god himself, gigantic offspring of a fantastic splinter.

In my rearview mirror I saw Freddie rearranging the lights on the wooden rainbow man's face, moving them away from his blind eyes. Freddie then put his own face down beside the wooden rainbow man's and seemed to check where his wooden eyes were looking. Was it my imagination, or did Freddie shift the wooden rainbow man's position just slightly, to make it clear beyond doubt that his eyes, cleared of any lights which might have blocked his line of vision before, were staring at the Starr Building and no other?

I made it as far as the abandoned stone house, with its sign reading, Zoned for Antiques, before I turned around. Freddie was no longer there as I passed; only his sparkling cairn, pointing the way. I parked in front of the Starr Building. The third-floor light from the dance studio glowed,

126

honey-colored asylum beyond the reach of the chilled arm of the winter solstice.

Before I went up those stairs, in Rhinebeck, New York, on that frigid night so many years ago, I tried to make myself believe—one last time—that the emerging map of another Rhinebeck between fiction and life was a lie. It was my final attempt at clinging to a faith contrary to the one my soul recognized as its original one. I told myself there was no region between imagination and experience governed by laws of its own. There was no story emerging from the world surrounding me, no tale happening inside a Rhinebeck mapped by soul and in soul—no such Hudson Valley existed. I said to myself, You are as guilty of misnaming the inhabitants of Manda's asylum as Columbus was when he landed in America and called the native chiefs Indians.

It is time (I continued to lecture myself) to let the Chief in the story—The Murder Mystery—do what he is supposed to do: find Manda's victim. There is no other chief with a mouth which moves from one Rhinebeck through another through yet another, promising restoration every time you see it. You live in a real house which you rent from eccentric scientists who spend most of their time overseas studying what happens to the brain cells when it is as dark as the solstice. Manda's asylum is no fairy-tale cottage belonging to an owl and a dove singing on a tree that will yield fruit again only when your soul's story of your brother's death is told. You are a writer, Meem's writing The Murder Mystery, and you must follow the rules of the genre: Victims of murder are dead, the authorities find the killer, and no birds sing.

Yet my feet walked toward the Starr Building in defiance of my every effort to preserve my infrastructure from complete deterioration. My body had other designs for the story and other terms for the divinity my soul would embrace as its own. Before I knew it, I was standing at the outer door of the Starr Building and pressing down the latch. The door opened. My mind rushed to deploy reason against the emergence of a story constructed by no builder within myself. It is a mistake, I continued to preach at myself, a trick of sense that you believe a woman who has been murdered is upstairs in the studio, dancing. The blind eyes of Freddie's wooden rainbow man are no more capable of opening doors than you are of entering a mobile, wall-less labyrinth through the multiple open mouth of the Chief of Restoration Tragedy. No architecture exists, no physics allows, such an entry by such a body. This door is the front door of the Starr Building, constructed long ago, and no star on the chart of the destiny Manda says she has brought for you to chart, with your own names for its constellations. The name of this building is pure coincidence, a bad pun no competent writer would ever allow herself to put into her fiction, and no accidental symmetry of soul with surroundings.

I entered and stood at the bottom of the stairwell, slowly raising my eyes. If you find Her up there in the dance studio, remember—She's dead. Manda told you she killed Her, and she's told Daryl, and he has locked her up in jail, and Gwen has asked you to the funeral tomorrow. And just because she was killed on the bridge in a dream—and the railings actually broke—and you thought you saw her in the car—and the redhead never came back to the Y—does not mean a beautiful mouth ever opened after you saw a movie in this very building about an ancient murder in an ancient time and a murder in this one—

But my mind was impotent against my body, which was carrying me up the stairs, my heart racing with the expectation of a joy that would crack my being, utterly, at the sight of Her. Infrastructure deteriorated totally, my inner sermon proved heresy, when I reached the open door of the dance studio.

I stood at the threshold. A flash of rainbow-colored chiffon grazed my vision, the same swatch from my mother's closet that I would wrap around my naked body when I danced and danced in the afternoon sunlight of my parents' bedroom in Chicago. I stepped inside to see the rainbow chiffon rippling above me as the Dancer raced around the room, holding it behind her as I used to in those days when I awaited my brother's verdict about magnets and magic and me.

She whirled and let the rainbow chiffon wrap around her, spinning and spinning until She was cocooned in a little girl's idea of the utterly beautiful, the sensuality of the silk, and the thinness of the fabric where the light played through it all I ever desired for reality. From inside the chrysalis of silken rainbows I heard a voice saying, "Should I unwind for you?"

128

I said, "I never could figure out how."

"Watch me."

The Dancer performed the trick my own body never could, un-winding herself from the silk in a fluid unfurling, releasing the body from the rainbow womb of the beautiful into life. Where the music came from, I don't know, I only heard it moving inside my muscles as they once had, before the accident; and how many of Her there were, reflected in the mirrors around the walls, I did not bother to count, nor did it matter. That She was dancing, that She was here, multiplied in Her beautiful form in an infinitude of fluid grace, was all my grievous form needed to behold the rhapsody of women and dream and asylum.

I fed my starved bones with the sweet food of motion, filling my in-jured, sorry skeleton with dance the only way I could. I danced inside my still body with Her as She moved around the large room, coated in amber light, Her red hair loose. Scarves appeared, in the same colors and shape I had when I would dance for my brother. He always had the charity to applaud his little sister. I watched as the silken trailings of my adoration of my brother moved across Her body, feeling the silk on my girlish skin as it floated over Her womanly form, anguish mingling with joy, hollowness tickling ecstasy. I could have stood at the threshold forever, watching Her, and perhaps, in a way, I have for these many years; for dance has no permanence but what is held inside the heart and eye of those who behold it in the temporal bodies of those who make it during the time they are alive. Giving the Dancer this one scene, in Her asylum from the story of the body spoken by the mouth of death, is the only way I can arrest Her motion and align the dance of the cosmos into a line formed by words on a page, lending the gift of im-mortality that language alone confers to that elemental art that is so per-ilously mortal.

The music ceased, the scarves abated, and She stopped before the mirror. To Her own multiple reflections, She said, "You finally found me."

I could not speak.

"I told Freddie you needed some help," She went on. "Did he really light up that wooden Indian? He said you would know the improvised god when you saw him, and if you didn't . . . but we believed all along you would, in spite of that mind of yours, which always gets in your way." She smiled.

My bones turned to milk.

Then She said, "It is time for you to say my name."

I had been waiting for this moment, but now that it had come, I stalled. "What will happen when I do?"

She rolled a rainbow-colored scarf around Her long arms, twirling it through Her fingers with the simple, mute fascination of a child who seizes, in the moment her curiosity is ignited, the thing which has aroused her interest. She studied the way the rainbow silk wrapped around Her, a sleeve made of the lost wings of butterflies, forgetting me in Her rapture with texture and color and sensation.

Then the rainbow scarf dropped to the ground before Her. "It's already happened."

I closed my eyes against the assault of sorrow.

"Manda is—"

But I couldn't hear what She said about Manda, for the name alone, on Her lips, deafened me to all but my own terror and grief.

There was a silence between us before She said, quietly, "I don't have a chance unless you say my name."

"A chance . . . ?"

"At restoration."

She nodded quietly, Her red hair falling over Her cheek. Then She raised Her face to mine, pulling Her hair away (as Manda never did). I saw the green brilliance of Her eyes. They had the same phosphorescent glimmer as those of the foreign woman in the jewelry store who had killed the screech of Alvin, insisting that "life is too short for such ugliness." And they were the same eyes as those of the beautiful young man who had tended the fire at The Beek, where many travelers had sought asylum throughout this country's history. It was the rhyme of those eyes with a real woman, and the body with what my body had dreamed of becoming, moving the sinuous moves of Rulla, sister to the nameless Venuses of the ancient rock cities; and the rhyme of those eyes with a boy who had once been my young soul's inspiration to match his beauty with beauty of my own, now lost to me; and another who tended fires too, knowing without my having to speak out loud my need for things to keep me warm—together all these rhymes of Her body with the bodies of others formed within my soul a conspiracy of dancers breathing in time with each other in an immortal rhythm, and awakened the desire in me—despite the awful risk—to speak Her name. Knowledge that this dance goes on where we cannot see it with the eyes of life on this side entered me through the phosphorescence of her eyes and the eyes of others in Rhinebeck—all the Rhinebecks on all the maps—the green nerves of life radiating in all their faces. And I knew, without words, that the dance goes on inside the souls of those who bear witness to it but stops in the souls of those who will not open their eyes inside the mouth belonging to an authority beyond oneself. And when we stand before Her, and bear witness, we must find the courage to give Her the name we know Her by.

The Dancer nodded, able to sense my own thoughts as I was thinking them. "That's right," She said gently. "This is how Manda has done this, for twenty-seven thousand years. If you do not give me your name for me, Manda will finish what she came here to do."

"Kill you?"

"Manda kills the Baubo who dances life here, laughing through the pain. She kills the joy we possess for our own vitality, which we can neither protect nor defend—but can ourselves destroy, out of fear. That is why she has never failed, not in all this time. Her favorite method is the one she has used with you: to tell you that I am dead already. If you believe her, then killing yourself is nothing but an afterthought, a return after hours to lock the door between you and the dance. And the murder of your own soul will feel like a dream from which you awoke too soon to find out who the murderer was."

"Suicide which feels like a murder," I said as I saw the red-headed guide through the maze plunge from the bridge, a long-armed woman capable of holding all of life in her arms. The spontaneous lexicon belonging to the world of my friend and Benjamin and me, the world of short-armed and long-armed women, Eternal Dew, floating pianos, Queen Pink and Mother Queen Pink, skies crying to make slugs before rainbows.

She nodded, able to dance with my mind as I had swayed with Her body. "Yes," She said. "That is what Manda kills: not the part of us that loves life, but the way life loves us. That's why the children are so vulnerable to her."

"Not—"

"Benjamin? He is a strong one. He knows Manda is here." I shook my head in horror. She tossed a scarf and let it float softly down into Her open hand. "Why do you think he brings you things to keep you warm? He knows better than you how dangerous your coldness is now that you can no longer dance. He may survive. He may not."

The memory of my brother pierced me, sending out from my grief a flare of anger. I wanted to fight Manda and use my own eyes and their truth—She was here in Rhinebeck and She was dancing—as my weapon against the Panther. But I was afraid that if She told me Her name She would be in terrible danger from the Panther Herself. Again She nodded, my thoughts not my own. "Once you speak my name," She said, "Manda will know I am here and try to kill me, as she already has, countless times." The reflections behind Her in the mirrors stirred, silk remnants of cosmic breath. "She doesn't know yet, for certain, if you've found me or not. She thinks I'm at the Y, across the river, which is a problem for her. Not the river, but the stone and the Dew—she is afraid of them."

She waited, Her phosphorescent eyes upon me. Finally I could not stand the lie any longer—my Cretan lie. I broke down and admitted what I had hoped to keep secret, even to myself. "I know your name," I said.

"Freddie told me you did. You were just scared."

"I am," I said. "Terrified."

She tilted Her head, thoughtful. "That's what happens when Manda reaches your kind before I do. It used to be that I always showed up first. But that was a long, long time ago. She has been gaining strength all this time, while I . . ." Lexy sighed and gestured to Her body. "I've been dancing for so long."

"You can't stop."

"Oh, every dancer has to face the day when she can't dance anymore."

132

She raised Her lovely arm and let the rainbow chiffon slip to the floor. She began gently and slowly to tuck in the sides of the fallen rainbow chiffon with Her foot.

I dropped my head in my hands, closing my eyes against the vision of Her. "I will go mad," I said. "Like Freddie. I can't defeat Manda."

"You don't have to do it alone."

My heart leapt away from me. "You'll fight her with me?"

"Hasn't Manda explained to you? We can't take the test for you. But I will continue to send you guides to help you."

"How will I recognize a guide?"

"You will feel as though you are with me." She finished tucking in the sides of the rainbow chiffon, forming a deep, enfolded nest.

I thought for a moment. "Do guides mean what they move, like you?"

"Yes," She said, smiling. "Guides must be able to move in two directions, yes."

"Like Freddie on Main Street."

"Like Freddie on Main Street."

Another silence, another stirring of Her silken glass forms in the mirrors behind Her. Then the Dancer broke away from the mirror, to the other side of the room. She looked out the window and then turned to face me. Those eyes, the color of electric life inside the ocean, fire in the dew of the sky, source of original food, darkened for a moment, a shadow moving over them. "It's time," She said. "You have to say my name out loud. You must do it tonight. Before the solstice passes through us. Which will be in a few moments, at this latitude."

I had believed the test of my courage, my heart strength, would be to call out the Panther, welcome the murderer into my house, listen to the story of the voice with boots on that kills. But these were easy acts, common terrorist fodder to feed the modern psyche of an educated woman like me. Psychosis, horror, killing, obscenity, the lashing voice of Manda's contempt—these were impotent cant compared to the quaking awe I felt standing before my soul, asking me to give Her real, mortal life.

My lips would not move. I could hear Her name pounding inside me to be released into the air which circulated through all the Rhinebecks on the map—but I could not risk letting Manda kill Her, as she had done so many times before. But this time, when she came for Her, the murder would be my murderous suicide of the way life loved me. And, when Manda was done with killing my vitality, she would step over the corpse of my soul to the next obvious victim in the Rhinebeck lineup: Benjamin. I trembled, standing before Her, the rainbow chiffon nest at Her feet, a holy vessel waiting for my sacrificial offering, Her green eyes shadowed with sadness as though She were seeing what I was seeing. Manda passing through Benjamin, after she had killed his soul, to my friend, who suspected nothing as the Panther crouched, ready to spring, delighting in the thrill of the ambush.

I was about to say no, I give up, I won't do it, the test of giving my soul real life, here, now, is too much for my battered, modern self, not even for the sake of the two people I love most in the world, a radiant friend, her joyous scavenging son, I do not have the courage to let life love me, fully, the risk in this Manda-world is too great—when I felt my brother hovering beside me. I looked at my soul in waiting for the naming. She raised her fingers to Her lips and shook her head to warn me not to look at the source of the voice of my brother, else he would disappear. She seemed to hold my gaze in Her eyes to protect me from the temptation—fierce as only first love can be—to see his face again. I let myself be locked into Her eyes as his voice whispered to me (I felt his breath on my ear, smelled the mineral smell of his bedroom), Didn't I remember? He was the one who would know. And he knew that I was ready for magic now. That was why he was going to let me play with the magnets today. My soul and my heart and my body would be fastened together forever now, I was ready for the alchemy of air which would join the Dancer to me for eternity.

I believed everything my brother ever told me. If he said I was ready for the magic of my soul, alive, then it didn't matter what I thought, or felt, or believed, or feared, for this was the voice of my brother, the magician, the Ace with the magnets.

"You are Lexy," I said. "Law of the Y."

Her silken reflections vanished, Lexy with them, and I was standing in front of a Panther.

The Panther

Not *a* Panther, Summacious. When are you going to learn how to write? *The* Panther. The only Panther that was ever seen in the northeastern United States. *Yours.*

You are my Panther.

For your eyes only.

Why did you come back?

The Messenger doesn't do Why. Just tells the story.

How? How did you come back?

Ashes, of course. Remember that haiku you wrote in fifth grade? No cherry blossoms for you. You were going to write something original. All the other little girls were talking about petals and perfume, but not you. You wrote about the skins flying off the backs of the burning children and the soldiers mistaking them for angels, precisely the correct number of syllables each line, even though the truth, Eraserface, is that you don't know what a syllable, a.k.a. a breath, is to save your life, let alone the lives of those children.

How come I can talk to you? Me, ashes. You, ashes. Ashes to Ashes. Come on, Summacious, don't look so sad. This is good news, for once. Wouldn't you rather be a Child of Ashes than a baby boomer? So much more elegant. So much more resonance. Child of Ashes—this, a soul can work with. Trust me; I have a feel for these things—take Vishnu and the

Bhagavad Gita over Spock and the Census Bureau. Even if the only Vishnu you have isn't the real thing, just Oppenheimer's funky translation. He's standing there looking at the bomb go off and he's saying, I, Robbie, am the form of forms, death the great bringer of life, he's doing poetry about the atom bomb too, Miss No Cherry Blossoms for Me, you and Oppenheimer, waxing moony over ashes.

Summacious, I am doing a very interesting routine here. Key, I'd say. The big clue. Me. Manda. The thing that can come out of the same trees you gotta dive down into and swim through if you are ever going to get your soul safely on the side of Main Street without splinters—but: I can kill you before you reach the underground river of stars to pick up the packet with the instructions for how to do Eleusis on them, hallucinate the seed inside the dark—Ashes to Ashes Me turns out to be your one and only Panther. At least crack a smile, for once. You gotta laugh at something this scary. You don't laugh, you're gonna wind up like my sister.

Dead.

Think of it as evolution, Summacious. If I can run twenty-seven thousand years and crack open a mouth in the cosmos and turn into a Panther so that I can find the woman who means that she moves—one more time—just think of how much you're going to have to evolve to get to her first.

Who knows where your Panther is, waiting for you to call her out and turn you into a Child of Ashes. Mine was in Vermont, that green shard of New England which seems to belong to the original map of the asylum my ancestors imagined this land could be. In Vermont, the skin of the earth is so dense with the life on it that nothing, not even the dark winter solstice, can erase the verdant green. As the December dark approaches there, at the edge of the horizon you can see a vivid vein of phosphorescent light, electric in its intensity, liminal life held at the edge.

There was another green from my time in Vermont, as permanent and undefeated as the green of the perpetual skin of the earth. But this other green was unnatural, or, worse, posing as natural, spreading over the floor of the insane asylum as if it were grass. The mental institution was a huge, tomblike brick building perched on a hill, with tiny windows to let in prescribed fractions of the view across the White River toward New Hampshire. The antiseptic smells within barely masked the swampy sepsis of the men and women incarcerated there. In that denatured building they seemed consoled by their own stink, as if solace could only come from the scents which arise from below.

I was there as an apprentice to the resident dance therapist, on a work-study project for my senior year at a nearby boarding school. This dancer who knew how to heal was a woman in her forties (as I am now) with a gentleness and courage I despaired of ever attaining. She was utterly beautiful to me. One of the elderly patients who had lived in the confines of this brick mausoleum since her infancy once said to me, "It makes me feel good to see her moving."

"Yes," I had replied. "Me too." And then, curious in a clinical, superior way, I had said to the crazy woman, "What do you think makes her move so beautifully?"

The old patient had looked at me with that special astonishment the insane reserve for the stupidity of the sane. "She means what she moves," she said. "People who don't mean what they move," she added, apparently feeling that illumination of a snooty eighteen-year-old girl was required, "it never comes to them."

"What never comes to them?"

"It," she said, stupefied that I, someone from the outside, did not know.

A description of the dancer's face will do you no good, for it was not in her face. And no matter how many words I might find to conjure up the shape of her body in your eyes, they are useless too. For It was not of the eye. It was of some organ for which we have no name, like the missing spleen of Chinese anatomy, there but not there. It was a quality of being she possessed, and the only words that ever captured it for me were the patient's—she meant what she moved. And because she meant what she moved, she saved my life when the Panther attacked me.

Soon after that brief exchange with the patient there was a big dance event bringing the elderly men and women together. There was much excitement among the patients at the prospect of being able to touch the opposite sex. The women, all over fifty, the same age as Freddie's chosen ones, giggled like schoolgirls as they came into the room where the men either sat in drugged stupor or jerked like marionettes.

As the group of women entered, the oldest and the stinkiest and the ugliest of them all, Isabel, with horselike yellow buckteeth and red wisps of hair around a freckled bald spot, went to the middle of a circle that had spontaneously formed. She curtsied. She turned. She grinned. She lifted her grease-stained flowered housedress to reveal her wrinkled, flaccid genitals. Blissfully exposed, Isabel announced that she was the

Queen. As she paraded her genitals for all to see, she instructed them that they'd better behave for the Queen. "Isabel is a French name," she said, with imperial authority through her great teeth. "And I am the Queen of France."

The Woman Who Means What She Moves quickly rushed in to stand beside Isabel before any of the white-coated orderlies could take Isabel away. She bowed to the Queen, her graceful movements conveying respect and reverence. So would Aphrodite approach Baubo—with reverence for her ugly sister whose silly dance lifts from the goddess the burden of representing perfect form as, together, they shimmy and wiggle and tease all of life, in all its forms, to the dance.

In a loud French accent, the Woman Who Means What She Moves asked the Queen if she would like to have the first dance. But Isabel turned from her and sat down, pouting. For all of the grace with which she had intervened, to participate in the hallucinatory reality of an Other requires, I now know, some sort of invitation, and the dancer had not been invited into Isabel's French court. "Madame la Queen," said the Woman Who Means What She Moves, "I zee I have offended you. I am zo zorry. Pardonnez-moi, Queen Isabel," she said, and dropped to her knees before the seated Isabel.

The orderlies retreated.

It was said that when Isabel was eight years old, and first brought to the asylum, she had tried to escape. She had slipped by the guards one summer night, dressed only in a nightgown, her feet bare. They had just noticed her gone and were planning pursuit when they found her, curled up into a tight ball, rolling, holding her bare feet in her hands off the ground. They say she was screaming, begging to be taken back inside. Now she was seventy-three years old, this Queen of the Asylum, and she had not taken off her shoes since (except in violent protest and with her eyes squeezed shut and her body wracked with the dry heaves of panic).

Isabel looked down at the bowed head of the Woman Who Means What She Moves and said, "Off with her shoes!"

The Woman Who Means What She Moves immediately began to remove her shoes. Isabel looked at her court gathered around her, asserting the truth of her absolute power. The Woman Who Means What She

Moves held her shoes out to Isabel, her entire body crouched in apology and shame. Isabel stared.

And stared.

The others around us grew restless. Barks and a few random melodies escaped from their mouths in a volley of querulous notes. One of the younger men was over at the stereo, and before we knew it, the sound of the Viennese waltz filled the room. Realizing in an instant that there would be chaos if she did not assume control as herself, the Woman Who Means What She Moves tossed aside her shoes and, in her bare feet, began to lead the inmates in the waltz.

The legs of the women were either scrawny and ridged as birds or pebbled with fat and veins compressed inside nylons tied at their knees with navel-like knots. Underneath the sound of the music I could hear the shuffle of their slippers as they moved. These women were like the walking dead, yet the dead had more dignity and status than they. The dead had the privilege of having had their experience; these were women for whom the simplest of experiences—grass—was not only denied but undesired. It seemed cruel that their minds had to carry around their bodies, that they had been given flesh and nerve yet no access to them, walking ghosted Drings without the skin of experience, and no way to mean what they moved the way life had intended the human body to move.

Isabel waltzed alone. In an affected nasal voice she addressed the air, explaining to nothing that the waltz was not French but German. Confusion. The war. "I have no country! I have no country!" she shouted.

The waltz swelled, unto itself, as they danced. Smocked and flowered and pajamaed elderly women moved in strange sways like algae tossed in a gentle ocean with sporadic spasms erupting from them at random. Many were locked on the sidelines in the rocking rhythms of their psychosis, and it was my job, as apprentice, to see if I could introduce into their psychotic bodies the rhythm of the waltz.

I chose a group of three old women who were hunched and as indifferent to the waltz of the sea algae as you might imagine the ancient Fates to be, too busy with their weaving of the threads of individual destiny to have time to worry about communal plankton. The dance of their fingers weaving the web of humanity was all that mattered, and so it seemed with these three crones: Their fingers worked inside their hands with a mysterious, frenetic purpose. As I approached, one of them, Fran, saw me and instantly clapped her hands into her armpits, making her look like a child imitating a chicken. She worked her elbows frantically as if to ward me off with a ritual gesture simulating the flight of escape.

I sat down next to Fran. I took one of my hands and tucked it under my armpit, hoping that gentle mime would allow Fran to think of me as a benevolent presence. I wanted to mean what I moved, like the dancer; I had wanted to mean what I moved ever since I could remember. I did not love to dance; dancing itself was love. Dancing was how love would find me. Dancing was how my body would be ready when he did find me. My imagined beloved would recognize me as his when I meant what I moved: These were my facts of life.

But Fran was not easily converted to my faith. She abruptly wrapped her arms around herself and began to rock vigorously in another ritual attempt, at self-comfort, trying to protect herself from my strangeness. I began to rock like her, slowly. After some time, long enough to have the waltz turn into a rumba and the sea algae metamorphose into human confetti tossed spontaneously around the room, Fran seemed aware of me. Slightly encouraged, I continued to rock, gradually building up to the same intensity as Fran's.

As she and I rocked together in the regular rhythm of the primal motion of the infant, I sensed her with me, sensed that she was ready to trust me. I began to move my clasped arms. I now tried to see if, by gradually releasing my arms with each rocking motion upward, I could get Fran to let go of her embrace of herself and direct her attention outward. I worked slowly and patiently as the music changed again, and the Woman Who Means What She Moves began to lead a line dance around the room. Fran seemed utterly oblivious to the change in music, and her large brown eyes rolled at me cowlike as she lifted her arms away from her body in imitation of my own.

I was excited. I felt I had reached her. I moved my arms a little farther away, and Fran did the same. We were both excited by the discovery that we were able to lift our arms, and our mutual excitement made us rock faster. Fran seemed, to my young mind, thrilled, and I thought that I was displaying exceptional skill, evidence that I had the magic to heal that I sensed in my mentor. I was not only meaning what I moved, I thought, but I was changing the meaning of how Fran could move. We rocked, our arms beginning to fly away from our torsos, and when they would return on the downward motion, we were both making a marvelous "thwack" against the tops of our thighs with our palms. We had almost reached the point when our arms would open as wide as wings, fully extended away from ourselves. Only a few more rocks, I thought, and she would be there—free, I believed, from her need to huddle and protect and comfort her abandoned body. Once, twice, on the next upward motion it would happen.

Fran opened her arms wide, imitating mine. A smile of triumph began to form on my face as I stretched my arms outward in the posture of flight and of embrace, of escape and of welcome. In the split second before Fran's body could mirror mine, her cowlike eyes clouded over, yet her arms obeyed mine, so locked was she in my body that she had no choice but to do as I was doing. At the moment her arms reached outward, her entire face capsized in anguish. My own arms were still wide open in what was now a mockery of freedom as Fran folded herself into herself beside me. And it was at that moment, with my arms held wide to embrace whatever might come, that the Panther burst into the room.

The waves of elderly men and women parted for the Panther. The line dance fell away, like cooked meat off bones, as they retreated. Across the room, I could hear over the music the pumping of her breath inside her chest. Her smock vibrated with life and fury and determination. She stood at a distance, her head moving back and forth as her black hair swished across her face. Then she saw me. She crouched, low, a hand on the ground, another, and froze.

Male orderlies rushed in. I heard exclamations that she had escaped from the violent ward. I saw them frantically handing something to the largest of them, a man as burly and bearlike as any I have ever seen, and to my horror I realized it was a straitjacket. The bear-orderly was rushing toward the Panther, holding the straitjacket out. I felt the fear rippling through all the institutional staff about "her." Whoever "she" was, she was someone. To have identity of any kind in such a place is a sign of power. Someone called out that the straitjacket wouldn't work. Something about not being allowed. Made her worse. She'd been known to. The Panther jerked her head, saw the straitjacket, and leapt toward me.

She now crouched, swaying back and forth, so close to me that I smelled her breath. It was sweet, minted, and the sweetness of it scared me more than the expected foulness, for when one's enemy is lovely, one is in real hell. Her skin—what I could see of it beneath her black curtain of hair—was pale, perfect, unmarred by any craters or scars. She shook her head, the black hair shimmied, as if to snarl without sound at me and invite me to fight.

Behind her the bear-orderly stood, paralyzed, the straitjacket in his hands, while behind him went on a furious argument about whether the straitjacket was permitted "with this one."

Then, with the same invisible swift grace she had embodied with Queen Isabel, the Woman Who Means What She Moves positioned herself between the Panther, the bearlike orderly, and me.

The Panther crouched even lower and began to sway from side to side, alerted by the commotion around her. The Woman Who Means What She Moves squatted in a deep mime of the Panther which carried not only the posture but the feeling of aggression. She whispered to me, "Very, very slowly, just your arms." Somehow I managed to move my arms downward. The bear-orderly took a step forward, the straitjacket held out before him to trap the beast.

"Freeze."

People who mean what they move have voices of great power, for he stopped on command. At the doorway, there was still chaos and shouts. I heard something about "her medication," followed by cursing.

The Panther had not moved her face from where it was locked onto mine. I was not only the same age as the Panther but also her size (roughly) and perhaps even resembled her in a superficial way. My hair was dark, though not as dark as hers. My body was muscular from years of modern dance training, and I sensed that she could feel in me a physical match of strength. But I wore clothes; she wore a smock. Costume alone conveyed to her my status as a member of reality, allowed to go "outside."

"You're not supposed to be here," the Panther snarled at me.

"Look at me. Not at her."

The Panther turned, sniffed. The Woman Who Means What She Moves was moving back and forth, in her crouched position, Panther herself. The Panther lifted her head and studied the dancer. The Woman Who Means What She Moves swayed in slow, tender circles as the Panther's eyes, hidden behind her black hair, followed the motion. Then, slowly, unable to resist the first motion of life, the rocking in the hammock of sway in which we are made, the Panther began to dance. You could barely see it; only her bones were moving in tender rhyme with the Woman Who Means What She Moves; it was an inner motion of skeleton, a tentative exploration of what her anatomy might feel like if she were to let herself be seduced into the girdle of life and join the human tribe.

I watched them—this took only a matter of seconds—and the desire to join that same circle, to enter into the swaying girdle of life, tickled my bones. I was not even aware of my movements, hypnotized as I was by the desire to enter into the circle with my animal sister and mean what I moved. I stood up, stepped forward to join the dance of life.

The Panther sprang, her muscles energized by the otherworldly force of madness. She landed on me and knocked me down to the floor, toppling the chair. Her hands pressed at my throat. She growled. Before I could do anything to protect myself (presuming I even could) I was aware of another body and another growl. Louder than the Panther's. An invitation from one of her species to fight. A hand swiped the air—I do not know whose it was. The Panther looked up. Another swipe of human paw above me. Had she sprouted claws, had linoleum turned savanna, the walls of the institutional ballroom rock and fluorescent, streaks of primordial dawn, I would not have been surprised.

A roar went up from the Woman Who Means What She Moves. Time trembled.

The Panther, her body still over mine as if I were the kill she was about to eat, made a low, threatening sound at her rival. I felt her nails digging into my neck. *Food. She is my food. Mine.*

The next thing I knew, the Panther was ripped away from me. Her nails would not release me, her kill, her food, and as the bear-orderly tried to force her off me, the skin on my throat stung. The bearlike orderly yelped; "Goddamned bitch!" The Panther had bitten him. The moment he let her go, the Panther dropped her entire weight on me. No one was going to take her food from her.

I was aware of the face of the Woman Who Means What She Moves on the floor beside mine. "Roll toward me," she whispered. "Just roll right into me. As hard as you can."

"I can't."

"Pretend I'm your mother. You're a baby. And you just roll to me because you can't help it, you love me and I love you and your body doesn't know anything else—now. Now!"

Surrendering to the helplessness of my love for the source of my food, I rolled toward the breast of the Woman Who Means What She Moves. My hunger for food and love and the sound of my mother's voice was all I knew, my fear was so great.

The Panther came with me.

"Quick—move away—out—"

I slid out from between them, scuttling to the side, and sat up. Before me the Woman Who Means What She Moves had locked the Panther to her with her arms and legs wrapped around her. She was saying to the Panther, "Shhh, shh, shh, I'm here, I'm here," as she began to rock back and forth, back and forth. Seeing the Woman Who Means What She Moves embracing this young woman who was like my secret twin, burdened with carrying in her spirit the rage and animal power I dared not carry in myself, filled me again with the desire to invade their partnership. I wanted to rupture their fierce embrace and claim for myself the blessing the Woman Who Means What She Moves was bestowing upon the Panther. To sacrifice my body to prove that love will triumph over fear—not to speak it or pray it or promise it or mumble it but to *move* and to *mean* the originating passion of humanity by holding against my breast the beast; risking not damnation but injury, death, pain; to grab the beast and pull it to me and keep it there, crooning to the terror a lullaby—canceled all formal faith inside me. The Woman Who Means What She

Moves proved compassion a matter of muscle and nerve and skin, texture and pulse. Her courage stunned my soul.

The Panther's soul too was shocked out of fury by the force of the dancer's hold on her, for she slumped, unable to resist the rocking in the embrace of the one who was just "here." Who knows what face the Panther was seeing, what smells she was remembering, what sounds returning to her; I suspect none. What mattered was only that the loving soft-touching thing that was "here" was all the food she had ever been hungry for.

I reached out my hand, an impulse upon me to stroke the Panther and test my powers to soothe the beast with my touch. The Panther's eyes locked onto mine; my hand reached; and the next thing I knew, she was screaming. The orderly had grabbed the Panther's black hair and jerked her head back. The orderly grabbed for the Panther's smock and pulled it tight against her neck as he hauled her up, making her seem even more like a cat clutched at the scruff, her face distended in pain.

"No! No! Stop! You're hurting her!" The Woman Who Means What She Moves reached for the Panther's hands. "Give her to me! Give her to me!" The Panther clutched at the hands held out to her, and they held each other. The orderly was yelling at his assistants to help. The Panther kicked the orderly. The Woman Who Means What She Moves kicked at him too, their hands never letting go of each other, the dancer begging, "Just let me dance—please—just let me dance with—"

He kneed the Panther in the back. Her eyes flew out of her face at the pain. She fell forward into the arms of the dancer. But before the Woman Who Means What She Moves could catch her and hold her again, the orderly had grabbed the Panther's elbows and forced her arms back up behind her. The dancer had to let go or else the Panther's arms would have broken.

"You bastard. You stupid bastard!"

The Panther arched in agony, her black hair falling away from her face, and a sound came out of her, a howl of rage and anguish resonant with eons of suffering past counting in any human system. The Woman Who Means What She Moves watched, helpless, tears falling down her face, as they dragged the Panther away by her elbows. I remember nothing after that except seeing the Panther's Carter's underwear where they showed at the back through the slit in her smock.

Ten years later, she would stand before me, her white smock tucked into her pants, black leather jacket hiding the uniform of those condemned to live inside forever.

I awoke to a searing blue sky, as buoyant and filled with cheer as the pulsating Santa Claus had been the night before. My first thought was to pray to the blue to protect me from the Panther. I lay in bed in my loft, I confess listening for sounds of Manda in the main room—not that she ever made any with her body. The phone began to ring. And ring. It was the era before answering machines, and so I was still able to tell an urgent call from an indifferent one—and this was urgent. The phone ceased for a few minutes and then started up again. The third such sequence, I sprang from the bed, the sudden thought in my mind that it was my friend telling me Benjamin had been killed. For while I had spoken Lexy's name out loud, and turned the magnets of my soul, my body, and life back around so that they would stick to each other, I was about to discover that it is one thing to name one's soul and quite another to hold on to it against the vengeful return of the Panther.

It was Gwen, calling to ask me if I were coming to the funeral. "Do you think Aristotle will be there?" she asked me.

"Aristotle?"

"The Chief," she said. "He was so kind," she went on, "when I went to tell him she was . . . gone."

"You went to him?" I said.

"Oh, yes. Didn't I tell you? That was how she . . . I had to identify
. . ." Gwen's voice drifted off. "Ari was so . . . he's a very unusual man, for
a chief. Taurus, but he's got this Cancer moon playing tricks with him.
He said he would . . . but I don't know . . . if . . . Would you?"

"Do you think Freddie will be there?"

"Oh," Gwen said, "if they let him . . ."

"I'll pick you up."

I hung up the phone, an unwelcome jealousy upon me that Gwen
knew the name that went with the mouth I needed now, more than ever,
to lead me to restoration. Not to mention the slimy sensation I had,
knowing it was my desire to see Freddie, maybe talk to him, that had
made me agree to what I would never have found the courage to endure
before the previous night. I had vowed (I was young) never to go to a funeral again. So I shook away the jealousy, and a little sister's oath, and,
with determined Puritanism, pulled my hair tightly back in preparation
for cleaning the house. I spent the morning dusting, washing, throwing
away, clearing out, in part to cleanse myself of funereal memories, in part
to exorcise the Panther. Not that I believed it would be that easy. But I
found the activity distracting. I did not know how to think about the
Panther, and Manda, and Lexy, and the threat to my friend and
Benjamin. When I would try, my brain would implode. Cleaning was
what my ancestors had relied upon when they had been seized by disturbing magic and their firm conviction that there was evil, and it was
alive, in their small town by the river; and I was more than happy to let
my honest legacy of ancestral denial have its way this particular morning.

The blue seemed to have heard me, breaking its code of cosmic indifference to human biography, for Manda did not show up. Maybe it
was enough revenge for the Panther that I had to break my girlhood
promise and attend a funeral. Maybe (it flashed through my mind) it was
the Panther's plot to tempt me to a funeral to contact Freddie, Manda's
way of letting me know that—well, that the sky makes slugs before rainbows. As I was cleaning up the bathroom, I found the rusted shower stall
consoling, for so long as it was unusable, then I would have to go to the
Y. I found myself cleaning faster, thinking that I might sneak across the

bridge to the Y to see that Lexy was, as She had said She would be, safely inside the impenetrable Dring where Manda could not reach Her.

It was in this spirit of hope—seeing Lexy, in daylight, as it were, inside Her sanctuary of Dew—that I went through my closet rapidly, looking for something suitable to change into at the Y so I could go from there directly to pick up Gwen, and from there to the stone church near the retreat of the Carmelite Sisters, along the river. The only appropriate black clothing I had was a pair of loose harem-style rayon pants with a black floral pattern. I put them on to see if they fit. The only shirt formal enough was a man's tuxedo shirt on which an artist from Woodstock had painted irises—the same Woodstock on the far side of the river where Pat Edwards had staked her ancestral claim to the Baubo in her. It was too cold to wear just the shirt, but a sweater was not formal enough for a funeral and wouldn't go over the oversized tuxedo shirt. I rummaged through the closet and found, tucked away in the far reaches, a man's jacket in a dark tweed.

A wave of sadness surged through me, so intense I had to sit down, as unwavering, concentrated, and fixed as the sadness about the Drings, the failure of Mihalyi's magic words, hungry, so hungry that I felt I had looked into a Dring and was falling into it and disappearing. The jacket belonged to a man I had once loved, still loved, always would love, a journalist from Nebraska. I tried not to think of him, and most times I succeeded. But the jacket undid me. I took it out and slipped my arms into the lined sleeves and wrapped it around me tightly. Then I sat on my bed, rocking, holding his jacket to me, remembering and not remembering at the same time. He was living in Lincoln, his hometown. We spoke occasionally on the phone, never talking about it, the love or the reason why we were thousands of miles apart, me in my cottage in the woods, he in Nebraska, pretending, as he put it, "like all journalists, to describe a whole world in three sentences. My editor would prefer it to be only one."

I could describe every world there ever is anywhere in one: The Eaners always come.

In our last phone call, I had joked with him that I had found another man. I had heard the quivering in his voice, the old love and the old fear of the love he had for me, when he said, "Oh yeah?"

"Yeah," I said. "He worries about making sure I stay warm."

"So do I," he had said, the shake of tenderness and withholding tenderness in his voice. "A lot."

"He's five years old, and he brings me firewood. But he is setting a precedent," I went on, forcing my voice away from tears. "From now on, men have to bring me things to keep me warm."

"I'll make a note of it," he said.

And so it was left between us, with neither one of us knowing whether there would be a next time, and if it would be warm.

I rolled up the cuffs with the same entranced fascination as Lexy, the night before, had wrapped the silk around Her arms, revealing the beautiful black patterned silk lining. I sat there lost in memories not of what was, but that other kind of memory, which clings to lost love, the memory of what was not but always hoped for, the unfinished story of an imagined future holding me in its embrace, teasing me to hope, again, for what was not to be.

I heard the crumbling sound of a car coming down the dirt driveway. I looked up, out the back window behind my bed. At first I thought it was my friend driving her white Toyota. But then I remembered: When she moved out of the house, her husband had demanded that he keep the Toyota and had given her the Ford with the broken trunk that jammed shut sometimes. My heart pounded as I realized it was not my friend but her soon to be officially ex-husband pulling in and stopping at my cottage.

My first instinct was to hide in the back of the closet, protected by my prairie lover's tweed jacket, and pretend that I was not home. But it felt childish, and I did not like to imagine him finding me there, cowering in fear. He and I had spoken little in the years I had been friends with his wife. He saw me as one of those muddy, indecisive, creative types, in desperate need of a mental scalpel to remove my offending immature spontaneity.

He looked so like Lenin that I called him by that name in my own mind. His eyes were set at the same oblique, hawklike angle as Lenin's, the same curved bald head, the same poky beard. I even pronounced Lenin in my mind with a Russian inflection, more like L-yen'n, for this slurring Russian y-glide conveyed to my senses his slippery, off-center, unpredictable nature. For though he was the kind of person who would think that his son had brought me twigs, which of course he had not (Benjamin's mortal lilac bush was his own soul on the funeral pyre of the death-no-death that is divorce, and the hope against hope that he would, in such a cold, be warm), this Lenin replica had underground passages filled with turbulent passions that would flood when one least expected. As my friend would point out, with the particular bewilderment that belongs to the divorcing, who never imagined the story ending this way, in the beginning he had loved her, and loved her splendidly. What had eclipsed that love in Lenin for the artistic woman he had married, whom life could not help but rush toward and love, none of us knew—not she, not Benjamin, and certainly not I.

I heard the car motor go off. Swiftly I moved from my bed, down the stairs, then stopped. I sat on the stairs situating myself where I could see most of the main floor of the cottage, but a large post hid me from view. I waited for a knock on the door.

When the door slid open, slowly sinister, I moved up a step, where I was all but hidden by the post. I could see less of the room this way, but I saw enough.

He came in and looked around. He called my name, but softly, as if he were trying to ambush me. I didn't answer, but held perfectly still. He looked around the room, his hawklike eyes searching. From where he was standing, he could see up into the loft that was my bedroom. I saw him look up, and a strange expression came over him, disgust perhaps, though I couldn't see clearly—I didn't have my glasses on. He then looked around the main floor, and his eyes landed on the manuscript for The Murder Mystery.

He walked over and leaned over to read it. No amount of fear will overcome a writer's absolute terror of anyone reading their first draft, especially if the writer knows that it's a mess. I stood up and ran on the stairs, to make it sound as if I were just coming down them.

He looked up and saw me. "I called," he said.

"I was in the back of the closet."

He looked me up and down, slowly taking in my severe hair pulled tightly back, no jewelry, no makeup, the man's jacket, the untucked man's tuxedo shirt, and he saw what he had come to see. "And now I see you've come out of the closet," he said.

It wasn't that I missed the joke. It was that I couldn't put myself into the joke he was making.

"Is that how you dress when you go out with my wife?" he said.

I still didn't get it. I said, "This is how I dress for funerals."

"You think I'm dumb, I don't get it?" he said. "In mourning. How cute. That part of you that is normal is the part that's dead," he snapped at me. I was, I confess, lost, unable to fathom his plot at all. "I knew you were the one who plays the man. The butch, isn't that what you call it? No, no, the dyke," he said, proud of himself for knowing the term. "I thought so. I knew my wife was the woman."

I felt my entire body flush with heat. No words would come to me. What use would they have been? I was constellated in his soul as something I was not, and (as Manda had taught me) just the words wouldn't work anymore. Nothing I could say would unfix what he had fixed in his mind.

"You think I don't know what you do? I know. I know. She's sick. Because of you. Ever since you two started going to that Y, that steam room," he said. "That's when this sickness started, this disease you gave my wife. You and that steam room are what gave it to her." His face was red, and his voice was rising to a hysterical pitch. "It's all your fault, you and that goddamned Y, you ruined my marriage. You fucking ruined my life, you cunt," he said. I stood there, paralyzed by his hate flying onto me. "Except you don't even deserve to be called cunt, you freak. If it wasn't for you, I'd still have a wife. But you, you perverted her, you—" he sputtered for the right epithet—"you lesbo," he said.

I stood facing him, my mind racing, my stomach churning. "Your wife and I are not lovers," I said.

"Well, what the fuck do you call women who are naked with each other all day?"

Rulla's joyous face and the smooth pink bronze skin of her body in its fold upon fold of flesh filled the inside of my eyes. "Sisters," I said.

He stared at me, and his resemblance to Lenin, which had caused my friend and me to howl with rueful laughter at times, lost all of its comedy, all of the strange alive comedy of names matching the souls of people.

"She keeps going there with you," Lenin's double said. "And she loses Benjamin. Loses him, you understand? I'm not letting my only son be raised by a pervert. And you and I both know that no judge is going to let him be raised by a pervert either."

If he'd any spit to spit, he would have. But he was a dry man, a man of ashes, a Lenin cardboard cutout, so there was no spit. There was a final looking me over in my masculine costume. Then his lips wrapped themselves around the word "sister" like hungry maggots around a corpse, and he was gone.

Everything about the funeral was bizarre, as if Bergman and Fellini had joined forces. There was the isolated stone church on the hill, the sun casting dense, fixed shadows over the rocks behind it, pure Bergman—for he is the artist of solstice extremity. Yet pouring into it, as Gwen and I arrived, was a group of people who belonged to Fellini, itinerant circus types. They were dressed in everything from frumpy housedresses to black leather pants, including a rainbow tie-dyed Grateful Dead t-shirt, sneakers under a long skirt, a small flock of flannel plaid shirts buttoned tight at long necks, and one woman in what looked like an old-fashioned wedding dress. The woman had shaved her hair off to within a quarter of an inch, and the tall young man in the black leather pants who seemed her escorting groom had hair to his waist. In their mixed-up clothes and intermingled sexuality, they looked like every sincere, impoverished theatre group I'd ever been a part of, artists without a means to their art.

But not to Gwen. Gwen stared at them. She was seeing a dead young woman as a member of this tribe from the local asylum for the children no one wants—like a sister who is a sister and a niece, both. I wanted to grab her by the shoulders and say, the Panther can make you believe her stories about how people die because she's a better storyteller than any of us mortal dreamers. Because she's the dream and the dreamer, both.

As the tribe approached, Gwen pressed herself back against the church wall. She was wearing something soft and long and gray and woven with wisps of the soft wool about her like down. Her eyes, usually the color of the sky, were softened to a steely slate color. Everything about her was subdued, cloudy, feathery, as if she were the ghost of a bird. As she pressed her downy self against the gray stone of the church, the impression intensified of a frightened baby bird, a mourning dove backing away into its harsh stone roost.

Their supervisor must have been used to seeing reactions like Gwen's. At the threshold, she stopped and spoke to Gwen. "They're harmless. And very heavily medicated. Are you the mother? You look just like her."

Gwen shook her head. "I am her aunt—sister, " she whispered in a halting, ashamed staccato, the word barely audible. "Her mother—"

"I know," the supervisor said, touching Gwen lightly on the arm. "It must be horrible for you, to have lost them both."

Gwen bit her lip. She looked at the supervisor, then at me. "I have no sisters left," she said.

This modest stone church on the hill pulled me toward it, seeming to offer not so much solace or sanctuary as protection against the forces of the dry, ash-filled Lenins of this world. I wanted to be inside something hard, thick, and impenetrable to shield me from the poisonous words that had just wounded me. Words work, I wanted to say to Manda. But only the poisoned ones. Of course, Manda knew better than anyone the poisonous power of words. Her voice was her weapon.

Gwen grabbed my arm as we entered, making me feel even more like the masculine creature Lenin had said I was. I was acting the hero prince for Gwen, but inside, if I let myself touch what was inside, I found something so soft and sad and silent that I was afraid to give it a name. I felt like the baby bird Gwen resembled.

As I entered the church, I was thinking only of the Y, of that refuge which had been my salvation from my own grief and was, for my friend, the same. It was the one place where she could put away her own sorrow at the end of her marriage. It held out for her the hope of becoming another kind of woman; the alchemy of the steam room was the place where she could let the wife she had been die, confident that she would emerge from that piquant womb where women of all kinds left their essential, nurturing Dew behind, reborn a new woman. It was a steaming away of the false skin, a process in which the skin of one's self was gently opened like the surfaces of the Drings were opened, and any hungry human could then find inside all the food and words and love his or her soul needed. The lost Dew of the cosmos in which you can find an infinity of rainbows, not the monumental architecture of one. And Lexy was there—beyond my reach. Not here in the Panther dark of the funeral.

The sermon washed over me as images of the Y crowded my mind. I saw Rulla lowering her huge body into the middle of the whirlpool and shimmying as the old men with their spindly legs dotted with spiderweb veins broke into spontaneous applause; the secretaries perched along the mirror, their gossip tossed up like confetti in easy celebration of what matters (how you are touched—or not). I saw the prenatal swim class, those protean female hippos as they gently bounded their full-bellied forms, letting the waters rock their bodies as their own placental waters rocked the child within them. I saw the Irish widow with the rose tattoo on her navel, her husband's grave, killed by the IRA. Tears sprang as I remembered seeing Rulla the Iranian and the Irish widow embracing, tears falling down their cheeks for dead men, both killed by the rupture of one man's independent spirit against the tyrannical force of another. Oh, Manda was right, the Eaners always came; the Clyks needed their black wind to thrive and destroy. Nobody knew the songs anymore. The poetry was lost, the poetry that worked to keep the Drings alive, it had been lost, and all the kings are King Pain.

Within me a moment opened like a flower; I could not tell you when it happened: Rulla pouring lotion into her palm to rub her skin. My friend watching as Rulla struggled to reach her back. Rushing to Rulla and then, with a decorum utterly unlike my friend's innate comedy, asking Rulla if she could "have the honor." Rulla's smile filling me up. My friend, stroking Rulla's back, saying, with the spontaneity of those who refuse to outguess life but just meet it, wherever and whenever life seeks them out, irresistibly drawn to the clowns of this world, "Rulla? Is your skin real?"

And Rulla, winking at me, "Real, sure. This is America, no?"

The minister droned on, his words utterly meaningless, as I sat there next to Gwen, staring ahead at a coffin holding the body of one young crazy woman, sister of a daughter who was a sister, possessed of the illogical but potent thought that if only she had found the Y, she would not have died. But now that Lenin had delivered his curse, not even the Y was sanctuary anymore. The only asylum left for women was the one Gwen's sister had died escaping. Gwen was holding out to me her lace handkerchief. I shook my head. No. I would not cry. I met Gwen's puzzled look. I shook my head; I could not explain. Gwen grabbed my hand and held it, to comfort us both. We gripped each other tightly, the two of us lost in our grief at the death of the sister inside us, killed when they died. Neither of us able to cry, the hollowness within so vast, so deep, we had to wait before the tears would rise up to the surface and spill over. To be in the steam room, where the walls grieve for you and with you—yet even the rites of mourning Lenin had taken from me, us, as though even our weeping were a threat.

The pain from her grip seemed to bring me out of myself. I looked around the church. I now noticed that on the other side of the church from where we were sitting, the crowd of Felliniesque inmates behind us, there sat a man, all alone. He was old, his hair thick and white. I looked over and his eyes met mine. They were the same crescent blue eyes as Gwen's. A shiver ran through me. I looked back at Gwen, who nodded.

"It's him," she said. "Father." Not "my" father, the possessive pronoun dropped to save her own soul's possession by him. Her hand was ice cold. There was not a tear on her face, and her body was utterly still. Her hand gripped mine harder, but I didn't complain or move. Through that grip ran the stream of her rage, passing it through her and into me. It took every ounce of will and determination for her not to scream. I could feel the ancient terror inside her passing from her hand to mine. She stared ahead at the coffin, the minister's pointless words washing over her as they did over everyone, as though drawing strength from the mute, lifeless form of her dead sister, willing herself to be that dead, that cold, so that Father would no longer want to touch her vital, warm femininity.

She kills the joy we possess for our own vitality, which we can neither protect nor defend. I heard Lexy's words inside me and shuddered, my being itself a solstice.

A gulping sob filled the church. Gwen closed her eyes. I looked over to see the father weeping and weeping. Gwen's hand squeezed mine so tightly at the sound of the father's sobs that it was all I could do not to yelp. The father's sobbing only intensified as the minister continued his sermon, punctuating his insipid stock remarks with titanic moans. Evil was weeping, and I could not move. It was as if my body had filled up with the same cold rage as Gwen's, passing from her hand to mine, and as I listened to evil sniffling like anything human cries, evil having to blow snot from its nose just like any person, the words coming through his tears only sent another wave of cold through me.

"Forgive me," he was crying. "Forgive me."

Gwen started to shake. She released her grip and grabbed at the rim of the bench ahead of us, resting her head. "I'm going to be sick," she said.

The minister had no idea that the sobs were the sobs of evil seeking pardon. He thought they were the sad, mucal tears of love and loss, which may be the same thing, and they fueled him into a climactic round of sincere cross-gender Christian solace about the earth receiving the dead girl into Jesus's bosom. Behind me, as the sound of the sobs of evil changed into halting animal whining, the inmates from the asylum were themselves beginning to cry, strange words coming from them, mumblings and whispers, a staccato shout, a groan like a cello out of tune.

The minister now seemed to be talking only to talk, to hold at bay these mumblings and strange words and the urgent, repeated, "Huhhsssh!" from the bald bride in the old-fashioned wedding dress. Gwen was still leaning forward, swallowing down the bile of her rage and shame, as the minister continued ranting about peace and dust and God's womb and Christ's bosom. Then a shout came from one of the inmates, and I turned to look.

I don't know whether she came in late or whether I had missed her when we entered, so absorbed in my own desire for invisibility from Lenin's vengeful glare I had not noticed her. But as I turned, Gwen taking deep breaths of air beside me, I saw a woman wearing a wig so conspicuously fake, so ornately blonde and curled, that it seemed to have no more connection to the story behind the dream than the minister's sermon. Her eyes were painted in thick black eyeliner, her eyelids shaded brilliant blue, and her lips hot frosted pink. Her features were barely detectable under this layer of makeup, and with the curled fake blonde hair above that heavily masked face, she looked like something out of California in the '60s. Or would have, if the black eyeliner had not streaked down her face in great black tracks. She was sitting next to the bald bride, silently weeping tears the color of crude oil.

Then the father said, "I loved her so much. She was my little princess."

The minister stopped speaking. All froze, church sudden tomb. Gwen vomited.

The blonde with the dark lines on her face began to mumble, a great current of words rushing out of her, faster and faster, building momentum and sound until they seemed to break from the stone casement in a flood: "Moon, don't lie down, moon, don't lie down I told her don't lie down skin season woe woe woe skin season moon I said, I said, moon, girl, Moongirl, don't, don't do this, don't murder the seed, please, please, don't murder the seed of moon in you moon girl, come back to me." She was crying now. "Moongirl! Come back! I have the seeds! I have the seeds inside me! Moongirl! Don't murder the seed! We can plant moons together. Come back and plant moons with me!"

The supervisor tried to subdue her—in vain. She wiped at her black tears, smearing her face, crying, "I have the seeds! Bring back your skin, Moongirl, bring back your skin to me!" It was then that I saw Melina Mercuri's blonde hair, the tears of her kohl-embroidered eyes streaking her face into a mask of grief and terror as she listened to the corporate wife telling her story in prison, the movie of Medea I had rushed out of and into Aristotle's mouth.

"I am cracking, Moongirl, cracking!"

"Shh, " the supervisor was saying to Melina Mercuri's double. "Get control of yourself. Did you take your medication? Listen to me. Freddie! Did Lorely give you your medication this morning?"

I turned to see Freddie staring at me. "Have you met Moongirl?" he asked me.

The supervisor grabbed him and hauled him up.

I nodded.

Freddie threw his arms around the supervisor and held her close in his huge arms.

All Gwen could talk about in the car on the way back to her little house was my pants. She apologized profusely for soiling them, insisting that I let her pay for the dry cleaning. She explained to me that she
hadn't felt well that morning, but she thought it was "just psychological."
She really had no idea she was sick. Must be a flu, she was saying. There
was a flu going around Max's jewelry store; she must have picked it up. It
was as though the funeral had never happened. The hand holding as we
locked ourselves together to mourn the death of sisters; her father on the
other side; the sound of evil weeping; Gwen trying frantically to wipe up
her vomit with her tiny lace handkerchief; above all the shock of Freddie
Van Heusen, creator of the rainbow native god whose blind eyes had led
me to Lexy, looking like a cross between Melina Mercuri and some latter-
day '60s California dreamer—none of it had happened. It had all been a
bad experimental film. All Gwen could focus on was ruining my pants.

I took her into her house, up the crooked, narrow stairs, and made
her promise me she would get right into bed. She rummaged in her
kitchen; the same dirty dishes from months before seemed still to be in
the sink. Then she handed me a paper bag and told me that I was to put
my dirty pants in this bag and leave it for her at the bottom of the stairs,
just inside the outside door, for her to take to the dry cleaner. I took the
bag from her, promising I would do exactly as she said.

164

As I turned to leave, she said, "He sounded so much like a woman. But it must have been Freddie who called me." She raised her dark blue eyes to me. "You don't think . . . Freddie knew . . . who I was to her? No," she answered herself, sighing. "Just another one of his lonely old women."

I couldn't help myself. "They say he reads from a Swedish sex manual. *The ABZ of Sex,* I think it's called."

Gwen's eyes widened. "That was no sex manual. It was . . ." Gwen shook her head. "Like how he was today. Sort of . . . radiant. You can't hang up; you can't resist it. And he uses this voice. . . ." Gwen shook her head. "She was such a joyous, alive woman," Gwen said. "You can't imagine. She should never have been in that place. Ever. She was like Benjamin, your friend's boy. One of those very special people who you think . . ."

"Life is less for losing."

Gwen nodded. "You're so lucky she's your friend." She looked down at the paper bag in my hand. "I'm so sorry."

"It's all right," I said. No one sighs as Gwen sighs. "Aristotle will call," I said. "He is the Chief, and I'm sure he does what he promises to do."

"Not for long. It's in his chart. He's already quit in his heart. It's just a matter of time."

"But—"

Gwen raised her blue eyes to me.

He has to lock Manda away. "Get some rest," I said.

It was closing in on five o'clock when I finally reached my cottage in the woods. The place was swaddled in darkness. But as I pulled up in my car and turned off the headlights, I saw that a light was on inside. I didn't remember turning on any lights when I had left in that cruel sunshine. Even more peculiar, it was the bathroom light. I entered the cottage, turning on other lights on my way.

There, in the corner, was a pristine, sterile, blazing white shower stall. Pinned to the curtain was a note from my landlords.

Returned from Germany earlier than expected. Too much political violence to trust our neurophysiological S.A.D. data. Neo-Nazis contaminating our results. Couldn't reach you by phone, so we came over and installed shower while we were up here. Returning to city tomorrow. Your rent is a week late.

I took off my soiled pants and dutifully folded them up into the paper bag Gwen had provided for me. It was a long time before I could remove my prairie lover's tweed jacket, but eventually I did, telling myself that he had always brought me something warm, and though it was not the vital warmth he had wished, he had given me his fiery masculinity, and the jacket was proof and palimpsest both. Slowly I stripped. Naked, I stepped into my new shower stall and turned the water on as hot as I could stand it and cried tears I did not know I had left in me; I had cried so much in my life I believed there were none left inside me for anyone or anything, ever again so long as I remained in the realm of the living and my brother in a realm I could see only with the eyes of the dead.

The Y closed for winter vacation. Christmas came and went. New Year's too, the gatherings and ceremonies moving around me like planets in a solar system whose sun never shone on me. I moved to the rhythm of some other calendar, in hock to a Panther sun that held itself poised in perpetual eclipse. There was little snow in January, no white cloak to soften the brittle branches scratched into the sky. Brief thaws immediately followed by frigid single-digit temperatures melted what snow there was and then froze it up again, forming layers of ice on the roads. The bridge was frozen black, crossed only by the intrepid. And I was the last one to trust its railings.

I wrote nothing of The Murder Mystery. I was the murder mystery; to write on paper was a poor surrogate for the story being etched onto my own flesh. I sat inside the cottage, locked in ice, unable to write, to think, to move. The Y reopened, but every time my friend called to suggest we go, I gave excuses: the bad roads, the bald tire on her car she couldn't afford to replace, a fabricated flu.

"But Meem, don't you miss Rulla? And the steam room?"

"You know, I read that steam rooms have all these weird viruses. . . ."

"Meem, you're scared, I can hear it in your voice. What is it?"

How Manda can make someone believe her dreams of violation are true stories. How Lexy insisted She was dead as She was dancing. How I need guides, but the only one I've met so far is a lunatic. How names, in this story, can kill you. What I said was, "Your husband is living up to his imaginary name. He's acting like a paranoid tyrant, not Benjamin's father. He thinks the Y . . . well, you know what he thinks."

Her husband's fantasy that his wife had a secret behind her unbounded enthusiasm for life in all sizes, shapes, and genders was well known to her. His distrust of her passionate temperament had been the source of their widening estrangement. "Because of the Y?" She laughed, but then immediately sucked the laugh back into her. She was silent. And then she said, "He's going to sue me for custody, isn't he?"

"It was just a threat," I said.

She said nothing, whispering good-bye to me in a voice at a far remove from her own.

Her silence blossomed into another silence as the ice encased the trees. Manda had not appeared since the night I met Lexy and Manda's identity as the Panther was revealed. I thought I had known grief before, when Lexy was only "Her," the anonymous feminine Manda had killed, but now that I had seen Lexy in the dance studio, that grief seemed vapor. This was flesh ripped from me, Manda like the eagle which returned to gnaw every day at the revealed liver of the impaled Prometheus, the man who stole from the gods to give humans the knowledge of fire. We humans could warm each other now around our own hearths, telling our own stories, free from our dependence on the gods for the basics: food, words, love. And like the body of the god whose wounded organ was renewed every night only for the eagle to pluck it out again the next morning, my dreams were filled with visions of Lexy dancing in the rainbow chiffon of my childhood, only to awake each morning to Lenin's curse, the impassable bridge, as the Panther threw all of Rhinebeck and the river environs into the prolonged solstice chill from her fatal breath.

One morning, I awoke to the predawn dark, my body shivering with cold. I had had a strange dream about a lizard that had been crawling over a dark red glazed urn in the classical amphora shape. The lizard had fallen down into the mouth of the vase and been unable to get out. When I went to the vase to rescue the lizard, there were slugs all over it. I stared out the window, the early light just appearing at the horizon, the linger-ing sensation of the slugs on the vase filling me with disgust. The sunrise began to fill the sky with the same dark pinkish hue as the color of the vase in the dream. Blood at dawn, I heard myself saying, and then my body went electric. *The sky has to make slugs before it can make rainbows.*

The dawn air was chill and fresh. I sensed that it was strategic to upset the rhythms of my life to work effectively against the Panther's seizure of the season. Instinct told me to touch life at times I had not touched before. That it was dawn, and I awake, no coffee or cigarettes in my system, was just the kind of jolt out of my stupor I needed to begin to develop the psychic muscles to defeat the voice with boots on that comes to kill how life loves us.

The driveway was rutted ice, and the main road no better. As I passed the abandoned stone house, which marked the long upward climb to Rhinebeck, past the asylum where Gwen's sister? niece? had been in-carcerated with Freddie, I despaired even of reaching town, let alone crossing the bridge beyond. The heater in my car refused to cooperate, and my fingers, frozen on the wheel, were almost too numb to drive. The car skidded, and it was all I could do to keep it on the road. I whirred my wheels as I passed the asylum and was about to give up when Freddie's wooden rainbow man came into view at the top of the hill. He was look-ing straight at me, and I could not help but feel that he had been keeping a vigil southward, in the direction of my ice-locked cottage, the entire time I had been under Manda's spell. The car scraped up the long, wind-ing hill past the asylum. As I came within full view of the wooden rain-bow man, the car engine died. I rolled through the deserted intersection, the road level and the ice now my escort to the gas station just ahead, on the other side of the real estate office which had—at last—removed Rudolph. In his place was an oversized plastic heart with an arrow through it.

The car rolled to a stop in front of the gas station. I read the sign on the door; it opened in two hours. As the light began to reveal the colors of the houses, I got out of the car thinking I would walk on to my friend's house and bang, very loudly. I began walking in that direction, which took me past the Starr Building. I almost did not look, and I still believe that I would not have had it not been for my desire to avoid Freddie's wooden rainbow man. I felt ashamed before his gaze, and turned swiftly away. The yellow light of the dance studio penetrated the violet hues of February dawn, beacon of honey. When it met my eyes, my heart, not at all plastic, was pierced as by the arrow. I raced across the street, knowing the door would be open as it had been the night I found Lexy there, and that She would be waiting for me.

I was already at the door before I smelled that sweet gas from Manda's old-fashioned lighter lingering in the air.

"You know what your problem is, Summacious? You're smart—just not at the right time."

Manda was sitting in the only chair in the studio, which she had placed in the middle of the dance floor. I slumped down against the wall and closed my eyes. "Where's Lexy?"

"Go ask your resident Medea. Or Venus. Or whatever name Freddie and his golden fleece are going by today." Manda twirled the chair in a circle, stopping with her back to me. The windows of the dance studio were the color of bruises. Manda seemed to be waiting for something. As the light filled the windows from below, morning like liquid, I heard the *coo—coo—coo* of doves. Manda looked up at the ceiling of the dance studio. The Starr Building was known for the perfectly preserved, architecturally-pure cupola on the roof just above us, a white clapboard tower perched exactly in the center of the square building. "If you knew anything about birds, Summacious, you'd have known there's no such thing as an owl and a dove in the same place. It's *unnatural*. Like your local Adonis. It would be a freak of nature. You put an owl up there, in the old cupola, even a plastic effigy owl, cousin to Rudolph and that plastic heart across the street, and all the doves, they'd disappear.

"Weird, about birds," she went on. "There's this critical period in the life of a songbird when it has this architectural event inside its mouth, and if the blueprint of the song doesn't have the right foundations, know what happens? Gets killed. By its own species. I must be feeling very sentimental, Summacious, to be telling you all this. Letting you know what happens when the words of the song don't work anymore and Baubo realizes it's time for her to pack her belly in cold storage."

I jumped up. "Where is Rulla?"

"Now, cranes, they're another story," Manda went on. "Those Japanese, whose syllabic abacus you so admired that you tried to fit burning children into the math of a haiku that was supposed to be about cherry blossoms when you were in fifth grade, wasn't it, Summacious?— the Japanese believe that cranes—"

"Rulla," I screamed at Manda. "What have you done to Rulla?"

She whirled around to face me, her black hair fanning out as she did. "You owe me," she hissed. "You owe me for that dance you interrupted. You don't know what happened, 'cause you had fulfilled all your requirements for that exclusive boarding school of yours. I, Summacious, was not there on a work-study program. That was my *life* you bent. I bet you never even thought to ask what your goddamned hunger for your own food cost the Woman Who Means What She Moves."

I stared at Manda, the Panther, my sister, inside. "She was fired?"

"Turned to ashes. She was history—while you graduated with highest honors from your precious high school. Those orderlies, they didn't exactly like being dressed down for forgetting to lock the door to my ward. Took their time getting back at me. Dragged it out for months. Never let me know, for sure, which one of them was going to do it to me, when. Mustard," Manda shivered. "They all smelled of mustard."

It was out of my mouth before I could stop myself. "Stay away from Rulla. She never did anything to you."

"Summacious, Summacious, get a grip, calm down," Manda said, her voice cooing like the doves above us. "I'm talking compassion. Courtesy."

Manda had stood up and was walking toward me. I backed into the mirror, wishing myself able to pass through to the other side to the familiar dimensions of a world I had lost long ago. "Do we have to do some remedial work here? After all this time? Don't you remember? I got stuck in your murder mystery. Yours, Summacious. My story, the story I've been waiting twenty-seven thousand years for somebody to tell—roll with me here, Summacious, just roll with me—my story is a love story."

"Love—"

"Happy Valentine's Day." she winked.

"Meem?"

"What are you doing up?"

"Art," my friend said. "That's my excuse. What's yours?"

Had a bad Valentine moment with a Panther, I mean, the Panther. "Bad dream. Do lizards regenerate?"

"Benjamin knows about lizards. Was that the bad dream? A lizard? You look . . ."

Thinking maybe the lizard was a guide who fell down (down), but I'm awake, so I can't ask him. Have to ask his ambassador about the laws of lizard land, and if maybe he could collect some of the slugs from around the vase for me. "Is Benjamin here?"

She grabbed my arm and pulled me into the upstairs apartment, toward Benjamin's room. He was asleep in his bed, making more noise in his sleep than it seemed such a small body could, the covers tossed around exposing his bare feet, covering his face. "Is he okay?" I whispered. "With the covers like that, I mean; isn't it dangerous?"

"Benjamin always sleeps like this. Meem, you really need a trip to the Y to the steam room. To regenerate."

I looked at my friend. "Did you say art?"

"Since four this morning. I keep on waking up before dawn, these pictures inside me." I took in her appearance. She was wearing pajamas and a sweatshirt and over that a kitchen apron, covered in paint. On her feet were hot-pink fuzzy slippers in the shape of rabbits, with open backs. They were much too small for her feet. "Benjamin would kill me if he found out," she said, following my gaze. "But I have to wear them when I paint. Meem? Did you hear me? I said, when I *paint*."

I had to piece together the verbal spinnerets of her enthusiasm until I had the story. Over fresh coffee in the kitchen, it came out that she had been drawing, in secret, at night, ever since the piano had floated up the stairs—the day after Manda's arrival—I thought; and with that thought attended to my friend's story differently.

No, she couldn't tell me, it was too "scary and delicate and real," she said. Pastels. Pastels of the women at the Y. Did I remember the day that beautiful red-headed woman showed us the steam room? The one I bumped into while she was staring at the secretaries in front of the mirror?—Yes. So. And.—That's when it started, that day, the pictures in her head. Again. After all that had happened. And the wet spot and everything.—What wet spot everything?

When Lenin had been courting her, dazzling her with his electronic wizardry and making stereo installation into an orgasmic experience ("Until whatever it was that happened that made orgasm like stereo installation"), she had been accepted for a one-woman show at a gallery in New York. She had been barely twenty-one. "Please don't ask how come I haven't told you yet, you'll get it in a minute." I remained silent and listened. She had an appointment with the gallery owner about the show. "My one-woman show. Except I didn't want a one-woman show. I wanted . . . I don't know what I wanted. I was nervous. I wanted some other women to pad it for me. Not so naked. Not that anything was naked. I was into this abstract stuff. You don't know, and you don't want to, I think. It wasn't at all naked. But I felt naked and. . ."

She went to speak to her art teacher. It was her art teacher's curse to be known as "the guy with the bed Frank Zappa slept in." After he had calmed her down and told her a lot of things she forgot even as he was speaking them, because she found his voice and his mouth soothing of themselves, she asked to see the bed. "This has nothing to do with Frank Zappa. It's about mothers. And it's all real. I was doing this Polaroid thing long before anybody, taking pictures of my bed at various times, like after we'd made love in it, before, everyone else was doing abstract and so was I, it was what you were supposed to do, but I had this weird Polaroid obsession with my bed. In the morning, night, empty, just . . . you know, 'Make your bed and lie in it.' That's what my mother always told me, still does, why she hates this divorce, nobody's accepting responsibility for making the bed, I mean—you know what I mean."

The bed was big. It filled up an entire room, she told her husband-to-be, who was just finishing his residency in surgery at Columbia.

"You asked this man to see his bed?" he said.

"Everybody wants to see his bed."

"I'm asking you."

"It was about my art."

"You asked a man to see his bed for your art?"

She should have known then, she said; it was a fight to end all fights; it was a raging, crazy, unfounded jealousy, and she should have walked away from him right then and there and never come back. But she'd never known him to be so animated, so flustered, so at odds with himself, so caught up in his feelings that the man who could always, but always, join the wires in the right places became a different man. And all her fear that he was too good at joining the wires the right way melted away as she watched his face turn red and his words tumble out of him in the wrong order, and then, in his stuttering, spluttering jealous fit, after he had just delivered his ultimatum that she'd better separate art from beds right now if they were ever—

"I'd just washed the floors and he found the one wet spot, and he went splat in the most classic pratfall I'd ever seen. I laughed hysterically, I couldn't control myself, and he just lay there, perfectly still. And then, slowly, he smiled and he began to laugh. He did once laugh at himself," she said. "That once. That was the only time, ever. I went over to him and . . . well, we made love on the wet spot and it was wonderful, and I never went to the gallery for my appointment for my one-woman show."

Her eyes were sparkling (green) as she grabbed me and pulled me into her living room. Everywhere I looked there were sheets of paper—on the floor, tacked on the walls, and completely covering the piano.

"I had to go to the Y, somehow. Aren't they wonderful?" she said—there was no arrogance, no boast. It was the women she had drawn, not the drawings themselves, that she wanted me to love, and in the spontaneous enthusiasm of her passion for them, she was inviting me in to share in her art. "Go ahead—just don't step on any." She had been modest when she said they were pastels. They were pastels, but she had glued all kinds of objects to them (a few I recognized from Benjamin's sacred stash). I walked around the room, the morning light falling here and there on the brilliantly colored panels. They were wondrous, spontaneous, funny, poignant celebrations of female flesh. There was the rose tattoo, in intricate realistic detail, above a spontaneous orange fuzz of—"It's one of those copper scrubbing pads. Used," she said. I stared at her. "Meem, it *is* used. The IRA *used* her. But you can't say that because artists aren't supposed to have opinions and being political is the kiss of death, so what you do is you don't say it, you let the stuff say it for you. You just take what you find, from around, and, well, I can't explain it, you always find something better than what you thought you needed. Where did you think Benjamin got his scavenger genes from—Lenin?"

I stopped to look at a large composition of women in various stages of dress and undress at their lockers, each one revealing to my friend's loving hand a part of her body, a huge hip, a gargantuan leg, a fleshy arm, a dropped, full, suckled breast, a sloping, smiling, folded belly, such that the women, taken in by the eye all at once, lost their distinct selves and became like one great multiple feminine. The mothers-to-be in the pool like hippos, their bellies under water, the babies inside their own placental pools. It was Dringing; my friend was making pictures of Dringing and Honeytime. She had drawn the whirlpool, with the spindly, spider-veined legs of the old men gathered around Rulla, submerged, her body drawn as if it were made of water, a great ruddy magnification of submerged flesh, the tiny men around her. My friend had called it *The First Day,* which, I now remembered, it actually had been; yet the drawing, especially Rulla's watery form, conjured the first day woman appeared, born of waters, the old men battered warriors who had suffered without her. Yet even this evocation of myth had intimacy and humor in it.

175

Then I came upon the woman in pink. She had called the drawing, *Queen for a Day*. My friend broke into wild laughter. Queen Pink's face was so unabashedly orgasmic, and my friend had had the audacity to make the belt around her hips break with the sheer force of her ecstasy, so that she and the machine seemed about to blow apart. All around the edges she had glued '50s advertisements from old *Life* magazines for all the products that were supposed to make being a housewife a regal experience. Over the top of the picture she had placed, central to the eye, a fragment of an ad for the cream that would end the "heartbreak of psoriasis." It was as ecstatic and hilarious a picture as I had ever seen. There was nothing poignant, or mythic, or poetic about this woman's ecstasy; it was comedy, pure comedy, as only my friend could have done it.

But I could not see the comedy. All I could see was evidence. All the evidence Lenin needed to confirm his fantasy about what the Y was.

I reached for another picture, face down, but my friend stopped my hand. "Oh, those are not part of the Y. They're not finished. They really shouldn't be in here." She threw her arms around me and hugged me to her. Tightly. Powerfully. "I love you so much. So much." And squeezed me tighter. "I would never have had the courage to do this if you weren't my friend. It was amazing, drawing them," she said. "I'm showing up, Meem. I'm finally showing up. Naked. That's what I'm going to call the show. *Show Up Naked*."

"What show?"

"There's this woman who owns this gallery in Woodstock. I have an appointment. Today."

"Woodstock's across the bridge."

"Meem, I've crossed it tons of times." She smiled a smile like her son's, a boat loaded with all the food and words and love anyone would need for a journey across water.

"Are you sure you want to do this?" I said, the instant the words were out of me feeling my whole body collapse, like a Dring when it was pierced.

My friend stared at me. "Am I sure I want to get my soul back from Lenin?"

176

I fumbled. "I mean, now. Do this now. Maybe it would be a good idea to wait until . . ."

"Until what?"

"Until . . . until everything's final and the custody issue is settled and it's safe."

My friend went to the piano and slid an oversized portfolio out from behind it. She then carefully began to lay the paintings inside, with sheets of tissue splotched with all the colors of the pastels between each one. She was shaking her head to erase my words, which had landed on her like the ashen words they were.

"Since when is art safe?" She shook her head at me. "You think I don't know how dangerous these are? You think I don't know how dangerous it is to show up naked? You think I don't know what the Y is? Not what it is, Meem, what it is. I don't do this, he wins. He owns me forever. I need the me I got back in the steam room. That's what these are," she said, touching the bulging curve of the portfolio. "These are the woman I found in the steam room, the woman he didn't destroy."

"I know, I know, but . . ." *But I just got a valentine from the Panther, and I have a feeling Rulla's dead, and what lizards can do isn't enough to bring her back.*

In a quiet, distant voice she said, "I thought if anyone would understand all this without me having to say anything out loud, it was you." Her voice was curled at the edges, retreating into itself, like one of those tropical plants that recoils when touched. She then said, "Meem, you're the one who went after her."

The redhead, the long arms, the perfume, materializing inside mazes only to disappear. My friend was zipping up the swollen portfolio, then gave up; it was too full. "None of this would have happened if you hadn't followed her to the steam room, and my soul would still be whatever it's been, which wasn't what it was destined to be."

"But Lexy—"

My friend's eyes popped open. "Lexy? Is that the long-armed redhead? Do you know her? Meem, tell me you know her and you know her well enough so that I can paint her."

"Mom?"

"Benjamin! What are you doing up? It's early, Pumpkin."

"You say the weirdest things sometimes," Benjamin said, rubbing his eyes. She gathered him up in her arms to carry him back to bed, leaving me alone in the room with the unzipped portfolio. I sank down onto her couch beside it. As I reached out to touch it, something cracked inside me, a parting of my bones, and from the chasm between my friend and me where Lenin's curse had sliced through us and left both our souls battered, exposed to the elements, She bloomed. She was dancing everywhere, over the entire surface of the cosmos, an atomic, quarking, spontaneous energy of pure movement. She was dancing on the scruffy beaches of the Atlantic, the pale suede of the Pacific sands, rocky crags of Corfu and Maine. She was cascading through the wind drifting apple blossoms of orchards over the sloping hips of the mountains of Vermont and the sumptuous, velveteen buttocks of Washington State and New Zealand's sheep-dotted waves of green which lead to the turquoise sea. I saw Her arise and race out into the sun and whirl and whirl, the wings of a brilliantly colored kimono flying off Her long, lean body till She seemed like a dragonfly in the sunlight. She traversed through time backward to the source and became a native goddess, dancing in a clearing as Spanish conquistadores peered over the horizon of a hill, shocked by the sight of a tribe of women, naked, performing a private rite. Then—but it was not "then" so much as it was a simultaneous event, the atomic dancing Her able to be all places at once—She appeared out of a fog of tulle, a membranous net of ballet costume draped over the cosmos, and as She emerged the tulle metamorphosed into the hide of a white buffalo, the ballet dancer a free maiden, porcupine quills at her breast trembling as she swayed.

She reached upward into a tree and plucked a fruit, for she was hungry from eons and eons of dancing. As the fruit separated from the tree, she fell into the peril of selfhood and I saw Her body enter into the body of Lexy. Lexy, wrapped only in a sheet, moved around the garden ripping out the roses, every single one, flowering, budding. Her hands bloody from the thorns, she removed the sheet and laid it on the ground. She threw all the broken roses into the sheet and folded it at the edges. Then Lexy walked on the thorns and the petals in her bare feet.

I watched her as she unfolded the sheet, dotted with her blood. She gently spread the crushed roses and lay down, stretching her long, naked body on thorns and petals alike. She lay utterly still, it seemed for centuries, her pain, her sadness, and her beauty having stopped the pulse of the cosmos. The changeable compass of light and dark which is season was stunned by her corpselike pose in the sweet time of her life when she should have been dancing, and the roses opened their faces to her in receptive joy. Lexy lay there like the dead, and the sky was too sad even for tears. I thought, She's stopped dancing, as She said She would.

"Meem? Benjamin says yes. They do."

I pressed my hands against my eyelids to push away the sight of Lexy surrendering to the fate of all dancers on this side, the side of history. "What did you say?"

"Regenerate," my friend said. "Lizards. So we're going to be all right, you and me. We'll get through this," she said. "Whatever it is that's taking you away from me—we'll regenerate, won't we?"

The guys at the gas station shook their heads. Engine was fine, they said. Must have just been too cold this morning, didn't warm it up. They had given the car a long-overdue tune-up, and they strongly recommended that I replace the tires, especially with the roads the way they were. About four hundred dollars later, I was on my way to the Y, alone. My friend was on her way across the bridge too, the unzipped portfolio in the trunk of her car. Her interview at the gallery was at eleven. Benjamin was going with her. There had been mumblings about lunch in Woodstock, maybe. Or maybe she would come to the Y, and I would still be there. She'd check in . . . just to see. If I . . . but she had Benjamin . . . so . . . lunch really would work better. That place Benjamin liked, the Middle Eastern one, where he was allowed to eat with his fingers. Didn't I want to join them? It was Valentine's Day.

Not even spending Valentine's Day with Benjamin could deter me from finding Rulla. I said, "Why don't I go to the Y and see if Lexy's there and ask Her if She'll let you paint Her?"

My friend gripped my arm. "Would you?" I nodded. "See? I told you. I told you we would regenerate, Meem."

The senior women's locker room was its usual hum of flesh and song, the women easily gossiping to each other as they dressed and undressed. I stood at my locker and pulled my sweater over my head just

180

as I caught sight of a movement near the large mirror on the wall where the secretaries preened and fussed. Red hair, quick, vibrant under the gray fluorescent lights of the locker room, sudden as the fox in the moonscape when I went to tell Aristotle She was dead the night Manda arrived. I pulled frantically at my sweater to get it over my head, but the neck caught in a hair clip and I found myself snared by clips and hair and wool in a vicious tangling. The edges of my clip had found their way into the knitting, and I could not see to remove it. I stood there, struggling, my head encased, unable to see, while I worked blindly with my fingers.

I smelled Rulla before I felt her soft fingers on mine, that blend of vanilla body lotion and the pure scent of her pheromonal self, the continual moisture of her body creating a chemical mist about her that was unmistakable. "Rulla help," she said. I was flooded with joy. The instant my head emerged, I reached out to touch her.

Rulla clucked at me. She was holding a bottle of body lotion in her hand. She held out the lotion and pointed to her back. "Rulla help sister, sister help Rulla," she said. I took the bottle of lotion and Rulla presented her back to me to be rubbed. My hands were shaking as I squeezed the cold lotion out.

"Rulla? Have you seen . . . the redhead? She was just here."

Rulla grinned, touching her own tufted nest of hennaed hair. "I am natural redhead," she said. "My sister, no. She is not natural."

"Where is your sister?" I tried to reach into Rulla's idioverse with my own.

Rulla sighed, indicated the bottle of lotion with her head. I poured the Jergens on her pink back. "Oooh, that's cold," she said. Her skin shimmered. It seemed to have small flecks of sheen in it, glitter, an extraordinary thing, the color of peaches and roses, with the shimmer of these coppery shards running through it.

I said, "The other beautiful redhead. With the long hair. I thought I just saw her. Your sister . . ."

"She dance for the shah," Rulla said in an impatient tone of voice.

I scrambled in my mind. "Will she return from dancing for the shah anytime soon?"

Rulla shivered again. Then she said, "You come to Rulla's belly-dancing class."

I rubbed the lotion in circles over her broad, soft back while the bevy of maiden secretaries streamed out. "I can't."

Rulla turned around slowly. She stood as high as my own breasts, her body a great round bronze cherry. Rulla huffed, her folds of flesh rising and falling like the tidal events of flesh they were. She grabbed the bottle of lotion and shuffled off. I felt a mild apology would help restore me to the Queen of the Y's good graces; some acknowledgment of her supreme position was called for. As I watched her broad rump retreat into the labyrinth of lockers, I called out, "I need to know when it is. Your belly-dancing class—so I can come—Rulla?"

But she was absorbed in her imperial disgruntlement and seemed quite content to let me suffer for whatever sins she was convinced I had committed. She rounded the corner and disappeared into the banks of anonymous lockers.

I was startled by a voice close to mine. "She doesn't have a job. She's homeless, you know."

I looked over to find the voice. Before me was a tall woman, her arms and legs long and bent, with short graying hair, small upsloping eyes, and a hooked nose. She was at least six feet tall, and she held herself with dignity and decorum. Among the sliding flesh of the other women, this new visitor seemed like a bird in the wrong flock. I had never seen her before.

"Rulla teaches a belly-dancing class across the river," I said.

The gangly woman's sturdy eyebrows raised. "Is that what she told you?"

"I know the owner of the studio," I said.

"Have you attended her classes?"

"No. But. But I can't dance anymore," I said. "I . . . I had an accident."

"So you don't know for certain, do you?"

Not even whether people who are alive are alive, people who are dead, dead, nor where a story happens, and whether it's a murder mystery or a love story. The Panther hoards sun to herself in revenge, a woman rises at dawn to make art she thinks will regenerate her but could destroy her, and owls and

*doves break nature to restore the cosmos to meaning what it moves. And . . .
and you are not a woman. You are a crane.*

Crane Woman found my silent admission of doubt to be entirely sat-
isfactory, for it was congruent with the facts about Rulla (I might say the
nonwhirlpool facts) as she knew them. "She used to clean house for an acquaintance of mine," Crane Woman said, scrupulous to distinguish her
categories of intimacy. "She used to just sit around all day and watch television. This acquaintance of mine had no choice; she had to fire her,"
Crane Woman said, and you could hear the semicolon in its proper
grammatical location as she spoke.

"Rulla made a terrible stink out of it," she continued. "Cried and
cried. She ruined my acquaintance's blouse, crying on her. Crying on
her," she repeated, as if repetition could convey the full measure of this
lapse of decorum. "Rulla told this acquaintance of mine she had nothing,
nowhere. This acquaintance of mine gave in. She's a very sentimental sort
of person. Well, the same thing happened, of course." Crane Woman
lowered her voice just a touch. "She had to fire Rulla a second time. It was
terrible. Rulla hadn't paid rent for months and months. She was sending
all of her salary back to her sister, she said. She's not all here, you know.
Personally, I am convinced that this sister of hers in Iran she talks about
all the time, this princess, is a complete fabrication. That woman is no
blood relation of an Iranian princess, trust me."

Crane Woman was dressing throughout her account. She was now
pulling on her pleated navy blue and green skirt over a full slip. She buttoned the skirt, the elbows of her long arms like flying buttresses, then
reached into her locker for a white button-down blouse. I offer these details not to embellish Crane Woman's character but because the clothes
she was putting on were replicas of my elementary school uniform. This
uniform had encased my body when the hormonal surge inside me
forced gaps in the seams which the authorities condemned in a brutish
system of discipline. I could not fathom how a woman who went to the
Y could dress herself in such punishing clothes.

"She lives here," Crane Woman said. "I caught her one morning. I
was the first one in here," Crane Woman went on. "Betty wasn't even in
yet, I remember. I had to wait for her to arrive to unlock the locker

room." Crane Woman paused while she pulled on a navy cable-stitched cardigan and adjusted her blouse underneath it, sending a shiver of kinesthetic memory through my own arms. I hated the feeling of the short sleeves inching up my biceps and scrunching at my shoulders. It must have been how Kipling's rhinoceros felt when the Parsee filled his skin with bread crumbs (I had developed a peculiar fascination with rhinos, especially literary ones, when I was cast to play one in our school production of Benjamin Britten's opera *Noye's Fludde*). The slip would work its way up my hips and collect there, only to make the ballooning worse, and the kneesocks would fall off my calves, snaking down, and no matter how much I pulled them up, they would slip down again, gathering at my ankles, where they tickled me in the most aggravating tease.

"Rulla was in here when I got in," Crane Woman was saying. "Well, naturally, I reported it to Betty. But Betty is in on it." She brushed her already perfectly cropped hair, vigorously, and then she removed all the strands and cleaned the bristles by blowing hard on them. "I think I really should report her." Crane Woman sighed, looking off in the direction Rulla had gone. It was the sigh of a woman who was disinclined to fulfill duty without the reward of martyrdom. "I would prefer not to have to get Betty into trouble. Though, of course, she does in a way deserve it."

She smiled at me, one of those cracking smiles that come and go in a second. "It's really not good for her to be here all the time," Crane Woman said, buttoning her trench coat and tying it at the waist. "Of course, you should warn your dancer friend if she really is thinking of offering Rulla this dancing job. Rulla is illegal. Utterly. According to this acquaintance of mine."

I watched Crane Woman, not a wrinkle on her anywhere, depart. A shudder passed through me. I wracked my brains for what cranes symbolized to the Japanese, but I knew nothing. I cursed myself for interrupting Manda in the dance studio when it seemed she was about to drop me one of her infamous "clues." If only I hadn't been so worried about Lexy—

I walked up and down the corridors of the lockers. I peeked into the pool, where the big-bellied mamas were just beginning their prenatal swimming class. I passed the whirlpool, hoping to find Rulla there, if not

Lexy with her, my heart straining against cranes and Panthers. The whirlpool was empty, the old men with their thin legs gathered around it, listlessly moving their parched ankles back and forth. The scene brought back my friend's painting *The First Day,* but as though its hilarious center had been removed.

There was only one place left to go.

I lay alone in the steam room and let the walls cry for me, spent within, the well of grief dried up. My mind wandered, avoiding questions I could not have answered anyway until I found myself entering into the memory of the irritation of that uniform from my past. The first year I was required to wear the uniform was the same year Mr. Bates gave us the assignment to write a haiku. I had endured years of that uniform by the time we were cast to perform as animals in the Britten opera. By then, the hunger to be allowed to take on some other shape than the required one was all I could think, every morning, as I pulled the recalcitrant kneesocks on, only to have them slide down the instant I stood up from the bed. Whatever I was, whoever I was, I was not this creature encased in blue armor, and my whole soul strained against it.

When they had assigned us the animals, they broke us down into groups: the fourth graders were to be rodents of all kinds; the fifth graders insects; the sixth birds; seventh animals with fur; and eighth, my class, those with hooves. As they handed out the deer mask to my archrival, the teacher's pet, and the stag mask to the son of the senator, Mr. Bates presented the rhinoceros mask to me. I wore glasses, he said, and the rhino was known for its nearsightedness, ha ha. Lying in the steam room I remembered fighting back tears at my fate to be cast as a rhino, when Mr. Bates handed the male rhinoceros mask to a boy with dark hair and full lips who was also nearsighted. He had answered a passionate, big-footed, ugly girl's silent prayers. My spousal rhinoceros had long, thick lashes, a full mouth, a head of beautiful hair he had finally let loose in eighth grade to explode into waves of black. He was the first of many reincarnations of the type of man whose zenith I had found in my Nebraskan journalist. If the only way I could be married to this boy was as a hoofed and horned and nearsighted hulk, then I would surrender to a mutually monstrous matrimony.

I lay in the dark in the steam room, seeing the face of my husband rhinoceros on the inside of my eyes. Deep, alarming music swelled inside me. It was the flood coming, surging. Noah's bold, muscular baritone ruptured the ominous cellos, rising and falling, the tide of the flood coming. We were each in our animal group, our masks on the tops of our heads bowing forward as we rushed to the Ark for sanctuary, waiting for our cue to be called out from the vast flyways of the Washington National Cathedral. Noah's voice rose above the tide of the orchestra, drums beating, the sound of thunder and lightning rending the stone halls. The rodents broke out of their hiding places and scrambled frantically toward the Ark, squeaking their *Kyrie eleison* as they climbed up and over people and around, panicking as they scurried toward Noah. The volume increased and Noah's voice strained to overcome the flood of the strings as he called to the things of the ground, and the insects and worms and spiders and slugs came humming and buzzing and crawling from where they had been hiding, racing toward the Ark as their young voices repeated in a soprano hysterium, *"Kyrie, kyrie, kyrie eleison"*; the violins and cellos were joined by dark bassoons, worried oboes, frantic clarinets as the flood rose—creatures of the air, Noah beckoned, his baritone rising higher in pitch as the orchestra swelled. Birds burst from their outposts in a desperate riot of plumage, descending in frenetic flapping toward the haven of the Ark, the voices of the children rising into song as they fluttered out from behind the pillars of the cathedral, their high sopranos flitting over us all, *"Kyrie eleison,"* they sang, *"Kyrie eleison!"* And then Noah called the beasts, and the lion roared, the tiger pounced, the Panther stalked toward the Ark in heavy padded rhythm to the kettle drums which beat the sound of the rising waves, the thumping beasts. Noah raised his voice higher, higher into the upper registers of fear as he called to us, the animals with hooves, pleading with us to come, quickly, as the dark vibrato of the strings shook the pillars of the unfinished cathedral. My heart was beating as I watched Noah and his children hustle the strays into the Ark, the great hoofed animals of my group calling out from where we had been posted in the full throttle of our voices on the verge of adulthood, responding to him to let him know we had heard his call. *"Kyrie—"* I sang, when my mouth was covered by something so soft that I thought I would faint and drown in the flood and never make it to the safety of the Ark, my legs were so weak, Noah pleading with us to hurry, the floodwaters were rising, the Ark already beginning to lift up and away, hurry, animals, as my rhinoceros husband kissed me full on the lips and told me he was in love.

My eyes were seared with a blast of white. The steam room lit up, detonating my memory of my first kiss. I was surrounded by white vapors bleached with light and sound. The instant the room lit up and the steam billowed around me, the hiss seemed to increase, and with the hissing came the annoying and invasive sound of a group of women all talking at once. They ooed and aahed that it was far, far too hot, you couldn't even see the benches, oh dear. And while they were making their bleats of alarm, I seized the opportunity to put my bathing suit back on before they caught me naked. The wet nylon stuck to my skin like the sweaty bunching nylon slip under my rhinoceros uniform.

The women had settled themselves on the benches, the light of the steam room sent up great puffs of white smoky steam, the glare of the tile searingly white, and in the corner, for the first time, I saw the source of the steam. A delicate nozzle was visible, its chrome showerhead peeking out from the pale vapors like a lizard.

The bleating women were in the middle of a conversation, and they resumed where they had left off once they settled down. I was waiting to see where they positioned themselves to make my exit without stepping on anyone, wanting only to get out—away from history, this invasion on the crest of salvation from disaster, and the hidden pain inside me that there was no one but my friend who would have found a way to make me laugh about my first kiss being not only from a rhinoceros but under threat of utter annihilation of my hoofed kind. But the steam was so thick, and the lights so bright, that the women's bodies kept appearing and disappearing and I could not make out where they were. I caught a glimpse of a leg, a knee, a head, as the hissing clouds of steam rolled around their voices from the showerhead.

"Can't because of some holiday. They don't even have the same holidays we do."

"She isn't . . ."

"You don't mean . . ."

"But how could she be? Her son's in Germany. Isn't her son in Germany, at the air force base there?"

"You think the army doesn't have Jewish soldiers?"

"Now, Pat, don't start getting . . ."

"He's not in combat. He works in security. Codes."

"Oh, well, they say they're very intelligent."

Silence. Hiss.

"She's a friend of mine, and I think it's rude of us to have a women's bridge club tournament without her. I think we should change the date. It's no different from our Easter."

There was silence, but for the steam.

Then one of them said, "Pat. It's the opposite of Easter. They don't believe in the Resurrection."

"I tell you, they're different," another cardboard voice chimed in. "Even the way they smell."

"Muriel Stockard, you should apologize for that comment."

Hiss.

"Well, all I can say is, you've changed, Pat Edwards. You've changed since you went to Woodstock and bought that silk underwear."

"Pat!"

". . . Edwards!"

"Woodstock!"

"Silk," said the voice of Muriel, turning silk into treason.

I picked my way over the limbs, stumbling on one anonymous thigh. It was all I could do not to turn up the steam nozzle as I was leaving. As I shut the door behind me, I heard Muriel say, "I've seen her before. She used to lie here in the dark naked with this other . . ."

I felt a wave of steam behind me as Pat Edwards opened the door. She walked briskly past me, saying nothing.

I saw her again in the locker room. My nerves rattled by visions of showers, I watched surreptitiously as she dressed. My hands were shaking. As I pulled on my clothes, I felt a terrible sense of guilt rising up inside me that I could get dressed, as if the mere act of putting on my own clothes after the hissing white clouds engulfed the shower room were a sign of a privileged status I did not deserve. I could not erase from my mind the images of the women's body parts, appearing and disappearing in the steam, and the uncanny rhyme of their conversation with the only image such a sight could awaken. I watched Pat Edwards dressing, desperate to know if she was feeling any of what I was. I wanted to let her know that I was not a member of the tribe of women in there, to remind her of our brief exchange what now seemed many lifetimes ago when she had joined me in the dark and said something about how we were all women when we were naked. I wanted to remind her that we belonged to each other beyond history and to turn off the lethal lights so that the Dew of us could form again in timeless, ecstatic benignity beyond the reach of history.

Pat Edwards pulled on her ice-cream-colored polyester pants, and over them a sweatshirt decorated with ducks. Her lips were straight as she put on a bright turquoise parka. She tugged at the waistband, tried to get the zipper into its slot, but the waist was too tight. She pulled again, a small grunt coming out of her, her lips folding in as she struggled.

Then Rulla appeared, as if out of nowhere, and watched Pat wrestling with the coat. I was now dressed. Rulla caught sight of me. She mimed Pat's struggle with the jacket perfectly, her naked bronze-pink flesh jiggling hilariously as she pulled a jacket of air tight about her waist and huffed and puffed.

"Don't you ever wear clothes?" Pat snapped at her, grabbing her purse and leaving.

Rulla turned slowly toward me, her eyebrows lifted at their centers, two straight lines pointing to the middle of her forehead. She looked like a round rubber clown, with her large green eyes and her straight brows and her spikes of wispy red hair. She performed another perfect mime of the flustered Pat Edwards, this time adding at the end, "American."

"Get dressed!" I said.

Rulla's whole face froze so quickly that it seemed her cheeks quivered at the suddenness of the motion. She looked at me, an alien cast masking her eyes, as if my reaction had hurled her into the idiosphere of her vast memory, into some private orbit of self where I lost her. My movement away from her, my shout, propelled her into the past where someone, somewhere, had done what I just did, moved away in repulsion, leaving her alone in the solitude of her ridiculous, exposed flesh. She turned slowly and shuffled in that slow lisp of her feet, moving neither up nor down, a sort of halting glide away into oblivion.

I was instantly filled with remorse, the way one feels when one yells at a child and the child bursts into tears. I ran after Rulla to apologize. "Rulla—wait! I want to know—when you teach. The belly-dancing class. When is it?"

She turned her body slowly around at the sound of her name. She stood before me, quite still. Rulla stared at me for a long time, her eyes vacant, as if I did not exist. She was lost in whatever place I had thrown her, and as I stood there, I could not help but feel that not only I had been wiped out of her mind, but also the Y, the Hudson Valley, America. She was on the far side of an ocean within her.

"Rulla?"

Her eyes blinked, and slowly I saw myself coming into her consciousness. "Hallo!" she said, smiling her broad smile. "You are here with your sister, yes? So wonderful. So beautiful. Sisters."

She smiled again, bowed to me slightly, and turned away, disappearing around the corner. I waited for a few moments before I slipped around to follow, dreading what I guessed I was going to see. She was sitting on the bench, her body collapsed in despair. She seemed to be sinking down, down. Down.

"Rulla?"

She stirred, but it was barely perceptible. She looked around on the bench, dazed, her movements uncertain. She found the bottle of Jergens. She looked at it for a moment, then she looked up at me. She picked up the bottle in the same hand as before and held it out to me. She then pointed to her back, exactly as she had done when I first saw her that morning.

My hand was trembling as I took the bottle from her and she turned around, presenting her back to me. I squeezed out the lotion, this time onto my own hands. I put the bottle down, rubbed the lotion and my hands vigorously together to warm them and the lotion. But as I put my hands on her back, Rulla shivered. "Oooh, that's cold!"

She shimmied all over, the tiny lines of coppery glints in her flesh quivering in her shudder of the memory of whatever the cold thing had been. I rubbed the lotion in slowly, very slowly, rubbing it all the way into her skin until I found the track of the scars, where the history of her sister was etched into her flesh and the tissue had erupted in luminous crimped fossils from the beatings, the burnings, the whips, the probes, I cannot tell you what they had used on her. For I am an American baby boomer who refuses to become a Child of Ashes and let history touch me. I do not know the names of the tortures inflicted on my foreign sisters ever since Scheherazade began dancing tales out of her body through the night to keep the tyrant amused, and herself—alive.

Spent by sleeplessness, art, and Nazi steam, as soon as I reached the cottage in the woods I made myself something to eat. I stood in the kitchen, not sure if I were relieved or the opposite by not finding Lexy in the Y—now that the Y had allied itself with Holocaust.

"The answer, Summacious, is neither."

I turned around. Manda was sitting on my couch, the smoke from her cigarette whirling up in evil spirals. Her legs in their Gestapo boots were stretched out across a wooden chest I had inherited from my maternal grandmother when she died a few years before. The chest was battered, scored with long, deep marks, and held together by wooden pegs. No nails. No metal. Only wood.

"Don't put your feet up on that," I found myself saying.

Manda lifted up her legs and held them suspended over the chest. "Don't like the idea of your Panther touching the sacred ancestral box, Summacious?"

"That's right," I said, my voice harsh. "Off."

Manda removed her legs in slow motion, melodramatically bending her knees and putting her boots on the floor with a definitive stomp. She exhaled. "Feel better now, Eraserface?"

"I feel like hell," I said.

"Thought so." Manda played with her hair, teasing me with the possibility of seeing her eyes. "What color were the roses, Summacious?"

"What roses?"

"The ones in Lexy's rose garden in Connecticut. My own advice is to make the roses pink. In honor of the dead queen mother."

"They were red," I said, regretting the words the instant I spoke them.

"Funny thing about how lizards regenerate their bodies," Manda went on. "They can only regenerate themselves. Repeats. Summer reruns. " She crossed her legs over the chest the other way, and grinned.

Sea chest, I now recalled. It had been a sea chest on the ship which had brought my first maternal ancestors, the Stokeses from Stokesay castle, across the ocean. Their daughter had married a man named Oliver Wolcott. Their child was the first Stokes born on this side of the ocean. The chest had been filled with sea biscuits. Dry, flat, tasteless, I could see them stacked inside the chest as it tossed on the ocean. My mouth was dry. I filled a glass with water and drank it down, then another.

"Aren't you curious, Summacious, why your peculiar brain chose to put Lexy in a red-rose garden in Connecticut?" I looked to see Manda tapping her cigarette ash on Oliver Wolcott's ancestral sea chest. My body shuddered. "You want me to say the name of the town in Connecticut for you?" Manda said.

"Madison," I said slowly.

"Street address of this fatal rose garden where the Dancer stopped dancing?"

I could see the address of my grandmother's ancestral home as I had seen it on the thick stationery of those letters she would send me. The memory of the birthday letters stirred something more inside me, and, not at all certain what I was looking for, afraid to find it if I did, I crossed the room to my writing table, where the Selectric sat. Held between two bookends made of carved soapstone, which had also belonged to my grandmother, were my journals. I wrote in them sporadically. I seldom recounted the mundane events of the day. I would not find in those pages any record which might have helped me to track the rhyming metaphors of Benjamin's twigs, Lexy's roses, and Manda issuing to me from trees. Nothing about light, golden or the spectral stuff outside the windows this chilly February afternoon. All that I would find among my so-called literary notes that might help me through the murder mystery Manda insisted was a love story was the date. If I were lucky.

It was an intuition, but when I saw the date in my own handwriting, I felt my bones wobble and I had to sit down. I didn't need to look over to the couch to see Manda gloating; I could feel it from where I sat reading the entry I had written the day Manda appeared.

November 10, 1981.

Manda had arrived on the exact centennial of my grandmother's birth.

Forgive me; I deceive you. I left out the one word which this story demands I insert in that sentence. So let me, awkwardly, give you the sentence as it should read: Manda had arrived on the exact centennial of my insane grandmother's birth.

Manda was a girl who was a Panther I had encountered in an asylum for the insane. The rose garden of my vision of Lexy lying on the bloodied sheet, rehearsing Her role as the corpse, was a garden inside the house where my mad grandmother was born, Oliver Wolcott's ancestral home. And the young woman who fell, Gwen's sister who was not her sister? Freddie's friend? Moongirl? What was asylum to her? Or to Medea? Rulla, who had found in the senior women's locker room of the Y sanctuary from a story of torture in which her sister had died at the hands of a tyrant. What was her fate, now that Crane Woman had appeared? The dance studio had proven no asylum for Lexy that very morning, which seemed many lifetimes ago. And I—who had for months sought asylum from the harangue of the Panther by leaving my cottage in the woods to cross the river to the steam room—I too had lost my asylum from Manda this Valentine's Day as the source of Eternal Dew turned living hell itself. There was no safe place from Manda left —not for any of us.

"There's hope for you yet," Manda said, a diet cola materializing in her hand. I stared at Manda and my pulse began to race. I was filled with a hate so huge that I thought I would burst. Hate for the Panther holding the diet cola, her legs stretched across the sea chest. My eyes were locked on the diet cola in her hand—the medicine, the dreamkilling medicine—and I all but reached out for it, to swallow the imagicide that would wipe her out of my mind forever, when I heard a dull, thumping sound.

A dove was beating at my window, mistaking it for air. I jumped up and slid the glass doors open. The dove flew in, and the diet cola dematerialized as the bird swooped at Manda, who crouched and swatted at it. The dove then flew past my eyes and out the window.

"Damn birds," Manda said.

And I knew what I had to do.

I sat down at my desk and turned on the hippo-Selectric. It kicked into motion, far more reliable than my car.

My Panther, recovering with a cigarette from the perpetual pack, sprang from the couch. "Summacious—what are you doing?"

"Writing the story."

"Whose story?"

"Mine."

"We have to talk. You can't do this. Summacious, the dove was a perversion—"

I laughed. "You calling a dove perverse, Manda, that's the only really funny thing you've said."

"It's February. The dove was unnatural."

I looked at Manda puffing. "Exactly."

"Exactly what, Miss No Cherry Blossoms?"

"That dove was a declaration of war."

"Do we need to repeat Symbolism 101, Eraserface? Doves mean peace."

"Not in our story. Yours and mine."

"What, suddenly you're the Audubon of the psyche?"

"No. Suddenly, Manda, what I am is the author of this story. Not you. Not anymore."

I put a sheet of canary-yellow newsprint into the Selectric. Into the inside of my eyes came the bridge, and the space in the railings, the red thread on the pylon. And instead of seeing a long-armed woman falling down (down) into a Dring, or a portrait of a sister from the Y that Lenin could use as his evidence against my friend, I was seeing evidence to make my case against *fiction*—Manda's.

"Wait—"

"It's over, Manda. You are going to be locked up, do you understand? Locked up by the authorities for murder. Of some woman whose name I don't know—a secretary. No more anonymous woman in America than a secretary. The woman who broke through the railings on the bridge."

"But I didn't do that."

My mind was racing. "Sure you did. Your murder weapon was the deteriorating infrastructure of America."

"Very clever, Summacious, but that is not a Cretan lie. It's just a lie."

"So, I'm going to pretend, Manda. That's the answer to the riddle about the Cretan liar: You have to pretend the truth. And I am going to pretend very hard and very well and very thoroughly that the real story is there, on the bridge, in the gap in the railings. I'm fixing the story in that gap. And I'm giving you all the sorry bones of all the ancestors that came over here to help you kill a woman nobody cares about. The Chief's going to put you in jail for it, Manda. Not his deputy, or me, your deputy—the Chief is locking you up in my murder story about you."

Cigarettes tumbled out of Manda's breast. She lit up, paced, fumed.

"This is not your destiny. Listen to me; I'm being sincere. I take back everything I ever said about how stupid you are. You're right; the story does have to go into a gap. But Meem," she said, calling me by that name for the first time, "it matters, it matters more than you know, what gap you put the story in. And you can't just decide. You can't just say, I want the story to go in that gap on the bridge so I end up with a valentine instead of me, the Panther, this walking, talking ransom note telling you the difficult truth your kind does not want to hear. You have to forfeit your self to get your soul. I know you're scared; every one of you baby boomers is too scared to do the Eleusis thing now that Oppenheimer's declared Fat Man and Little Boy the next Prometheus and signed the papers to form the Ashes Corporation. I swear, Summacious, I swear to god, this gap on the bridge and using the Chief against me—it's not the way to Eleusis."

"Who says I want to go to Eleusis? Who says I even can?"

"You have to have faith."

"First it's a dove, now it's faith. You're losing that Panther touch, Manda."

"The tape, listen to the astrologer's tape, you don't believe me."

I looked up at Manda, her hair cutting across her eyes. "You advised me against amateurs. I am not impressed. Quote unquote."

"Summacious, what did I do to lose your faith in me? I am trying, trying with all I am, to get you to bring the story back here. Right here. "

I stared at Manda. "Let me see your eyes."

Manda's head fell forward, her hair falling down. "You're not ready yet."

"Ready?"

"And you were so close, Summacious. So close."

I hesitated, wavering, as Manda's black hair swung back and forth, teasing me. "When will I be ready?"

"When you stop fighting what the story is and give me Lexy to kill Her like you have wanted me to do from the beginning. Then I show you my eyes."

"No deal," I said, my voice like surgical wire. "From this moment on, Lexy is no longer in The Murder Mystery. I'm taking Her out. You never killed Her. You never even knew Her. But you did commit a murder, Manda, a *different* murder, which is going to lock you up forever. And Lexy . . ."

Manda stomped. "You still don't understand the first thing about what's going on here. Not the first thing."

I lit a cigarette and adjusted the margins on the Selectric. "Call me stupid. I don't care anymore, Manda."

"You must care, Summacious," Manda said. Had her voice not been—suddenly—quiet, I would not have looked up at her just then. "Gwen," she said, in the same soft voice. "On the tape. She tells you what she saw in your hands, Summacious. The hands which are writing this story. What she couldn't make sense out of her names for stars. And what she saw in your hands was me."

"You?"

"In the stars, she saw that a teacher was coming to you. But in your hand, she saw the gift your teacher brought. And I'm that teacher, bearing you the gift."

"You're my *teacher*?"

"I'm the most important teacher you will ever have in your entire life." She was sitting at an angle to me, her face toward the trees. Something about her voice made me pause. I looked at Gwen's tape, a film of dust over it, and then up at Manda, who was staring out at the trees. "How many times do I have to tell you, Summacious," she said in a voice made of its own ashes. "There's a way to sing about Her, the song you want to sing more than any other, trust me, I know what I am talking about. I want to sing that love song to Lexy as badly as you do. But this owl-dove combo is not it."

My voice was choked by rage and grief in equal measure as I burst out at Manda, "If you can do all these other things that I swear you are doing, somehow, why can't you do the simplest thing of all—rewrite the story? Change the plot? Turn your murder story into a love story and not kill Her?"

"My murder story is a love story, Summacious. And I can't rewrite the plot line of *what was, and is, and always will be* any more than you can write your brother's magic out of your life story. Do you think that because I'm a Nazi, and a Panther, and a murderer, and twenty-seven thousand years old, I don't grieve for the beautiful I, myself, am fated to kill, over and over again, for eternity?"

Memory swept into me. The same year I had been cast as a rhinoceros, I was doing spelling homework. I was an excellent speller and never missed a word. I sat in my room at my desk, my rhinoceros mask in front of me, the words for the next day's spelling quiz before me, my eyes welling up. I began furiously copying out the words for my spelling test. "Decision—Decisive. Ravine—Ravenous. Authority—Authoritative," I wrote down, resenting my teacher for these stupid pairs with their dumb tricks. "Beautiful" was the next word on the list.

B, I wrote. E. But then the letters scrambled, my heart pounded, as my eyes filled up with the rhinoceros face. I scratched out B and E furiously and started again. B. E. A . . . T . . . More furious scratching as tears dolloped the page. I grabbed my notebook and rushed out of my bedroom into the hall. My brother's bedroom door was shut. I went to it and knocked.

"What?" he called.

"I need help with spelling."

The door opened. "Since when do you need help with spelling?"

"How do you spell 'Beautiful'?"

"B-e-a-t-i-f-u-l," he said.

I bit my lip. I knew it was wrong. I went back to my room, opened my notebook on my desk, and dutifully wrote down my brother's misspelling. "B-e-a-t-i-f-u-l." I looked at the word on the other side of the pair: "Beatitude." I wrote: "B-è-a-u-t-i-t-u-d-e."

Beatiful.

Beautitude.

These hieroglyphics of memory appeared inside my eyes, circled in red where I had misspelled them on the test. Forgetting Manda was there, I tested the words on my mouth to see how the misspellings would sound. "Beatiful," I whispered, and into my mind rushed the image of Lexy in the rose garden, beaten, fully. "Beautitude," I said, and She appeared in my eyes, dancing in the Starr Building.

Manda said, "Like I told you, Summacious, you want to do this story right." Her voice startled me. "You think writing this sterile murder mystery in a coward's fugitive yellow is how you're going to fulfill your destiny and climb up the ladder to literary stardom. But your destiny, Summacious, requires that you take a spelling test."

I looked at the blank page in the Selectric. But I saw no words. Into my eyes-inside-my-eyes came a long stone wall, overgrown with roses, snaking its way down the side of a hill. At the bottom of the hill was a tennis court, where my brother was playing in a tournament. I watched him toss the ball to make a serve. Ribbons of rainbow chiffon chased upward after it. My whole being filled with the sight of my brother leaning back, back, Lexy whirling beside him, the rainbow chiffon gathering into a cloud above them, the tennis ball enfolded inside the magical suspension of silk.

His beautiful body broke forward for the serve—

The diet cola materialized—

Ace!

I stared at the can in Manda's hand. I could hear the sound of my bones crunching in the accident, the can of diet cola rolling on the floor of the car. I leaned over and reached down for it when the car . . . filled up with trees. . . .

"*This way to Eleusis,* Summacious, that was a direct quote, and you know it. I am the one with the medicine."

I closed my eyes against the memory of the doctors' voices as they wove in and out of the dream of the painkillers while I lay there in the hospital, my pelvis smashed. *The only reason she survived at all was that she was in this strange position . . . but her brother . . .*

I heard Manda's raspy, ash-filled voice so close it seemed inside me. "Take the diet cola; Summacious. Reach for the diet cola; it's right here."

"*No!*" I screamed at the Panther. The rainbow chiffon shivered in midair in rhythm to the volley. The point went to my brother. Love— thirty. He took his racket and, as was his habit, plucked the strings with his fingers. The *dring—dring—dring* of the strings of my brother's tennis racket reverberated in my ears, drowning out the other sound, the bone-crunching sound of my pelvis splintering. I wanted to hear the *dring— dring—dring* of my brother's tennis racket to surrender to the anguished beauty of the impossible, time-bending melody of the Drings of a murderer's fairy tale merging with the *dring* of an American sister's history of losing the eyes of the one who knew the beauty of her inner magic.

"He came back to me. My brother. He came to me, in the dance studio, with Lexy. In one piece. He told me it was finally time." I swallowed my tears. "For magic. I am going to undie them both, damn it, and make them stick to life forever. The diet cola is poison, not medicine—you said it was imagicide. Dreamkilling. And I won't take it. I am going to dream them back, Manda. Lexy and my brother—I am going to dream them back here. He came to me and he told me I could and he always tells the truth, Manda. He never lied to me, ever."

"How does your soul spell the word 'beautiful,' Summacious? Answer that, and you'll do this murder mystery right."

I looked up.

The Panther was gone.

The trees stood vigil for spring, immobile, denuded skeletons of a winter that dragged on. Forgetting that Lexy had told me in the dance studio that I could not change the story backward, I pushed against the story Manda had told me, willing my imagination to go in reverse. I was less engaged in imagining a new plot than in disimagining the one Manda had already dictated to me when she had first arrived and seemed no more than a "character." I sought to erase all that had transpired since Manda's arrival on November 10, determined to undo our story, the story of Manda and Lexy and me and madness.

That radical, potent medicine was in order was no longer a question—not since Manda had stretched her legs over the ancestral sea chest, and I had discovered that the Panther had arrived on my insane grandmother's birth date. My sanity, I was convinced, lay in removing the rhyming pulsations in the warp of women and dream and asylum from Rhinebeck—all the Rhinebecks, putting up impermeable, blood-proof walls between each one. I trusted the Chief, as locked inside fiction as Manda, to be my guide from within those walls.

It was a sign, perhaps, of the true measure of the faith I had in my imagination surgery that I began to do the necessary errands of life to the south of my cottage, toward Hyde Park, rather than risk Main Street. I took back roads, shortcuts, anything to avoid passing through the intersection where the asylums in my soul's ancestral pilgrimage from madness to Her—The Beekman Arms, the Starr Building, the "home" no one called by its real name, and the two sides of Main Street—all met at the intersection where Freddie's wooden rainbow god, stripped, stood vigil outside the smoke shop. I avoided all contact with the places on the map of the other Rhinebeck where I was in danger of finding a chink in the blood-proof walls I was frantically constructing between them. I focused all my energy on reverting the Rhinebeck in The Murder Mystery to its singular status as a small town in a Hudson Valley anyone can visit, where the average American tourist would find no sacred chamber of Eternal Dew across the bridge, no floating mouth of the Chief of Restoration Tragedy, and no Main Street inviting the splinters of psychosis on one side and worship at the shrine of a local rainbow deity of the Phosphorescence cult on the other. Doves alone would coo in the cupola of the Starr Building, for the birds in that Rhinebeck recognize the songs of their own species and, unlike humans, are not each other's murderers. What could be easier than to restore the quaint, picturesque town with the pristine Main Street of The Murder Mystery? Certainly easier than restoring my soul from its shattered entrapment in Manda's murderous love story.

The thousands of words I poured into the manuscript of The Murder Mystery to unsay Manda's initial three—I killed Her—are beyond the reach of my memory to reconstruct, for it was not language I was writing. It was muteness. The only authentic reconstruction of these "Mutemouth" words I wrote during this time would be the seventeen years of refusing to tell this story, the one here in these pages. It seems I have been sitting my entire adult life with a story three spoken words long and thousands of written ashen words short of the tale itself.

Where were my surgical instruments? The Selectric was the authority now, the final phase of its transformation from apogee of technology to hippocampic tomb fetish complete as it conducted my fingers with its hypnotic, shamanic drumming to lead me on a journey through Lexy's tomb against my will. The Selectric had its own idea of the type of medicine my imagination required for my psyche's restoration, and it was the opposite of the one my ego prescribed for me. What was flying off my fingers was more terrifying than my storm trooper from trees arriving on my Grandmother Stokes's birthday. The same rainbow chiffon scarf which had slipped from Lexy's arm to fall to the floor of the dance studio, where She had gathered it into a nested shape, kept appearing on the inside of my eyes in tatters. Shredded, dirty, it hung on the branch of a tree somewhere in Hyde Park near the river. Manda had put it there when she finished strangling Lexy, teasing me to find the evidence I had been looking for all this time. The battered chiffon of my childhood entrancement with beauty was Manda's murder weapon.

In desperation to avoid the actual scene of the murder taking shape in my eyes, I would force my imagination to go backward in time, to before Manda arrived on the scene. I saw Lexy standing near the shore of the Hudson on the summer estate of an American president who had the ashes of the children of my haiku, the victims of Hiroshima, on his guilty hands. She lifted the rainbow chiffon to announce that Her dance was about to begin, as though She were Scheherezade, determined to dance the tyrant out of a war. I knew if She began this dance, it would change into Her death dance, and I knew that a death dance was what She wanted. I sensed Lexy's urgency to die, and, worse, I sensed Lexy joyous beyond measure to be the victim in Manda's murder-love story. It was almost as if my avoidance of Main Street, and the simple action of making a right turn at the end of my driveway toward Hyde Park, was the final act Lexy had been waiting for me to perform so that She could get on with the business of dying. I could not erase from my eyes the vision of Lexy dancing on that presidential ground no matter how hard I resisted this new horror being born inside me, knowing the fate of the rainbow chiffon before Her dance was through.

Her vitality as She danced Her death dance was anguish for me to watch, a vision of such breathtaking beauty and passionate energy that I couldn't stand to look—but neither could I bear to look away. I must have been feeling sensations akin to mortals in ancient myths who unknowingly stumble upon a goddess in her woodland bath and are struck dumb and immobile by the direct sight of her divine nakedness. There the analogy breaks down, for it was no naked bath in the forest with her maidens, no Lexy safely in the asylum of the Y to which I, a mortal liv-

ing in Rhinebeck in 1981, was bearing reluctant, entranced witness. But
I was about to make the attempt to bend the living story in that direction,
and it was going to prove to be fatal to me, not Lexy. She was a goddess
dancing Her own death dance, and dancing it with an exuberance beyond the powers of my human mind to comprehend, my eyes-within-
eyes paying homage to Her whirling dance of the dead on presidential
shores day after day after day at the Selectric shrine. Her naked feet
pounded the rocks, and as Her feet pounded out the rhythm of the dance
celebrating Her certain death at the Panther's hands in rhapsodic anticipation, my fingers pounded out a rhapsodic plot to the same ecstatic
pulse.

One day, when the trees were still refusing to break out into green, I
could bear it no longer. I unplugged the damned Selectric, picked it up,
and carried it across the room. I put it down on the round dining-room
table, cursed a few silent curses at it for having been the Panther's ac-
complice, and then walked back across the room. I rummaged in some
drawers to find an old but unopened pack of legal pads. I ripped off the
cellophane and settled down at the desk with a fresh pad before me
where the Selectric had been. I took a pen from a cup with a broken handle I kept on my desk and scratched out a spiral on the top corner of the
sheet. "Hah!" I mouthed at the Selectric on the far side of the room.

I looked down at the blank sheet, waiting for literature to come to
my aid. But I kept raising my eyes to the Selectric, perched on the table
where Manda used to sit. I threw the pen down, crossed the room again,
picked up the machine. The only other surface large enough for the machine was the ancestral wooden chest in front of the couch. I plunked it
down and then went back to my blank yellow pad at the desk. I picked
up the pen and looked defiantly at the Selectric on Oliver Wolcott's sea
chest. I thought, the Panther cannot stretch her legs on the chest and gloat
at me any more.

Then, Manda appeared, not as the Panther but in that other aspect
she had in the beginning, when I still believed she was a fictional character. She was a transparent figure whose legs stretched out and went
through the Selectric like a television trick ghost. Instinct and experience
told me that this Manda would not speak out loud, but the vision,

specious as it was, awakened something inside me. Before I knew it, I was standing in front of my bookshelf, thumbing through my well-worn copy of Shakespeare's *The Tempest*.

A scene formed, and I was back at my desk, writing by hand.

Manda was with her mother, Moms, in the kitchen of the apartment in Chicago the morning after her father left. Behind them, the bedroom was covered with the plastic sheets that flapped in the background, where my nearsighted eyes could not read the letters. Her sister lay in repose, utterly still, on the bed.

"It worked," I heard Moms say. "He left. God knows where to, and I don't want to know what God knows. But I made sure he knew." Moms finished washing the dishes and dried her hands. Then she reached under the sink. Manda looked up and bit her lip. She was expecting Moms to pull out the colander. But instead, she pulled out a large, worn volume. "Shakespeare," Moms said, putting the book ceremoniously before Manda. An eighteen-year-old Manda, roughly the same age the Panther (and I) had been when we first met in Vermont.

"Under the sink?" Manda said, reaching for it. She opened the flyleaf and saw the sticker for the Wilber, Nebraska, Library, the envelope with the index card still in it. Manda pulled it out as her mother went on. "Right next to the Wild Turkey. So your father found it every time he tried to sneak another drink. I know he knows."

"Knows what?"

"That I was destined for something better than him," Moms said, removing her apron. "We are both of us destined for poetry, Manda. You must believe that. Poetry is all that matters. Did I name you Pat? Betty? Good, respectable Wal-Mart check-out names? No. I gave you a name with a destiny. Miranda. Poetry. So he couldn't destroy you."

I looked at the name, "Miranda," in my own handwriting, studying my weapon against the Manda I had known for almost a year. Miranda, a name fashioned from literature, a conscious, vengeful strategy against an icon from the realm of soul, as if renaming her were the only way to disimagine the message she had been running twenty-seven thousand years to tell me. I looked up at the Selectric on the ancestral sea chest, and my stomach lurched. My throat went dry. The Special-Effects Manda was barely visible, a warp of air lingering around the machine. I forced my eyes to the handwritten page. Miranda, I read again, wreckage on an island filling my eyes.

Miranda. Daughter of an exiled tyrant, Prospero, tossed up on an island. This trick of a syllable was going to accomplish what thousands of words had not, and undo Lexy's murder?

Memory awakened from its slumber behind the blood-proof walls of fiction, and I felt an enormous claw scraping at me from within. I was eleven years old, a clunky, big-footed girl who had upset my teacher with my haiku filled with the ashes of Hiroshima. When my mother told my Grandmother Stokes that I had written a poem about the atom bomb, she said, "Well, dear, so have I. You must come visit, and bring her." My mother told me that my grandmother had been "a real poet," and that she wanted to see me. She lived nearby, and it was not long before I was standing in front of my grandmother in her garden room. She stared at me as though registering my existence for the first time. I stared back, not in defiance but to prove to her that I could take being seen by "a real poet."

She was the one who broke the stare, turning very slowly to my mother, who was the stage manager of this silent encounter. My Grandmother Stokes opened her dark black eyes even more, and her resemblance to an owl, with her round, astonished pupils framed by her white feathery hair, and the way she never blinked when she moved her head, confirmed my sense that I had just been put through a silent test in which my grandmother had penetrated into my soul, seeking evidence of incipient wisdom. She said to my mother, "I heard from Sister . . ." And launched into family news. I sat down, trying to compose myself. I had no doubt that I had failed my Grandmother Stokes's test and that my first meeting with a living poet was to be my last. Then, as we were leaving, she handed me some books of poetry, with no more ceremony than my brother when he tossed the magnets into my lap. She said, "The ratio of listening to writing is a thousandfold to one. The song you hear inside will always sound better than the song you sing. And there is no such thing as too much Shakespeare."

On my bookshelf in the cottage in the woods, in view of where I was sitting the entire time I was writing The Murder Mystery, was my grandmother's notebook of poems. It had been given to me at her death, five years before the Panther arrived. I had never read a single one of them for fear that I would find in her poetry what had been revealed to me only after her death: the extent of her madness. My whole being was shuddering now as memory crashed through the blood-proof walls of The Murder Mystery. I heard my grandmother's piercing, descant voice, saying, "Well, Sister said . . . Sister knows . . . Sister called . . . Sister . . . Sister . . . Sister," singing inside me, and the final thread of the fatal tapestry of Sisters the Panther was weaving appeared in the pattern on the loom of my ancestral destiny: All Stokes women called each other "Sister," regardless of relation. To be a Stokes woman was to be a Sister who was—and was not—ever since the first Stokes woman, gravid with child, had made the great crossing to America. She brought her copy of Shakespeare with her, secreted away where she hoped her husband would not find it, afraid of what this good son of a family that produced ministers would do if he discovered his wife's passion for poetry.

I dropped my head on the handwritten pages of the scene of Moms christening my murderer, Miranda. The name Miranda had taken me into ancestral madness, the blood legacy of Stokes Sisters. And the name Manda took me back around, circling, to the beginning of my story with the Panther. There was no way out of the maze where Sisters were in mortal peril when they meant what they moved as sisters. I was trapped in a dead end of the labyrinth that blocked me from crossing Main Street to reach the asylum on the other side, where Freddie's rainbow god pointed the way to a dancer who was the embodiment of the way my soul loved the life that loved me. My only way out was to retrace my steps.

I tried to say "Miranda" out loud. I couldn't. The Panther had my throat in her grip, and my will was impotent against those hands, which acquired muscle in sound, flesh in voice. I stared at *Miranda* on the page, as though my eyes could fix on paper what my throat could not, and with the handwritten word I could make this name stick to the murderer in my story—all of my story, emerging simultaneously in all the Rhinebecks.

I lifted my head back from the paper and stared at my own handwriting. What I saw there, in my own script, was "Manda." It was useless. I could no more spell their names the way my conscious will desired, and fix the dance of icons from the soul realm in the pattern my ego wanted, than I could live any longer in a sterile Rhinebeck in a literal landscape, its divine features surgically removed by my medicine of willpower vying against the mystery of Eleusis. And I could no more choreograph Her dance of meaning to subdue fear and terror within me at Her fate any more than I could stop Main Street's emerging from the other Rhinebeck, or remove Baubo from the steam room, sisters from fatal bridges, Freddie from his golden fleece, rainbow god, and crazy mother's idea he was created from a splinter, or change the history of names in my family and pretend Stokes women did not call each other "Sister."

There was nothing I could do to stop Lexy from lifting up the rainbow chiffon scarf to begin Her death dance on presidential grounds.

Part Two

No warning, no official authority announcing that the soul journey is scheduled to begin, no wise elder appearing in a vision, no certified shaman handing me a set of instructions for how to make my own silver thread to show me the way to—and back from—lunacy, no agency coming to my aid but my own soul, speaking from within, telling me to use the only instrument I, a deracinated modern woman, have to undertake the perilous mission of rescuing my soul from its own ashes—my narrative imagination. Story was all I had then, and all I have now.

I begin my descent into what we moderns experience as madness but the old wisdom knows as swimming in trees. It was my fate, however, to meet Manda before I met Lexy, and swim in her murderous tree first. And so the guides in my story will have to possess the strength for madness if I am to swim in the trees of wisdom.

The power to cross Main Street emerged from the story itself. Whether the patterns I can discern in my own accounting of my story of soul are enough for transformation of my soul in actual life, I do not know. But I do know that every time I interrupt myself to ask the monk inside the tree to tell me what the official system for counting breaths is, he tells me to get back to the process of breathing, that my destiny will be found only in my breathing, my way. It seems that codified wisdom won't work for me, if I am to believe the holy spirit inside the tree. And from this point on in my story, I am going to believe him.

I now speak the words that will take me neither to the Main Street of fiction nor the Main Street of experience, but to the other Main Street, with those other kinds of trees growing on either side, which are madness and wisdom, both.

Swimming in Trees

The landscape was painful to look at during the day, the grass brown stubble, the dregs of snow on north sides of streets and buildings the color of ashes. The trees seemed homeless, exposed without the shelter of leaves, starved for a green that refused to come.

I did not have the first clue where to look for my guides. I knew only that I had to find them if I were to finish the spelling test of my soul, and I would not find them sitting in my cottage in the woods, alone.

Nor did I have a clue where Manda was. She had not returned. I had no illusions of a successful exorcism having taken place. Our story wasn't finished yet. Manda was somewhere in Rhinebeck—the noumenal Rhinebeck—and its environs, stalking Lexy, and I had to find my guides to take me all the way into that dreamtime Rhinebeck to finish the battle with Manda for my soul—and all the way out.

I had been offered a part-time job as a teacher in the adult education outreach program of the local liberal arts college, up the river, north of the bridge leading to the Kingston Y. I had been hesitating, but now I decided to take the job. The class they hired me to teach was Autobiographical Writing for Adults. Whenever I looked at the faces of my students, I could not help but hear Manda's harangue that I needed "remedial make-up work." I wanted to say to them, "The art of autobiography is for you to spell the word 'beautiful' the way your soul does.

Then your story matters. Unfortunately," I wanted to confess to them, "I haven't figured this out for myself yet. I'm looking for guides to help me." Maybe my students were guides I did not recognize in my anxiety over teaching them what I myself did not know. One thing was clear, once I began to teach: I finally believed Manda's insistence that I wanted to tell the story "right."

As a quasi-faculty member at the college, I was invited to attend all their literary events. I went as seldom as the delicate politics of academic employment allowed. But I received in the mail an invitation to a ceremony I had no choice but to attend. It was to honor a Hungarian poet with a humanitarian award, to be given to him by a famous Czech poet who was visiting the college for the year. The college had been making a great public relations circus out of the ceremony. But that was not the reason I had to attend. The "invitation" was a folded copy of one of the posters plastered all over town for my friend's art show, *Show Up Naked*. My friend had written a note across the back.

> Remember the wet spot and how Lenin who wasn't Lenin yet made me laugh? We went to hear this poet read that same day. So far, only a threat. I think it's safe to go to the Y again. Together. Did you get a chance to ask Lexie to let me paint her? You have to come to this with me. Because of the wet spot.

The night of the event, I was to pick my friend up. As I pulled into her driveway, she raced in front of my headlights and opened her coat. She was wearing a brilliant fuchsia-colored satin blouse. She got into the car and said, "I got it at the thrift shop for eight dollars. You know, when I was little, my mother says she would buy me all these nice clothes, and you know what I would do? I'd trade them with my sister's used ones. And she said it used to drive her crazy because after the war, all she wanted was new clothes for herself and her family. I'm nervous, can't you tell?"

"What about?"

"Wet spots."

"On your blouse?"

"Of course not on my blouse. In my life. They got me in trouble the night I first heard this poet. And here I am . . . I think I live more dangerously than most people."

We wound our way north, along River Road, through dark woods under an indifferent moon. We reached the intersection where Route 9 crossed River Road, the bridge to our left.

"Did you get a chance to ask Lexy . . . ?"

"I haven't been to the Y for a long time. Her name is spelled with a y."

"How do you know how she spells her name? Are you like close friends now or something? Why haven't you introduced me to her? Except maybe you shouldn't. Maybe it's better this way. I think it is. I take it all back. I think I shouldn't meet her. I think I have to paint her without knowing her." I laughed. "Meem? What is it?"

"It's the way you think out loud, and can talk your way from one side to the other faster than anyone I know."

"I was serious," she protested. "I really don't think I could paint her if I met her. It's just this feeling I have."

As I crossed River Road, passing the turnoff to the bridge, it hit me. Lexy had reached my friend first.

"Paint her," I said.

She turned to look at me. "You sound so serious."

"I can't explain it."

"It's *that* serious?"

"It's even more serious than that."

"Do you know why I made you go with me to this thing tonight, Meem? It's the same kind of serious as you wanting me to paint Lexy. You need to see this man. I don't know why. I just know you do, like the way Benjamin knows you need things to keep you warm."

As we walked the long distance to the auditorium, I listened to the chatter of those walking with us. People had come up from New York on the train, driven over from Boston, down from Syracuse and Buffalo, and a whole flock of people from Chicago had flown out of a late winter blizzard, they were saying in halting English to our (very famous) resident novelist teacher who was their official escort to the event.

It was one of those gatherings where you smell perfume on the women everywhere you go, and there are glints of gold against sedate black, an occasional brilliant scarf, a shawl, and most of the faces are powdered or wrinkled and the hairlines sparse, retreated, on women and men alike. My friend's thrift-shop satin seemed like a tropical fruit amid the somber suits and elegant dresses of the visitors from all over. There were many deep voices in strange accents, and scattered throughout were the sounds of a language I had never heard before; it had music and rhythms all its own. English sounded lazy and impersonal compared to it, like a manufacturer's report in contrast to an ancient lyric chanted by the honey tongued and liquid limbed.

A hush descended over the auditorium by unconscious consensus without signal or sign. My friend squeezed my forearm and whispered, "I can't breathe." All heads turned to the podium.

The visiting poet who was to give the award came out on stage. He spoke in a rich, musical voice about many human things we had all forgotten, and would forget, were it not for the stories of men such as the man we were honoring tonight. As soon as the glint of the honoree's wheelchair caught the stage lights, the audience erupted into applause. But my friend and I stared not at this small, bent man furled like a pale fern, his head wrapped in white hair and beard as though he had been caught up in a wayward cloud. My friend grabbed me as the audience continued to clap.

"It's her," she said. "Meem, it's the Alvin woman."

She stood tall and straight, a dark tree behind his wheelchair, her short white hair like a fragment of the same lost cloud that had caught him up, her long arms like branches curved to provide him shelter. Glowing at her neck we could see the necklace she had purchased from Gwen, and as it had then, in Max's jewelry store, so the necklace now illumined her eyes. Even though we were sitting at the back of the auditorium, those phosphorescent eyes reached through tier after tier with their brilliant green energy, to reach us where we felt them land on our skin with a heat and power all their own.

We watched as her husband reached up for her hand. At the moment they touched, the audience quieted.

"She is so beautiful," my friend said. "She is just so beautiful."

The ceremony went by in a haze of admiring words, speech upon speech about the nature of suffering, the importance of poetry, the triumph of the human spirit, including a long speech by the college president about the arts, which was roundly applauded by a small coterie of faculty members. Throughout it all, the woman with the phosphorescent eyes held herself still, exuding a regal grace that needed no necklace to reinforce it. The only movements she made were occasional looks at her husband to see that he was comfortable. Once she adjusted the collar of his shirt. It was a gesture of such private intimacy, what one would do in a bedroom, yet done with no self-consciousness or awareness that she was on stage in a room with at least four hundred people in attendance.

The moment had come in the ceremony for him to give his acceptance speech for the honor being bestowed on him. The visiting poet brought the award to where the honoree was sitting in his wheelchair. There were a few awkward moments when he began to speak his thanks and no one could hear him. The visiting poet, flustered, was signaling for help from the stagehands to move the microphone. But Phosphorescence, a woman accustomed to handling everything, simply rolled her husband to the microphone. She then untaped it herself, the visiting poet rushing to help her, but she shrugged him away gently. She flicked the switch and then brought the microphone to her husband's mouth.

He leaned his large head forward and said simply, "I am here because of my beautiful wife. She should have this award."

She looked at him, shaking her head back and forth, slowly but firmly denying credit. His next words were not meant for the microphone. "No more fighting about it, darling. You are why I am alive. It is that simple. I keep telling you."

A shadow passed over her. Her head shook quickly, once.

He turned to the audience, leaning over to reach the microphone. "My wife does not want me to tell you. We had a terrible fight before we came here tonight. Yes, yes, even a man as old and crooked as me, I can still fight with my wife, like a real macho guy, yes?"

There was sprinkled, disquieted laughter, shifting in chairs, a few glances between old couples, and the visiting poet's face performed a whole circus of expressions in a few seconds. The college president's face showed only one.

"My wife, she is embarrassed by this story. But you good people here tonight, and my brother poet who is much more famous than I will ever be, comrade from that beautiful, sad place Czechoslovakia where I cry every time I visit . . ."

"Me too," said the poet. The men, compatriots in exile, smiled.

"You should know, this award, it is strange," the honoree said. "I do not mean to be rude person. But this is strange, to honor a man for living. That is all. I just lived. Any man, he can do this. So, I sit here where I have no choice," he said, gesturing to the wheelchair. "Asking myself, while you are talking . . . and talking," he said, bringing a warm laugh from the audience. "I am saying, why this award? What is this meaning? A man lives. So what the big deal? So, Stalin tried to kill me. And all my brother poets. And I live. That's all: I live. I am here, now, in America. And Stalin? Stalin, he is dead."

As the audience broke into applause, my friend's eyes glimmered. She looked at me, shaking her head. "I love him," she said. "I love this man completely."

His words, thick with his accent, seemed to undulate as if they were being pulled by the moon through water. He looked at his wife, standing tall, reminding me of an amphora. "All I did, I love this woman. Listen," he said, to stop the applause. "I am talking serious. Look at her. Is she not beautiful?"

Her face was at an angle, impossible to read as the applause broke out again. He raised a shaking hand, and the audience quieted.

"When I was in the camps," he said, and the last remnants of sound died immediately. "When I was in hell, every day, I thought of my wife. I did not know, is she alive? Is she dead? I have nothing to write with. They know what they are doing, these sadists. So what can I do? I want my wife alive. So I make her alive. I make her alive with a poem. There is no other way. This is what is interesting about hell," he said, his words falling unevenly on the shaking microphone in his wife's hand. "Hell, it makes poetry much more important, yes? Stalin—we owe him. We owe him for teaching us that poetry *matters*."

He went on, "But this poem, it is long, no? I have much to say about this woman I love. It is too long. No American editor would ever allow a poem as long as this poem I make up in my mind to make my wife alive for me in hell. But I am feeling, because this is hell, that if I forget this poem, if this poem does not survive, then my wife, she will not live. Very strange idea, no?"

Someone in the audience shouted, "No."

He raised his thick black brows. He looked at her. She stood perfectly still, nothing showing on her body or her face, only the quivering of the microphone betraying her. "I share my wife with the other men," he said, looking at her. Then, to the audience, he said, "Terrible husband."

At the edge of her eyes the sheen of a tear caught in the light.

"I give each man in my, how you say? Dormitory? Each man who is with me—factory, shoemaker, historian, yah—each man, I give a verse of the poem about my wife. To remember in his heart. The poem that is written on my heart in hell, I say, please, every day, remember her. Recite your part of this poem. This way, Stalin, he will not kill what matters in a human being. How he loves."

My friend's eyes were streaming with tears.

"Well, my wife, she is here," said the poet. "Right here. So. So what the meaning is of this story," he said. "Did my poem keep her alive? Me? Both of us? Mystery."

There were few dry eyes in the auditorium as the audience, slowly at first, and then with mounting fervor, filled the huge cavernous space with their cries and claps. The poet waved the microphone in the air. The Czech poet took it and said a few words in his native language, which generated a new wave of applause from the group that had flown through the blizzard from Chicago. He did not translate. The award on his frail lap, the honoree was waving his hand as if to wipe away the applause, but the audience would not stop.

"Speak speak speak speak speak," erupted from the crowd. The poet pushed the microphone to his wife. She looked out over the audience, her green eyes searching (we later said, much later, searching for us, my friend and me). She stopped when she saw us, and (we said) seemed to recognize us right then, that moment.

He said something; she gasped. He nodded. She looked around the audience, then back to him. He nodded more vigorously. Now she searched the audience openly.

The man beside me raised his hand tentatively. The poet signaled for him to rise. Phosphorescence turned to her husband. He held his hand out for the microphone. She handed it over to him slowly, in a trance, her eyes going back and forth to the man beside me and her husband.

Into the microphone, he said, "For you. On your birthday. Because if you had never been born, I would never have lived. I am praying all day, this blizzard in Chicago, it will go away." He indicated the man beside me and called out, "You remember the last verse?"

"Yah. I cannot forget. Every day, that was the bargain. Every day, I recite."

The honoree said, "Happy birthday, my darling wife."

The audience gasped in one gasp. My friend's hand was squeezing my arm so hard it hurt. My heart was pounding as the man beside me cleared his throat. Words poured out of him. Though he spoke in a language of which I knew not a single word, I knew it was the food of love, pouring into a gap of history, bringing restoration to a goddess of petrified wood. When he was finished, he stood utterly still before he slowly sank down into his seat, a man delivered of a lifetime burden.

Tears were streaming down the face of Phosphorescence as the earth at her neck glistened and sparkled. There was not a movement or sound in the audience. The poet held the microphone as he looked at her tears. With the faith only a poet who has lived through hell could possess, he clicked the switch of the microphone off, trusting the words of the song to be enough.

The reception was held in another building, Hilson House, the original residence of the family whose estate became the college. It had been, through the architectural incarnations unique to private colleges in America, transformed from residence to convalescence hospital (consumption) to a Red Cross station (the two world wars), then restructured as a women's dormitory, then as a men's, then as both, each requiring new plumbing, until finally a group of retired Red Cross volunteers had seized it as their personal mission to restore it to its original splendor. The college had not refused the offer; one of these women was the direct descendant of the founder, a spinster who was in her eighties, who smoked two packs a day and whose latest adventure had been to go boating on Norwegian fjords.

At that time, Hilson House was in the second stage of its restoration process. The eastern side of the house, where the original kitchen and servants' quarters, garden room, and downstairs parlor had originally been, were all blocked off. Women from the Hilson House Restoration Committee were in attendance, no doubt a requirement of the college legal counsel, to make sure that no one went into the blocked-off portion of the building. They were also there to oversee the catering and answer any questions about the house, convinced in their passion for restoration that anyone who came would be as fascinated by neoclassical balustrades

225

as they were. Above all, they came to these literary functions to provide directions to the restrooms, whose locations were as quirky and quizzical as the neoclassical architecture was not.

The women's room was up the second flight of stairs from the first landing, through the library door on the left, then straight back, where there was another small door leading to the servants' stairs. You went down those and then down the same two flights you had ascended, through a hallway back in the other direction, until you reached the women's room. It was actually located immediately off the main floor reception hall, but because of the reconstruction you had to take this circuitous, labyrinthine route which these avid retired women were more than eager not only to describe for you but to usher you there, if you so desired.

In the main reception room downstairs, the honoree and Phosphorescence were surrounded by the literati luminaries of academic America asking all manner of questions. Into this thick wad would occasionally surge a wave of friends and relatives, speaking their melodious languages, who would embrace the old couple, who in turn held on to them as if to lifeboats in this noisy American swell. My friend despaired of finding her way through to the goddess who had killed Alvin, so she waited on the stairs in hope of an ambush. "She'll remember us, you see, she will," she said. "Even the beautiful have bladders."

I went into the main room to get us some wine, leaving my friend on the stairs. As I entered, I saw the man who had delivered the last verse of the poem pouring a glass of red wine. I hesitated, fumbling for what I could possibly say to him. I could think of nothing, but neither could I let him disappear. I approached, wordless.

Courtesy is a kind of miracle in our country. Without any signal or word or sign from me he handed me the glass he had poured for himself, smiling, his full lips and pink, flushed cheeks radiant under his bright blue eyes. I could not put any age to his solid body.

"Thank you," I said.

"It is good. California," he said, indicating the lavishly illustrated label.

"You're from Chicago?"

"Well, no, I am from Hungary, of course. But after Stalin, many things change. I have a wife, I leave to come to America. I work hard, make money to bring her over. But . . . excuse my lousy English. I understand everything, I just do not speak."

"Do you know what your verse of the poem means—in English?"

He blushed. "Means, oh, well, yes, of course, I know what it means. But in English. Oh boy."

"I'm sorry, it's . . . it would mean so much to me."

He sighed, smiled, embarrassed, and said, "Well, it means. I try. I am not poet. I am factory worker. I make things, metal. Metal things. Not poetry. " He sighed again, sipped at his wine, smiled, sipped again, and then said, "It means, you are my hands, yes, but this is not it. Hands, they are your voice, my voice, your hands . . . I am so sorry."

"No, please, go on," I said.

Another man now joined us, about my age. He held out his hand to the factory worker from Chicago and introduced himself. "Marek," he said.

"Oh, you are Marek! So good, yes, to meet you."

"I cannot thank you enough for coming tonight," Marek said. "My mother has not been well, and I thank you for your gift." He too had an accent, but it had been softened at the edges and lost some of its foreign cadences. He had dark hair and the same green eyes as his mother.

"No, no, I should thank you for finding me, at last. I do try, you know. Really. To get home. So expensive, America."

Marek touched him on the shoulder. "It is all right," he said warmly. "It has all worked out perfectly."

The factory worker nodded to me, with his wine, and explained to Marek that he was translating his verse "very badly, I am so sorry. This nice young woman, she asked me, a metal worker. But you, Marek, you can do this translating of your father, yes?" He nodded emphatically at me. "Marek is educated person. Doctor. American doctor. Very, very smart."

Marek smiled a rueful smile. "And no poet, I'm afraid."

"It's all right," I said. "I shouldn't have asked."

"No, no," the factory worker said, determined in his politeness to fulfill my request. "Marek can translate. I will help you." He took a deep breath, and the words tumbled and fell and rose and blossomed in syllables and sounds. At their sound, Phosphorescence turned and looked in our direction. She walked over before the verse was finished and put her arms around Marek. She dropped her head on his shoulder, and he stroked her hair in a calm, absorbed lovingness. The factory worker finished and turned to Phosphorescence. "I tell Marek he should translate his father's poetry, no? This is good, I think."

Phosphorescence looked at her son, wonder and hope and concern mingling in her eyes. "Marek? Will you?"

Just then I heard the familiar Midwestern twang of the director of the adult education program saying in a loud voice, "Well, happy birthday to you!" He pumped the hand of Phosphorescence. "Many happy returns!"

Phosphorescence looked at me, a quick glance to the only woman at hand that conveyed volumes to us both about the odd ideas men have about what matters. She nodded politely at my sole means of employment, then excused herself abruptly, tears forming again in her eyes. She disappeared into the hallway, toward my friend waiting for her on the stairs. Marek caught my eye for a moment.

Wasn't it some evening? my boss said. Wasn't I just so moved? Touched? Did I know that Harvard had been in competition for this guy? But we got him. Harvard. Imagine. But he chose us. And did I know why? Wouldn't believe it. Trees. There's some sort of beech, or oak, or something, it grows here in the Hudson Valley and in—what is it now? Hungary? Never could keep straight which one of them was from Czechoslovakia and which from Hungary, or Poland, wherever it was, they have the same trees, that's all that matters, trees that Harvard doesn't have. . . .

When I finally broke free and burst into the reception hall, the stairs were empty. I ran up to the first-floor landing, where one of the Hilson House Restoration Committee women was standing on duty. She began to give me directions to the women's room when I interrupted to ask if she'd seen "a very short woman with black curly hair and a very tall woman with very short white hair; you couldn't miss them."

She thought they'd gone to the bathroom; did I know where it was? Yes. Was I absolutely certain I absolutely knew for sure where it was? It's quite tricky, you know. I surrendered as far as the library, when I could not help myself. I ran through, back, down, around, and burst into the women's room door to find my friend, her arms around Phosphorescence, who was sobbing onto her breast.

"Oh, Christ, Meem."

Phosphorescence sobbed and moaned as my friend stroked her and rocked her, reminding me of when she would hold Benjamin with patience inexhaustible. She was always so buoyant, so restless, so comic. But when she was called to be a mother, she became that steady rhythm of woman. I met my friend's eyes. She shook her head gently, and closed them. Slowly Phosphorescence's sobbing subsided, and for what seemed to me an eternity, in silence, they rocked.

Phosphorescence lifted her head and blew her nose into paper toweling, and made a face. My friend's fuchsia satin blouse was soaking wet. "Oh, no, look what my sadness has done," Phosphorescence said.

"It's all right," my friend said. "It is an honor. Besides, I always have stains, don't I, Meem?"

I looked at my friend. "It's just a wet spot, right?"

"Oh my god," my friend said. She looked at Phosphorescence, who was, understandably, baffled.

Only my friend would have explained. Anyone else would have kept it her exclusive private symbol, but not Benjamin's mother, levitator of pianos. "I was a painter, I mean, I still am, but I'm not as much of a painter as I was, because there was this wet spot on the floor, and my husband, he wasn't my husband then, and he isn't my husband now, exactly, but in between he was, and when he fell on the wet spot I knew he was going to be my husband and I wouldn't paint anymore and we heard your husband read poetry right after that. The wet spot, I mean."

Phosphorescence smiled, touched my friend's cheek, and then her mouth bent into itself and she was sobbing again.

"The door—Meem—guard the door."

I went outside and stood in the tiny hallway of the servants' quarters. I heard cries, then I heard soft voices, mutual, intimate, no words. I looked up at a sound to see Marek coming down the stairs. He said, "They did not want to direct me to the women's room. Is my mother in there?"

"Yes."

"Is she all right?"

"She's with my best friend," I said. The image of my friend rocking his mother as if she were Benjamin filled my eyes. I looked at Marek and absorbed his face into the image of their spontaneous pietà. He was staring intently at me. He said, "I am sorry I was unable to finish Mihalyi's translation of the poem."

"Did you say Mihalyi?"

He nodded slowly. "Mihalyi from Chicago, yes. I hope the music of my native tongue was enough to make it work."

I shook his words out of my head, but instead of dislodging them, the opposite happened. His voice entered into my own, or mine into his; I could not discern whose mouth was whose.

Can you hear me?

Yes. Are you a guide?

You sound doubtful.

I was expecting . . .

Feathers? Ceremonial robes? A mythical figure, with a better costume than Freddie's well-used fleece?

We were in a house undergoing reconstruction, in a subterranean hallway, outside a women's rest room. It was a very peculiar location to begin a soul journey, but it fit the requirements of the map.

I swallowed audibly, my heart racing so fast that I could feel the pulsations of my terror at what I was about to say clutching my throat. I closed my eyes. It was but a blink, as brief as the gap between the nadir of the solstice and the advent of spring. But that was all the time I needed to make my leap into dreamtime Rhinebeck complete. I slipped through the gap between real time and dreamtime, a fraction of a pulse.

"Mihalyi and I know someone in common, from Chicago," I said. "She's a young woman who lived in the same building with him, she was just a little girl, I think, when Mihalyi knew her. Her name was—"

Laughter cascaded out of the women's room and into the hall, tumbling. My friend and Marek's phosphorescent mother giggled out the door in pure girlish joy as I said the murderer's name out loud.

Many theories circulated through Rhinebeck to explain the peculiarities of that spring. Lack of snow was cited as the reason for the sedge-colored grass, which should have been fierce spring green. Others said it was the alternation between the frigid waves of air from the Canadian tundra and the surging warmth of the Texas Gulf Stream, conspiring to form the layers of ice. The seeds could not push through soil that cold and compacted and choked, people said. Others took the genesis of the problem all the way back to the previous fall, saying there was no battle of air being waged over the entire continent; in fact, there was nothing unusual happening at all. Dry fall, dry spring, they said, just like it's been before, how many times? And the old timers would begin checking off the dates. Spring of '44 . . . '52 . . . '63 . . . Still others, claiming the same superior local knowledge, said it was a wet fall that made a dry spring. Others made the first mental rustlings about "what we're doing to the planet." Mr. Bert, in the smoke shop, sighed and said, "There's no explaining it. Never seen anything like it. And I've been here longer than just about anyone. Parliaments, right?"

I nodded as he put a pack on the counter. I handed him a five. "That's for two packs," I said. Mr. Bert reached for another from the shelf behind him. "No—for the one I owe you."

"You owe me?" Mr. Bert made a skeptical face.

"It was from a long time ago," I said.

He shrugged. "If you say so."

As he handed me change, I said, "Doesn't Freddie usually work on Tuesdays?"

Mr. Bert sighed. "They say Freddie's too sick to be out and about. Hell. Just 'cause he's got bad taste in wigs . . . I know some lousy toupees myself. He was doing fine," he said. "Just fine."

As I was leaving, I patted the shoulder of Freddie's denuded rainbow man, as if to console him for the loss of his human attendant. I drove slowly home, passing the asylum no one called an asylum, heading south. Freddie, back inside—how could I not interpret it as a bad sign? Freddie's reinstitutionalization confirmed my unspoken fear that something had gone wrong in the hallway with Marek when laughter had all but drowned out my pronunciation of the murderer's name. I replayed that moment over and over in my mind, getting no further with it than spring was getting with itself. Had he heard me say, "Manda"? Had I heard him speaking to me without making any sound? I could not help but believe that I had botched a critical moment in my battle with the Panther for my soul.

I pulled into my drive and sat in my car, smoking. The fairy-tale cottage needed green around it, but the green refused to comply. It looked like an unfinished stage set for the performance of a fairy tale that had been interrupted during rehearsal. Inside, the Selectric remained on the ancestral sea chest. I stood at the door—the same glass side door through which the Panther had entered—telling myself to put the machine back on my desk and get back to work. I stomped out my cigarette on the porch steps and entered. I picked up the Selectric, returned it to the desk, poured myself a glass of wine, sat down. The handwritten pages, with Manda in my script, were mixed up in the typewritten pile of The Murder Mystery. I separated them, pretending to a sensible order during this season that would not yield to itself, slipping them into my copy of The Tempest, which also lay on the desk. I looked at Shakespeare with something like a prayer trying to form inside my eyes.

What is the magic I need? Show me how to keep Lexy dancing on the seashore of the island in Her yellow kimono after Manda kills Her. Show me how to tell that story as a true one. Make me believe it.

I don't know how many glasses of wine, how many cigarettes, before twilight came and I lay down on the couch, my head pounding. I dozed fitfully, moving in and out of a dream. I was traversing a mountain range in a foreign country whose name I did not know. The roads were encrusted with white patches of ice, and my feet, bare, were numb from the cold. I was wearing the white shift of the Panther—the girl in Vermont whose food I had been. A jeep filled with soldiers passed by, whistling at me. The winds from the mountains blew my shift and revealed that I was naked underneath. The soldiers stopped and offered me a ride. "Where are you going?" I asked. "This road leads to the Great Pass. We'll take you there," they said, leering.

I shook myself out of the dream before I could get into the jeep with the soldiers. I knew I was going to get into that car, and I knew what would happen to me in a car of soldiers wearing nothing but the Panther's shift. Mustard breath. I looked at my dark, empty cottage.

"Got your postcard, Manda," I said out loud.

Silence.

A surge of energy sent me out the door, into my car, back into town, and bounding up the stairs of the Starr Building. I stood at the top of the stairs, my head reeling, the tinny sound of "The Blue Danube" on an old record player imploding in my brain. I walked gingerly, holding my head perfectly still, to the dance studio door and peeked in. A man with sideburns shaped like hourglasses was leading an old woman around the room, shouting over the music, "One-two-three, one-two-three," as she bumped repeatedly against him. Her hair was piled on her head in a teased beehive, streaks of dark yellow and brilliant pink running through it. The hairdresser had not mixed the dye, and the effect was worse than Freddie's wig. As the man whirled her around, I caught sight of her face. She had glittery blue eye shadow, and her lashes were so thick with black mascara that little dabs of black stippling ran under her eyes. The rouge on her cheeks was the same intense pink as her lipstick, and probably was her lipstick. She wore a dress that must have been hanging in her closet since her first dance, an ornate creation of tulle and lace and satin with a new zipper she had stitched in by hand with white thread in crooked, stuttering lines down the middle of her back.

When the man saw me, he stopped abruptly. The woman lost her balance, and he reached out just in time to catch her. "Some waltz!" she said, pulling a handkerchief from her sleeve and dabbing her forehead.

"The waltz is utterly misunderstood," he said in a voice that matched her bad dye job. "It is not a dance for the fainthearted." He turned to me. "Please, come in. Beginning Ballroom has only just begun."

"Actually, I was . . . I was looking for . . ." *A murdered dancer to tell me how I can get my guide back before I do get into a car carrying soldiers to a pass where there is no bridge, you just drive off the road to the realm of the dead.*

"Bettina sold the place to me," he said. "Please take a schedule."

I thanked him, made excuses, said I wasn't dressed for ballroom. Before he could object, the old woman said, "You really do need the correct attire. It is inspiring."

I stood on the street corner reading the schedule over and over, willing myself to see words which were not there. *Belly Dancing with Baubo, midwife to life. Rainbow cocoon chiffon unfurling.* I threw the schedule away and stood facing Main Street. I glanced north, toward the fork leading to River Road and the bridge. Get it over with, I heard myself saying. Drive over the Great Pass and die. You know the Panther is going to win in the end; she already has won, every time, for twenty-seven thousand years. She's the professional, you're the rank amateur. Surrender. Get into the car with the soldiers.

A police car was headed my way, laconically, the lights and siren off. It stopped directly in front of me as the light turned red. When I did not cross the street, the Chief rolled down his window. "Can I help you?"

I shook my head. "No, thanks, I'm fine."

"Go ahead and cross," he said. "I'll wait."

I crossed Route 9 to my car, my feet heavy. The light changed midway. The Chief waited until I was safely across before turning down Main Street. I sat in my car, weak, hungry, sick. I couldn't bear to return to the empty, silent cottage. Manda was outside, somewhere in Rhinebeck and its environs, breathing onto the green fists of spring on the branches to stop them from opening. Of all the theories circulating about the strangeness of the season, my theory about the Panther's breath blowing on every living thing was the only plausible one for the Rhinebeck I was stuck inside, afraid that my guide, Marek, was gone like Freddie and Lexy, and that I would have to take the journey by myself, and hitch a ride with rapacious soldiers to get there.

My friend was the one who forced spring to open against the Panther's breath. The night *Show Up Naked* opened, the quickening of the season began as an event of air, a stream of faint perfume, familiar, evolving into the drama of color, pink trees, golden bushes, lilac twilight. And then, finally, it was the sensation of hurtful liberation as human limb and seed alike forced their way through cold to mean what they move. I drove through the unbearably supple evening, weaving under the tender fabric of the trees above me, heading north on River Road to the bridge. I had no choice this evening but to cross to the other side to reach the gallery in Woodstock.

As I turned left onto the bridge, the violet air caught me in its gauzy embrace, and I was, for a moment, grateful that the time would soon be upon me to take this journey I dreaded. Relief lasted but an instant as a most unlikely thought came to me. I doubted there was such a thing as a "Restoration tragedy." Wasn't the proper literary term "Restoration comedy"? I asked myself. And wasn't its literary counterpart "revenge tragedy"? What was the spelling my soul recognized as the correct pairing with revenge—the Panther's revenge against me for taking the Woman Who Means What She Moves away from her?

I reached the midpoint of the bridge, the shore of the Hudson sparked green, the river swollen, churning below. As I crested the bridge, my belly was suspended in midair, as though it belonged to a singular gravity apart from my limbs.

Revenge comedy, Summacious. After all the killing was done, they lived happily ever after.

They.

Lexy and I.

Lexy and I.

Still confused about the pairs on the spelling test, Summacious?

Still trying to learn how to dance, Manda?

Do me a favor and give your friend a special big thank-you from me.

For what?

She slipped into the trees again.

As I drove the winding back roads to Woodstock, weaving in and out of flowering trees, I sensed Manda moving in the same vital groove of the cosmos with me. The Panther was inside the greening of life, using petal and perfume to mask her lethal shape. I had only heard her, not seen her. She had been released from her Nazi costume by spring into a voice only, as mobile as the Chief's mouth, speaking to me from within the phosphorescent channel of Gaia herself. I had been wrong about the spring; it was not the Panther's breath that had paralyzed the branches for so long. It was Manda sucking the green stars of spring into her, shedding her leather jacket as she absorbed life. She needed the vitality of Gaia on this side, the side of the living, for the final battle against the life that loved me.

I pressed on the accelerator, panic upon me. Who knew what Manda had been doing all this time while I was trying to undo the story, disimagine the murder, and waiting for my guide to reappear?

I entered the main street of Woodstock and found a parking place off a side road. Afraid even to let myself think of what the Panther wanted me to thank my friend for doing for her, I rushed to reach the gallery as though it were the Y itself, where the Dew could console me and heal me as it had done so many times before.

The gallery was nestled in a curve near a bend in the stream that weaves its way under the main byways of Woodstock. As I reached the entry, people were crowding to get in, and the crowd was momentarily stalled. When I finally reached the door and was about to enter, I smelled the familiar vanilla of Rulla. It was the scent of hope to me, and I pushed past others to reach it. Rulla was standing just within the threshold, taking in the crowd. She was wearing a floor-length, long-sleeved caftan, again suspiciously like upholstery, her red hair wrapped in a flowered silk turban. I sidled up to her, against the wall, soaking in her smell. She did not notice me. I watched as this Santa Claus lover, creator of woman on the First Day, sister of a lost princess, goddess of the whirlpool, swooped across the room to my friend's open arms. My friend embraced her and then released her, presenting Rulla to the audience. Rulla slowly turned in a circle, the queen reviewing the royal portraits of her court. When she was facing the painting entitled *The First Day,* her own body in resplendent pink and coppery folds multiplied in the waters of the whirlpool, the spindly feet of old men around her, Rulla pointed and said in a loud voice, "That is me."

"That's you, Rulla," my friend said. "Queen of the Y." Rulla bowed. My friend raised her hands and began to clap. The guests followed her cue, and Rulla beamed.

I then stepped in as the crowd began to hum. I went up to my friend and touched her gently. "Did you buy Rulla's dress?"

My friend burst out laughing. "What's left of the dress I bought her from the thrift shop is around her head," my friend said. We both watched Rulla holding court before the paintings. People were gathering around her, and I promise you, Rulla wrapped in her upholstery was as naked to them as she was on canvas. "Rulla's dress cost me the rest of my leftover garage sale money, you know, Meem, what I stuffed in that boot in my closet? I used it to pay for the framing, and with the rest, silk for Rulla. I'm wearing something that belongs to my sister."

"You look beautiful," I said. "Where's Benjamin?"

Rulla shimmied up to us. She raised her small, childlike face, her eyes ringed in kohl, a regal smile pinned on her face. "My sister," Rulla said. "She is supposed to be here."

I gave my friend a look. I said to Rulla, "Your sister called to say she was delayed, and for you to please enjoy yourself."

Rulla shook her head and raised her shoulders. "Typical." She spirited herself away to the food.

"Lenin forbade me to bring Benjamin."

My heart fell down into a vacant place inside me. "Is he suing . . . ?"

"Not officially," she said. "But he just gets worse and worse the closer we get to the actual court date." Her eyes, which should have sparkled with unqualified joy, quivered with fear. I cursed spring for allowing panthers and Lenin into the phosphorescent region of my dreamtime Hudson Valley. Why couldn't spring be divided down the middle like Main Street, madness and splinters and murder on one side, with the wood restored into a rainbow god and the Dancer dancing on the other? Why did my journey require crossing back and forth? What was the trick to moving from one side to the other without going mad in the attempt? It was too dangerous to be caught stranded in the middle, exposed, confused, unarmed, the Panther stalking her way to murder through the veils of blossom where I could not see her.

My friend looked at me and just managed to say, "Benjamin should be here," when she was surrounded by women. It was the beginning of an oceanic swell of hurried stories delivered on the currents of her art. Women were thanking her, hugging her, laughing with her, shaking their heads at her with mischievous smiles. Women came to her with tears in their eyes, whether grieving for the body they had lost or joyful for the body they had found in my friend's images, one had to guess, for they were unable to say a word. Women grabbed my friend and whispered something in her ear that no one could hear, and then the two of them would raise their faces in wild laughter. I stood by, watching at the edge of these scenes, but even off to the side, I could feel a mutual elation that each woman had finally shown up, naked, as she really was, and found beauty in the life of her actual (folded expanding scarred tattooed magnificent mobile) skin.

My friend broke off and came over to me. She grabbed my hand. Tears swelled. "Is this bad?" she said, her eyes scanning her art. "Is this bad for my son?"

"No, no," I said. "It's good."

"I'm allowed to . . ."

"Survive real hell? Yes."

My friend held my hand tightly. Her eyes again searched her paintings. She blinked, and then she seemed to melt at the sight of something behind me. I turned, and there, coming in the door, was Phosphorescence. Around her neck was the necklace of petrified wood, earth glimmering with the colors of the cosmos, the brilliant green of her eyes reflected in the glinting at her throat. Marek stood beside his mother, his eyes fixed on me. My friend said, "Aren't you going to thank me, Meem? I asked them for you."

"Would you show me the paintings?" Marek said.

"The paintings."

"This is such a strange request?"

Marek came to a stop before the painting of Rulla in the whirlpool. He leaned over and read the placard out loud. *"First Day,"* he said in his melodious voice, tinged at the edges with his native Hungarian. "What is the story of this *First Day?*"

"The story?"

"Your friend tells me you are a writer, like my father."

And you are a guide, like your mother.

"It was the first day we went to the Y," I said, my throat dry. Marek paused. Then he raised his hand to indicate that I was to remain where I was. He went to the far side of the room, where there was a wine bar. He returned with a glass of white wine and a glass of red.

"Which one will help you to tell me this story of the *First Day*—red or white?"

"Red," I said.

He grinned and held out the red wine. I took a sip, but Marek nodded to me to take another. "Warming up?"

Iced over.

"So," he said, sipping generously at his own wine. "I think the story about this painting, this *First Day,* must be something wonderful, yah?"

I looked at the painting of Rulla, her naked copper-rose body under water, the eddies of the whirlpool multiplying her rotund femininity. I looked at her face staring at me out of the painting. My friend had rendered the delicate doll-like pathos of the Queen of the Y. "She is the Queen," I said. "And this is the first day of her reign. . . ."

"I can see she is the queen. Go on."

"She came from a land far away, " I said in a soft voice, which forced Marek close to me until I was half whispering. "This land was run by a tyrant who was desperately in love with Rulla's sister, a beautiful dancer."

"Beautiful, yah, go on," Marek said.

I glanced over at Rulla, who was beaming in the company of my friend. "The tyrant had many wives," I went on. "But none had been able to bear him a son. Daughters, daughters, daughters, surrounded him, wherever he went in his palace, his eyes were filled with girls. Girls dancing, girls singing, girls reciting the sacred poems, girls making charts of the world . . . All the tyrant could hear all day long was girls calling out to each other, 'Oh, Sister! Sister!' This beautiful dancer, the tyrant said to himself, will give me a boy. So the tyrant went to the beautiful dancer's father and demanded the dancer's hand in marriage."

Are you making this story happen inside me?

"Now, the father, he loved both his daughters, the beautiful dancer and the ugly one. But the love was not the same for the dancer as for her sister." Marek nodded, thoughtfully. "His heart would sing when he watched his beautiful daughter dancing. And his heart would twist in pity, and he could barely restrain himself from laughing, when his ugly daughter would dance with her. But . . ."

Marek caught my eyes. "But?"

"The father did not want to give away his beautiful daughter to a tyrant."

"But he did not want to give away the ugly one either," Marek said.

I looked at him. "You said he loved them both."

"He did."

"So he has a real problem."

"It's even more complicated," I said. I swallowed, trying to stop my heart from catching my voice. "Anyone who refused a demand of the tyrant was killed by this Panther who was magic. Nothing could kill this Panther. Not arrows or knives or poison—nothing could destroy it. Nothing except a magic which . . . which no one knew how to make, or where it could be found, or even if it existed at all. And the tyrant said to the father, if he refused, he would let the Panther loose and kill all his girl children."

Tell me you know what I am talking about.

People were pressing against me to see the painting. I gulped down the rest of my wine and handed Marek the empty glass for a refill. I followed him with my eyes as he crossed the room to the wine bar. As Marek was on the other side, waiting in line, a man came into the gallery. He moved through the middle of the room, on a straight approach to Rulla, his arms held out as if to embrace her. "I'm overwhelmed, I'm speechless," he said. He stood before her and kissed her hand. The beaming Queen of the Y took a swift look up and down to see if she liked what he had to offer. "Your work is incredible," he said, and Rulla, who had apparently decided that she liked what she saw, gave him one of those smiles of hers which sent her cheeks out into the stratosphere and held out her hand for him to touch.

"My sister," she said. "She will be here soon. We are twins. You cannot guess who has painted who! It is all a trick." Rulla winked at him. All it took was a touch of Rulla's skin and you were lost. Lost utterly in the softness of that glistening coppery pink radiance that formed the cascading rounds of her. She glided the enthusiastic stranger over to a corner, somehow levitating into her and his hand each a glass of wine, and then sat him down and said, "Tell me what you are feeling so very strongly."

Marek was standing in front of me, another wine glass held out. "I want to hear the rest of the story."

I looked back at Rulla and the man, then to the painting. "It's the first day of a new time," I said, frantic, scrambling. "The Panther was killed, somehow, and the tyrant defeated. . . ."

"The magic was found?"

244

Is that a clue? I have to find it? I thought I was supposed to make it up. You're supposed to guide me, not confuse me.

"The beautiful dancer? And her sister? What happened to them?"

I looked over at Rulla, remembering the scars on her back. "One died. The other went crazy, and believed she was the queen of a country that did not even exist."

Marek followed my gaze to Rulla, and studied her for a moment. Then he looked at me, and his face was grave, his eyes so clear and knowing that I could not look at him. In a gentle voice he said, "I am thinking this is a true story, and not make believe."

"It is a little of both."

"Are you all right? Maybe some fresh air?"

The air was agony, the trees floating above us. I could not find my voice for the longest time. Marek, his arm loosely and politely interlocked with mine, gently led me away from the lights of the town, wandering through the unlit roads, heading into the dark as the ground beneath us began to rise.

Finally I said to him, "You must live somewhere."

"Of course. Not so far away. East of here, I think."

"On my side of the bridge?"

"Other side from here?"

I nodded, struggling. "What . . . what brought you here?"

"Your friend called my mother—"

"I mean . . ." What did I mean? What was here? "America."

"Oh, well, what brings everybody. To study. Work. No, no. This is not exactly right. I could do what I do in my country, but . . . I need to leave. Something very sad made me have to leave. My wife died," he said.

"I'm sorry. I . . . didn't . . . know." *Guides could have dead wives. Wives. Sorrows. History. If you are a guide.*

"I like very much your story."

"It's a lousy story," I said. "It has huge holes." *Like all my stories. They all have panthers and gaps, and the beautiful ones keep on dying, no matter what I do.*

"It is difficult to make up a good story, I think. Even a true one."

"It's not supposed to be difficult for writers, though," I said.

245

"I think for writers it is most difficult."

I looked at him. "Why, Marek?"

"You say my name like a Hungarian woman! This is wonderful."

"I used to speak Russian."

"Ah! It is the same, and different. You've asked me a difficult question. Maybe it is because of my father, my mother. But I think only the impossible matters to artists." We walked silently into the darkness, the sound of the winding stream swollen with snowmelt, loud, then receding, as we meandered along the roads. "But maybe not only artists." Marek resumed speaking. "Maybe for each person, there is some impossible thing that matters the most to do in life, and every one of us must become an artist to do this impossible thing. For me, it is to live."

"Live?"

"After my wife died, it is that simple. I came to America, a small town called Stockbridge, in a place called Massachusetts because this is a name so different from the name of my home where I lived with my wife. A silly trick, no? To pretend if I change the name of home, I can change my own heart."

I stopped walking. Marek kept on a few steps, then, realizing I had stopped, he turned around to look at me. "Stockbridge?" I said. "Aren't you from Rhinebeck?"

"I work back and forth, two places, so I can help my mother and father while he is here, at the college. But it is the same work in both places."

Then you must be my guide after all. If you can move in two directions, back and forth.

"What work?"

"I am a psychiatrist," he said, in that "nice" tone therapists use which made Manda skittish when I used it with her, now unnerving me. "In Stockbridge, I work at—"

"Riggs," I interrupted him. "Riggs Sanitarium."

"You know this Riggs?" His voice was uneasy now.

"My grandmother was there," I said. "She thought she was a bird."

Beside us a dark field, with no boundaries but distant trees barely distinguishable from the night sky, lay, indifferent to human dramas. I

began walking toward it, drawn by its shadowy calm. I sat down and
began to dig my hands into the dirt.

"Please. Say something." Marek was beside me, on the ground.

My head was pounding from the red wine, my throat dry. Into the
earth, I said, "Why didn't you tell me you were a psychiatrist?"

"But I did."

"Before." Dirt gathered onto my lips. I had to sit up. "When we met."
And we talked without talking, and I believed you were sent to me by Lexy.
Marek began, "Your friend . . ." Then stopped.

"Did my friend send you to spy on me?"

"No, no, it is not like that. I am making a big mess."

"She told you I was crazy, didn't she?"

"She said she was worried. She was so kind, with my mother, that
night, I felt I should return the favor." He touched me again, a strange
bouncing motion, as though to quiet me and to reach me and yet aware
that he could do neither of these things. "I tell myself, as I'm listening to
your story, that I like you. And then you tell me your story has holes, and
I like you again. And then, when I realize you have been telling a true
story in this fairy-tale way, I say to myself, Marek, you are losing your,
you know, professional distance, you call it. But now, I think, because of
your grandmother, this is not good for you, my feelings . . ."

"My friend should never have asked you to do this," I said.

"Maybe. But I think she asked out of love for you."

Waves of dark fury passed through me, a pantherine wind. Love or
betrayal? Agency of Lexy or Manda's spy? Spring was conspiring against
my psyche, merging the two sides of Main Street, confounding asylum so
that I could no longer tell which side was sanctuary, and what the cost.
Was Marek guide or spy? Protector from the Panther, or emissary of a
storm trooper determined to close in for the kill? Or just a dark-haired,
bright-eyed man my friend knew I would be attracted to? Knowing I fall
for his type, part poet, part rhinoceros. The questions themselves seemed
proof of madness, the answers irrelevant. I had gone out of my mind long
before I knew it, and if there ever had been a path for my soul to take to
secure its restoration, I had long ago lost all traces of it. I was swimming
in trees, where the living and the dying, the mad and the divine, the em-

braced and the splintered, Panther and dancer, brother and sister, all swim in the same green channel of spring, Gaia's rhapsodic season, back and forth, back and forth, never stopping on one side or the other. I was not out of my mind; my mind was out of me, swimming in trees inside life before it gives us the faces we will have in our living story on earth, swimming in the green arms of Gaia where She holds us in Her arms and breathes Her vital phosphorescent breath charged with the sacred energy of life itself into us before we must be dropped (down, down, down) into mortal selfhood, and put on the face of our story, the one we will be wearing when we die.

I dug my hands into the black dirt. "What's Riggs like?" I asked. "Do the patients still make pots?"

"Pots?"

"My grandmother made beautiful pottery when she was there." I saw before me the pair of urns she had made, glazed a color called oxblood. It is a burgundy-copper hue considered to be the most difficult of all colors to achieve. Oxblood glaze requires a subtle level of suffocation when the pot is in the kiln. Too little air, the glaze turns to ashes that stick to the clay; too much, the glaze turns to ashes that fall off, leaving the clay charred. At an infinitesimal point of near suffocation between ashes and ashes, the glaze bursts into a rich oxblood color with the sheen of copper running through it. When my grandmother went mad and was sent away to Riggs, she produced two vases in the classic amphora shape, turning the air down in the kiln to that near suffocation point. I had all my life wondered how many times she had to try, how many pots she had made and lost to ashes, before she performed the miracle of the oxblood. No one knew the part of the story about the ashes; only the magnificent coppery-red amphora, emblems of a madness that everyone could pretend had never happened as they displayed the beautiful product of "that time she went away for a rest and did some pottery and poetry."

Marek was talking in a kind, simple voice, like a boy. "There is something I like very much. Riggs was once upon a time an apple farm. It is good, this smell, for the patients, I think. Pushkin, the great Russian poet, used to put rotten apples inside his desk. He said this smell, it made him write great poetry. Strange, no? Rotting apples, not fresh. I think I would be a great psychiatrist if I could figure out how to make Pushkin rotting-apple medicine."

I smoothed the dirt with my hand, forming a rectangle. I stared at it, seeing, not seeing, the shape dirt takes when a human corpse is inside it. I looked up at Marek. He had turned his head away. He seemed to be listening. I strained my ears. The sound of clapping in rhythm came through the spring night air from the middle of town to the rutted field where we were sitting on cold ground. Marek said, "Can you hear that?"

Hey-ah!

"It is Rulla," I said.

"Queen of the Y?"

"We call her that."

"Is she the ugly sister in your story? Or the beautiful one?"

"Isn't it obvious?"

"Not to me."

"You think Rulla is beautiful?"

"I can see how beautiful she must have been. And so can your friend. In the painting, the queen is exactly that—beautiful, once upon a time. Excuse my English. It has holes too."

Go ahead, Summacious, kiss him. There's no rule that says you can't have your murder story be a love story too.

He believes Baubo is beautiful, Manda.

Summacious, this guy is just another one of those dark-haired hazel-eyed men you fall for that all resemble that rhino who gave you your first kiss. You think a Panther is scared of a rhinoceros?

Not of the rhinoceros, Manda. What's in his horn.

Dicey bit of phallic imagery there, Meem.

Ancient medicine, powdered rhinoceros horn. Good for fertility and potency.

Are you telling me that if you kiss this guy who reminds you of your make-believe rhino husband in this dark field in Woodstock, it's enough to produce ancient magic fertility medicine?

If a steam room in the Y can produce Baubo, and Freddie can direct me to Lexy with a carved wooden Indian decked out in Christmas-tree lights, and my friend can paint Baubo and this man finds her as beautiful as Lexy—then yes, a kiss in this dark field in Woodstock is a medicine that will give me the power to give birth to a different story and change Lexy's murder into a love story.

It already is a love story, Summacious.

My love medicine from my rhino in my love story, Manda, which ends happily ever after when I dance, for eternity, with my soul, and mean what I move for as long as I am alive on this earth.

Summacious, you crack me up. Just when I think I'm so bored after doing the same thing for twenty-seven thousand years I can't go through with it another time, you do something so ridiculous, I actually begin to enjoy this eternal murder contract I'm under. I have never known anybody so hungry for magic to be real as you. Most of you people on the other side, I have to do something to get them to believe in the magic. But you—you make the magic up yourself, and it is hilarious.

That's why you chose me for your asylum, Manda. Because I make it easy for you. And you need something easy. You're tired. Weak.

Excuse me, Summacious, but aren't you forgetting your facts? Lexy told you She was tired, and believe me, She is. You and your Sisters on your side, you make Her do all the dancing for you. She needs someone to take care of Her, Summacious. Give Her a break, for once. Send Her someplace where She can get some real rest.

That's what they said about my grandmother, Manda, when she was put inside Riggs. That she needed a rest.

Summacious, you forget who you're talking to. You think your Panther from Vermont could ever send Lexy to a place like Riggs?

If it was the only way to get back the Woman Who Means What She Moves, then I believe the Panther would do exactly that. Because the Panther knows an asylum—especially a Stokes Sister's asylum—is the one place I'm the most terrified to enter, even if it is where my soul is locked up. But I am going to walk down Main Street, Manda. I'm going to walk all the way down Main Street and risk going mad myself to find Her, and take my rhino husband with me to bring us both out of it alive.

Summacious, I know how much it confuses you for your murderer to bring you good tidings of great joy, but I have to inform you how the love story is going to go. In less than a minute here, Marek is going to say what you know he's going to say. Something about how the world is ending and it's all up for the animals and people, and would you like to come into his Ark and lick his wounds and he'll lick yours? And because he is not only your guide but also your rhino husband, you are going to say yes, you want to be in the Ark with him bad, real bad, you happen to know a bed-and-breakfast up the road from the art gallery. Where—just to keep you posted—you're right, Rulla is doing one of her cosmic dance routines for the crowd and they are soaking it up, Baubo-in-Carpet. About the time you two finally stop making love, which is going to take you all night, there're a lot of dead people you're going to be trying to bring back alive in that bed, the songbirds will be singing there's land out there, the flood is over, you're safe. And I will have taken care of Freddie and Lexy.

Freddie?

Summacious, pu-lleez. Surely I do not have to explain this to you? Didn't Lexy tell you you can't know Her without knowing me? Freddie and I, we've been friends for a long time now.

You're what drives him back inside all the time, aren't you?

I keep on trying to get it through your thick overeducated skull: I'm a professional, the Panther, Madame Rhino. I am the one they never catch, ever, but slips away, living forever in the mind, making the mothers crazy with fear so they keep their children inside, making the fathers buy the guns to kill me—the hypothetical, the never-but-could, the unsolved crime, the unfinished murder mystery. But it's the kid that picks up the gun meant for me, instead, and the kid is never a hypothetical, the child is always life, so it's the kid who dies. Never me. I'm the Could Be a Murderer—murderer who returns, over and over and over again, as a maybe. A possible. The What If of the story. The Possible which makes you humans on your side close the doors on life and put on weird fetishist wigs because—as I believe Lexy explained to you in the dance studio—the only way you can make me go away is if you make yourself go away. I am the murder inside every suicide, and the suicide inside every murder. I am the one who makes a fatal accident fated. A brother, dead to a sister, a sister, dead to a brother. It all depends on what side of Main Street you're on.

"I—I have to . . ."

"Go back to the gallery, sure. We should," Marek said, beginning to get up.

I reached out to stop him. "No. To Stockbridge."

"Stockbridge?"

"It's only, what? An hour? Two? From here?"

Marek was silent, the sound of the audience clapping to Rulla's dance filling up the quiet between us. Finally he said, "Your friend was right to worry about you, wasn't she?"

"Yes."

"I speak as a doctor to you. It's awkward, but I must speak this way. I can take you to Stockbridge, and I can put you inside Riggs. I have this power, if that is what you want to do. But I must tell you, this would be a terrible mistake."

"No—I mean, yes!" I stuttered, tears finding me. "Being locked up is the one thing I don't want to happen." *I've been locked up all this time, with my soul's murderer. I want out, not in.*

"But is this not what you are asking me to do? Put you inside Riggs, because you're afraid you are going crazy like your grandmother?"

Tears streamed down my face. "I just want to walk down Main Street. And I want somebody to hold my hand when I do."

"Main Street in Stockbridge?"

"I don't know," I said, crying, confused. "I just know it has to be Main Street."

Marek fumbled in his pockets and gave me a cloth handkerchief. I felt like a little girl with her favorite uncle as I blew my nose. Marek said, "Riggs is at the end of Main Street, in Stockbridge."

I stared at him, dumbstruck. "It is?"

"More or less. There is a fork in the road. Riggs is located just where you must make the decision which direction to go."

"Take me. Please. I know it sounds crazy, and maybe it is crazy, but that is all I am asking you to do. Walk down the middle of Main Street, in Stockbridge, holding my hand."

"It does not sound crazy to me."

"But it is," I said, swiping at my tears with his handkerchief. "It is crazy of me to think that by walking down the middle of Main Street I can avoid going crazy like my grandmother did."

Marek shrugged. "It is a much safer kind of nuts than other kinds. It is no more crazy, I think, than me. I pretend I can erase my sadness by moving to a foreign country, so I do not hear my native tongue which I spoke to my wife when we made love."

I was sobbing against Marek's chest before I could stop myself. He put his arms around me and held me against him, stroking my head to help me calm down. When I had stopped crying, I sat up and said, "You are a very kind man. Thank you. I don't know what to say."

"What are you crying for? Your grandmother?"

"You know that Panther, the magic one, in my story?"

"That was make believe, and not?"

"Yes. I was crying about that Panther. It got my grandmother . . . and could get me, if I get too cold inside. Or . . . or choose the wrong direction at the fork at the end of Main Street."

Marek gently put my hair behind my ears. "I am feeling I should apologize. I should never have pretended I could play psychiatrist-spy. Ever since I talked with you, in that peculiar building at the college, I have felt a connection. It's awkward for me. I was not expecting to feel something for a woman again."

"I expected you to be something you're not," I said. "I thought you could guide me . . . through the . . . underworld." I paused. "Mihalyi is a common name in Hungarian, isn't it?"

"Yah. Like your Mike."

Marek and I held hands for a while. It was silent but for the sound of the water in the nearby creek. I said, "The Queen of the Y has stopped dancing."

"I am sorry we did not see her."

"Me too."

Marek inhaled the sweet air. "Do you know what the patients at Riggs like to do on spring nights like this one?"

"What?"

"They like to sneak back and forth across Main Street."

"Marek—"

"I am speaking the truth, so help me god. I was just out last night, in fact, chasing after this new patient of mine who had crossed Main Street to go to the Red Lion Inn. He told this social worker intern, on duty, that his sister was staying there and he had permission to see her." Marek sighed.

My heart leapt away from me. "Was she?"

"What?"

"His sister. Was she staying there?"

"Oh, no. His sister was killed a long time ago. He was just moved from Rhinebeck over to Riggs, at my suggestion. I don't know. Maybe I was wrong to move him."

My throat was dry. "Why did you?"

"His sister was killed in Rhinebeck. When he is there, he pretends he is her. You see, that way he believes she is still alive." He shook his head. "There, inside that gallery, is a crazy woman who has just danced, to everybody's delight. You know she is crazy, I know, I think maybe everyone knows. She hurts no one. This patient, when he pretends he is his dead sister, he hurts no one either. Why is she there, but he locked up?"

"She is locked up."

"She is?"

"In an asylum. Where she is safe. She lives at the Y, on the charity of a tough, chain-smoking, wiry woman who is the gatekeeper to the senior women's locker room. Marek?"

"Yes?"

"Take me to Stockbridge. If I don't go right now, I never will. And I have to. I have to finish the story. . . ."

"About the Panther?"

I nodded.

"What is this Panther?"

All I am is history, Manda had said. As I looked at the gentle face of this man before me, whom my heart trusted on this spring evening, in a dark rutted field watered by my tears, I saw the face of a real man my whole being yearned to have as my guide down the Main Street where a Stokes Sister had been laid to "rest." I allowed myself to say what I already knew but had been afraid to admit, even to myself. The history of the Panther went far beyond my own biography, farther than Vermont, all the way back to the original thirteen colonies which were asylum to my Stokes ancestors from England. Manda was the Panther passed down to me through the blood of the mothers of my mother who have been looking for the magic for centuries to kill the madness that has been stalking them ever since the first day a Stokes Sister departed from a country ruled by a tyrant to seek her freedom on the other side of the ocean. That Sister was carrying a child inside her, and her mother begged her not to go. The journey was sure to kill her in her gravid, vulnerable state. But she left; her love for her new husband and her desire for a new life was greater than all other loves. When the father of her unborn child, Oliver Wolcott, opened the wooden sea chest to give her a biscuit, he stared in horror at what he found inside. There, instead of the family Bible, was a copy of Shakespeare's *The Tempest*. His voice was sure and strong as he said to his pregnant wife, "You are mad, woman, to have done this to us. We are doomed. You have committed a sin against your unborn child."

She reached out for the biscuit. "Poetry is no sin," she said. "Please— a biscuit. For the child."

"I will not feed you, woman!" The ocean revolted against them, and their bodies crashed back and forth. She grabbed at the blasphemous Shakespeare and pressed it to her belly. "I denounce thee," her husband raged. He would keep his word and never touch his wife again.

Through the gap of his coldness, the Panther slipped in, and into the child inside her, and into hers, and hers, as the curse of the tyrant upon the first Stokes Sister making the crossing, carrying new life to the other side though she was certain to die, passed through all the Sisters to me. And still, the magic that could kill the Panther had not been found.

I, like my mother's mothers, knew only one way to spell "asylum."

But unlike them, I knew two ways to spell "beautiful," and one of them would bring my soul restoration, and the other the Panther's victory over another Stokes Sister—again.

An owl hooted.

Marek reached out his hand.

Main Street. Stockbridge, Massachusetts.

On one side, the lion rampant hangs on a wooden signpost for the famous Red Lion Inn, almost as old as The Beekman Arms, offering a safe place to rest for the many travelers who have passed through this town since my ancestors arrived in America. The rampant lion also happens to be on the Stokes ancestral crest. I believe it was the Stokes lion my grandmother saw from her bedroom at Riggs, across the street, where the smell of the apples filled her room every spring she was there. And she saw the six skulls lined up on either side of the lion, in two units of three, which complete the Stokes family crest. The three skulls for the three pregnancies that made her wish she were dead; and their doubles in life, her three daughters, who were born in spite of her desire to kill herself, murdering them inside her own suicide.

"What are you thinking about?"

"My grandmother's madness. She was like Medea to her daughters. She had magic in her, like Medea before she was used by one goddess to take revenge on another. A frightening, amazing earth magic. I remember when I was little being drawn into my grandmother's eyes, the color of the earth, and terrified by what I saw inside them."

"So it makes sense, your grandmother's pottery. Earth medicine for earth madness from earth magic."

"You don't talk like a psychiatrist."

"I am a son born from a poem. It gives me a peculiar perspective."

"I take it back. I do want you to guide me through the underworld."

"Only in springtime can a young woman do this, you know."

As we snaked through the back roads to Stockbridge, I saw my grandmother. Not the owl I knew, but the young woman in photographs airbrushed for a Pre-Raphaelite effect, her skin luminous, her enormous dark eyes dreamy. I closed my eyes, as round and dark as hers, and I began to imagine the part of the story no one talked about—the ashes.

My grandmother has been given special permission to go to the art area where her pots are being fired. She walks down the halls with an orderly, nervously reciting to herself the instructions for how to achieve oxblood. Flitting into her mind are images of an ox, its neck slashed, lying on an altar, a sacrifice to the gods. She will write a poem. A poem about the sacrifice to the gods called Art, when the poet must determine that precise point of suffocation required to attain the magnificent color of the ox's blood where it lies on the altar, exposed to the eyes of the gods and scavengers alike. Yes, she thinks, it is knowing just how much life has to be snuffed out, breath denied, if the muse is to breathe in you. That's the trick—to get the perfect hue for art's sake, you must suffocate the living things that turn your art into ashes.

"This way to the art area, Elizabeth."

"I know the way!" my grandmother protests. She marches into the room ahead of the orderly. She stands before the kiln. "What time is it?"

"Midnight."

"Precisely?"

"According to my watch."

"Your watch?" my grandmother screeches at the orderly. "What kind of a watch is your watch? Is it accurate? Who gave it to you? Do you take regular care of it? Do you have it cleaned by a reputable jeweler? What make is your watch? Give it to me this instant!"

The orderly removes his watch and hands it to my grandmother. "Oh my god, oh my god." My grandmother now panics as she stares at the watch, her enormous dark brown eyes fixed on the dial. She is mumbling unintelligible words to herself. The orderly moves over to the large black phone on the desk. "Get the doctor. Now."

"I would like to hear this story out loud."

"You're persistent, aren't you?"

"I like stories."

"It would make you too much like a professional."

"And you like a patient."

"I need to pretend that we are just driving through the spring night to Stockbridge, where we will walk down Main Street holding hands."

"But this is not pretend."

"It is all pretending, Marek; pretending I am alive."

"I have pretended I am alive too."

"I've been pretending I am alive since a car accident when I was younger."

"In a black car?"

"Why do you ask?"

"I was thinking of your Panther."

"It was a yellow car."

"Even the stories psychiatrists make up have holes in them."

It was the summer following the spring the Panther attacked me. My brother and I had been hitchhiking on the island where we all went every summer, my father allowed, for a few weeks, to be a Prospero before he returned to the business of running the country. We were picked up by the son of some colleague of our father's in his new BMW. As soon as my brother and I got in the car and we realized we all sort of knew each other through our fathers, I felt the driver tense up.

"Tennis camp," the driver said to my brother. "I remember you from tennis camp." My brother was an extraordinary athlete, very handsome, and this other son of a scion of Washington was neither athletic nor good-looking. The coach at the tennis camp had been mounting a campaign for years to persuade my parents to allow my brother to become a professional.

We drove for a few minutes before the driver said to my brother, "So, what are you?" In this era of Vietnam, he needed to say no more.

"I'm working on something," my brother said. "But one thing's for sure—no tennis. The military finds out I could be pro . . . it's tennis or death in the jungle," my brother said. "That's my story."

"I'm 1A," the driver said. "The car's a consolation prize."

My brother pressed himself against the seat, then turned and glanced at me. I was staring out at the trees, watching the way the light played on the stubby oaks of the island, with their pale green leaves and silvery bark, trying to erase the images of the dead in the black plastic body bags being carried out of the jungle, swinging from helicopters. The car swerved; a can of diet cola on the floor knocked my foot.

"We can get out right up ahead," my brother said.

"I'll take you all the way home," the driver said.

I noticed my brother playing with the door handle.

I don't know if my brother had an intimation of death or whether he was just scared to be with a guy his own age who wanted to go to Vietnam and resented him for winning every tennis match he had ever had to play to prove to his father, the girl he had a crush on, his pushy mother, that he was a man. I sat in the back seat, trying to roll the diet cola can away from me, noticing my brother's hand playing with the door handle, the images of Vietnam spewing from the television news cramming into my eyes. The yellow BMW accelerated as the driver said, "I know a shortcut," and turned off the main road onto what we called the Straightaway. I thought he meant a shortcut home, to our house. But he was seeking a shortcut to death to avoid death in the Asian jungle. As the speedometer passed fifty, eighty, struggling at the nineties as he forced it higher, one hundred and twelve, sixteen, counting out loud, at one twenty, my brother screamed, "Stop! If I wanted to die I know where to sign up—"

One twenty-two . . .

I watched my brother as he looked at the gearshift, at the pedal, at the door, trying to find a way out. "Stop," he said, over the hysterical whir of the engine. "Stop the car! Don't do this!"

The BMW broke one twenty-five and crept up to one twenty-six. The diet cola can was vibrating from the speed.

"Please."

The speedometer passed one twenty-seven, one twenty-eight . . . my brother said, "There's a curve—"

One twenty-nine . . .

"The curve—" my brother said.

The diet cola can shook.

One thirty . . .

I leaned down to pick up the diet cola can, stretching sideways across the seat, praying to gods by every name I could think of not to take my brother away from me. He is the only one, I told the gods, who sees the magic in me. Don't let him go to Vietnam. Please. Don't let him go. I can't lose his eyes, the way they see what no one else can see in me—do something so he can't go to Vietnam—a little hurt, enough to keep him here, on this side of the ocean—he's so beautiful, and so strong, they'll take him, they'll take him to that jungle, and I can't lose—

The car swerved as the embankment swelled and we were swimming in trees, where the dead are not buried and the living do not live.

The new, foreign doctor arrives in the art area. "Is something wrong, Elizabeth?"

"I explained it to you in detail," my grandmother says. "The suffocation procedure is crucial and very delicate. It must occur at precisely the correct moment. But no one knows what time it is! See? This man's watch and the clock on the wall and—let me see your watch."

The doctor allows Elizabeth to look at his watch. She raises her startled face to his. "It is going to fail. All because of the clocks. You know, doctor, I've been meaning to say something, but I did not want to offend my hosts. But none of the clocks, none of them, say the same time. It makes what I have to do all the more difficult."

The doctor nods slowly. "Explain it to me again, Elizabeth. I have forgotten why the timing has to be so exact."

"It was the critical moment between ashes."

"What ashes?"

"The ashes!" my grandmother screams at the doctor. "The ashes on both sides! That is why you have to be on the alert, and see in both directions." She moves her neck around, her dark eyes open wide. The doctor swallows as he watches her shifting her head like an owl. It is a bad sign. And Elizabeth was doing so well, he thinks.

The doctor pauses before he says, "Tell me more about these ashes on both sides."

My grandmother jerks her head still. "Too little heat, ashes. Too much, ashes. Why didn't you wake me like I told you? Everything's been destroyed. If you had only followed my instructions, I could have saved everything inside. I could have made it beautiful. But now it's all ashes. Because of you."

"Open the kiln, Elizabeth."

"Hold my hand."

"Tell me what you are imagining."

"Opening a kiln."

"And what is inside this kiln?"

"Either there is a pair of beautiful vases, and they are glazed a rich coppery red. Or the glaze has turned to ashes and ruined them. Or . . ."

Elizabeth stares at the closed door of the kiln, unaware of her hands on her belly.

. . . Nothing. There is nothing inside the kiln.

Every time Elizabeth swelled with a child inside her, she would see her mother again, walking into the sea, and hear herself screaming—nothing.

Not a sound. Not a word did little Lizzie call out to stop her mother as she walked into the swirling Atlantic. This sight was better than any dream she had tried to hide from herself, better than any hope she had not let herself hope with words, squeezing her eyes shut every time she would imagine her mother dying. There she was, right in front of her eyes for real, walking freely into her own death, singing her favorite hymn ("Where Sheep May Safely Graze") as the ocean, curling white at the edges of the waves, took her down, down, down. Little Lizzie just stared, and swallowed, and wondered if there were a god after all. She had given up hope in any god of any kind the first time her father raped her, and she screamed for her mother to stop him—before she realized that it was her mother who was holding her arms down, telling her to sing, just sing, that it would be over soon.

My grandmother's grandmother found little Lizzie way up the beach, her long dress tied up into a sack, filled with rocks and shells and long strips of (foul-smelling) seaweed. She took Lizzie back to the house, where she delivered to the girl the sad news that while she had been walking, her mother . . .

"I wasn't walking," Lizzie said. For she had been told never to lie to anyone, especially not to one of her elders. "I saw Mother go in."

"Oh, sweet Lord Jesus." Her grandmother enfolded Lizzie in her arms.

And so it happened that instead of saying what was on the tip of her tongue (that her mother deserved it for holding her arms down so her father could make sin with her and in her) her face was buried in the pink moiré of her grandmother's morning housecoat. She inhaled her perfume and was silent. Her story slipped into the weave of the pink silk shimmering over her grandmother's ripe bosom, untold.

Only to explode in her when she became herself a mother. Untellable. Unspeakable. Unknowable.

There had been gulls (she remembered, when the first girl of three was swelling inside her) flying over her mother as she walked into the same ocean that had carried her mother's mother's mother's mother . . . safely to this side, nurtured only on the stale sea biscuits in the old wooden chest held together with pegs. Gulls squawking overhead, circling her mother as she walked through the waves, out, out, and down (down) till there was no longer any sign of her, only the gulls circling where her long red hair had spread itself into a lacy fan like the seaweed little Lizzie would fill up her dress with and her grandmother would throw away.

Lizzie retrieved the sea fan from the garbage. She kept it hidden in a crack in the stone wall of the rose garden until it had lost itself inside the roses. Like the words Lizzie had never said when her face was muzzled in the abundant pink of her grandmother's soft breast, the sea fan became a thing forgotten which, when remembered, would turn inside out.

And instead of being a story about a little girl watching her mother kill herself, when the sea fan of her mother's hair came back to Elizabeth in the final month of her first pregnancy, she knew what she had to do. She had to become a gull, skillful in plucking food from the depths of the ocean, live food.

She stood up, shaking her arms into wings, when the first pangs of birth seized her. Miscalculation: The baby was coming now. She must fly before it was too late—

"Mrs. Stokes! You will come down from there at once!" the nurse said, speaking to my grandmother as if she were the child. Having disobeyed only once in her life, when she did not follow her mother into the rolling, spitting waters of the Atlantic despite having been told to do so, Elizabeth obeyed the nurse. She would obey from now on. Yes. That was the solution: to obey when she was commanded. No matter what the command.

She came down from the balcony railing and said, "Tell me what to do. The baby is coming."

After the birth, Elizabeth sat beside the bed. The nurse bustled. "Mrs. Stokes? Do you not hear the child? It is hungry. Listen and you can tell a hungry cry from a tired cry. . . . Mrs. Stokes?"

Every scream from the infant girl's throat was an accusation, calling her mother to come to her, now—as little Lizzie had not.

The second time she swelled up with a child inside her (my mother), Elizabeth developed acute laryngitis. Medicines were prescribed, and the signs of infection disappeared. Yet Mrs. Stokes could not speak. The only sounds that she could make were reminiscent of birds, strange hiccuping chirrups, and an occasional whistle in the same melody; it sounded somewhat familiar to one of the doctors, but he could not quite place it. (Years later, he would be at church, and turn to Hymn 454 in his hymnal, and as the organ began he would recognize the tune.)

The doctors referred Mrs. Stokes to another doctor, who was, in their expert opinion, the best in throats. He was, however, foreign. The foreign doctor was astonishingly young. He examined Mrs. Stokes's throat, observed her rounded belly, and made his radical recommendation. He had recently attended an extraordinary lecture about a new kind of "talking cure" for such curious feminine maladies as the one Mrs. Stokes was apparently suffering from. The head of the recently created American Medical Association himself, Dr. Putnam, whom it was his special privilege to know personally, endorsed this "talking cure."

My grandfather said, "What kind of a doctor would recommend a talking cure to a woman whose problem is she can't talk?"

And so my grandmother was taken back to the house to endure her second confinement with my mother, unable to talk her way to a cure for not being able to talk. There she sat for the entire remainder of her pregnancy reading a book. Much to her amazement, she read that the mother must never respond to that scream. And the book went on to say that the very worst thing a mother can do is to indulge her child when it acts "like an animal." Her responsibility as a mother was to civilize the infant, and if she were to succeed at this ennobling task, then she must do all she could to refuse the child's pleas for attention from the mother. It was when she read the sentence, "The child who calls to its mother is a child who has not overcome its animal instincts, and is doomed never to join the ranks of human society as a respected member," that my grandmother went downstairs and said to the nurse, who was having her afternoon tea in the kitchen with the cook, "From now on, all the children born in this house are to be put on a strict schedule. No more of this giving in when she cries. She must learn that crying is what animals do, not humans, and is *not called for by god*."

The nurse dropped the pink luster teacup, and it shattered.

My grandmother, carrying my mother inside her, went upstairs to her study and resumed reading the book avidly.

If I have another child, my grandmother said to herself, there will be more screaming. More screaming to test her commitment to civilization. My grandmother touched the swelling belly holding my mother. Air, she said to herself. If only this child inside me were air. And she a balloon. And that long-delayed flight across waters, scanning the ocean for whatever it was I lost.

A rose. She had lost a rose in the ocean, that's what it was. A red rose.

"Mrs. Stokes?" It was the nurse coming upstairs, the broken pink luster in her hands. "Are you all right now, then?"

Chirrup.

"Oh, sweet Jesus."

"Just some indigestion," my grandmother said. "I must have eaten something disagreeable. My stomach is terribly bloated. I suspect it was the oysters at luncheon. Tell cook no more oysters."

"Yes, Mrs. Stokes."

She looked at the broken pink luster in the nurse's hands. "I never did like pink luster. The way it shines. Pink is a terrible color."

When they found her sitting in the birdbath, the thin white nightgown soaked transparent and revealing her distended nakedness, waiting for the birds to alight on her and sing, they said that women sometimes did strange things when they were in this state, but she would be well once the child was born.

If only it were air, my grandmother thought. If only it were air. If she became air, she would give birth to a child of air. . . .

When she fell (down), the doctors said it was lucky she hadn't lost the baby. It would be best, they said, if she were to enter into her confinement early. No more social engagements. Visitors, a few. But no going outside the house until the child was born. And no more of this silly wandering about at night and jumping off porch walls, Elizabeth. Won't do. Simply won't do for a woman in your condition.

She would be a good mother. Follow the rules. She would not ever let herself think those terrible thoughts again. Child of air. Never again. No. She would be ever more perfect with this second one. She would be even more strict with the nurse. She knew the nurse was not adhering to the schedule as the book recommended, slipping in five, sometimes ten minutes early to fetch the first one. Not with this one, no.

Three weeks after my mother was born, the nurse thought she heard a strange sound coming from within the nursery. She checked her watch. Impossible that it could be Mrs. Stokes in there. It was not the right time. But something drove the nurse to break the rules and go in. She saw the older girl, in her crib, holding on to the railings. On the balcony, Mrs. Stokes was holding my mother as she tried to climb up onto the railing.

"Mrs. Stokes?"

Chirp.

"I'll have none of this chirping. Give me the child."

My grandmother turned to the nurse and said, "I must have forgotten. I'm supposed to go first. Then my daughter follows me. Because she is a good girl and does everything her mother tells her to do." She held my mother out to the nurse.

"Can't take her." The nurse pointed to her watch. "It's not time to be holding the child yet, Mrs. Stokes. The book says we must not touch her till four o'clock. And according to my father's reliable timepiece here, it's not yet two. Now, Mrs. Stokes, you listen to me. You take the child inside and put her down in her crib with her sister, and I'll make sure nobody finds out you broke the rules. I won't tell on you if you be a good girl now, yourself, and do what the book says."

My grandmother went inside and laid my mother down. The nurse came in and watched. The nurse noticed that my mother's sister was wet, and she began to change her. Elizabeth was up and over the balcony before the nurse could stop her. The nurse said it had seemed, for a moment, as if she were flying, when she spread her arms and her dress billowed. There must be some sort of bird in her, somewhere, said the nurse. How else can you explain landing without a scratch? Just a wee bit of a sprained ankle was all Mrs. Stokes suffered. All, that is, except for what happened to her voice.

"The bird sounds mean something, Mr. Stokes," said the young foreign doctor. "We just don't know what yet."

"But she's the only one who knows what they mean, and she can't tell you."

"Not with words, directly, no," the young foreign doctor said. "We must translate these songs. And if we are lucky, if I and my esteemed American colleague do the translation right, she will come back down to earth."

Main Street is just up ahead.

Summacious! Can you hear me?

No.

Good. Listen. Don't take this walk.

I like hearing you sound scared, Manda. Talk to me some more.

I'm trying to stop you for your own good.

I believe Hitler's mother used that phrase when she beat him.

Summacious, I take it back. It's a good idea, this walk down Main Street with Monsieur Rhino. Just don't walk down, you understand what I'm saying?

Lexy's here, Manda. I can feel Her.

She's sleeping.

Then I'll wake Her.

She needs the rest.

Not inside this kind of asylum, Manda. I'm taking Lexy to the Y, where Baubo will take care of Her.

How many times do I have to warn you—just when you think you are doing the story right, you've got it inside out again.

Not this time, Manda. Rulla is crazy enough to think Lexy is her dead sister finally arriving for the opening of Show Up Naked.

The song won't work that way.

I'll make it work that way.
When you start screaming at me that I killed your soul, don't forget—I warned you, Summacious. I am warning you now: Leave Lexy alone and let Her keep on dreaming.

"Which direction should we walk?"
Say up, Summacious. Up and into the Ark with your animal mate.
What is Lexy dreaming, Manda?
What She always dreams—that I come to Her.

"We'll walk that way, toward Riggs."
"Hold my hand."
"I am."
"I think maybe a little bit tighter. It gets very dark down there."
The only sound comes from the bar in the Red Lion Inn, its red rampant lion hanging brilliantly lit up before us. Marek and I pass by dark storefronts, the Red Lion growing larger and larger, down the middle of the empty Main Street. He holds my hand tightly, I his, and we say nothing.
I feel Lexy's presence growing stronger and stronger. I know She is inside Riggs, calling me to come to Her. I see Her sleeping. Marek slips his arm around me. The solution is so simple I am stunned. In Lexy's dream, it will not be Manda who comes to kill Her. It will be me, come to embrace Her.

Careful, Summacious.
Things getting wobbly for you now, Manda?
Do I need to remind you how the spelling test works? Pairs, Summacious. Inseparable pairs. Change one side, the other side changes. That's what happens when you walk down the middle of Main Street.
I have pairs, Manda. A pair of amphora, inside a kiln.

They're identical, Summacious. And the spelling test doesn't do identical.
It does similar. Derivatives. Variations. Ratios. Relations.
And you've been accusing me for weeks and weeks of stupid literary tricks.

Ahead of us, at the fork at the end of Main Street, the streetlights end
close to where the original apple orchard begins. I see Lexy deep inside
the darkness sleeping under an apple tree. I hear Her regular breathing
as She rests, exhausted by having to do all the dancing for all the sisters
on this side who have lost our souls and can no longer mean what we
move. It seems there is a lullaby somewhere near Her, as if someone were
with Her, singing to Her. Freddie, of course. Adonis crooning to his one
and only Moongirl— bonus, as Manda might say, wouldn't you, Manda?

You get bonus questions wrong, Summacious. It's a bad thing, Freddie
being here. Freddie, he doesn't exactly like it when I show up.
Who says you're showing up?
You keep on walking the way you're walking, Summacious, and I don't
have any choice. I have to get there before you do: That's how the plot goes.
Your plot.
Our plot, Summacious.

We are walking more slowly, Marek and I, our arms around each
other, the sound of laughter from the Red Lion Inn reaching us as we
draw parallel to its large, deep, inviting porch. Marek's arm pulls me
tighter, and I respond in kind as we all but come to a stop in front of the
sign of the rampant lion, symbol of heart strength, courage in battle. I let
myself close my eyes, surrendering utterly to Marek's powers as a guide,
and as I do, I merge with Lexy asleep under the apple tree. We will be
dreaming the same dream together, She and I.

Marek and I are folding our bodies into each other under the Stokes
crest, all skulls removed from sight.

"Open the kiln," says the doctor.

"I have an idea," says Marek.

"Will it keep me warm?" I ask.

My grandmother reaches out her hand to the kiln door as spring works a greater magic than all of us, opening all the doors on all the hatching, firing, nesting, creating, borning things seeking life between the ashes of the winter before and the winter to come. All I want is to go into the Ark and, for one night in my life, to be a woman who means what she moves in a quickening season. As Marek and I mount the stairs, I forget that Noah, like spring, does not discriminate and calls all the animals to the Ark to safety, the hoofed like us first, the great beasts following, then the solitary dove.

There are dreams you wish you'd never dreamt. Dreams that stick to you like wet dust, and although you awake and tell yourself it was only a dream, this doesn't stop you from getting into the shower, the sterile, pristine shower, and washing it away, scrubbing your skin to get the dream out of you, rinsing and rinsing to drown your skin so the dream won't float to the surface of your body again, and your cells remember what happened to them while you were sleeping. But your cells pulse the dream into your mind, and no matter how long you rinse, no matter how sterile your shower stall, no matter how red you rub your skin, your cells remember what happened in the dark.

I yearned for the steam room. But the memory of the scene of the holocaust in the steam room only made the dream renew its imagery inside me. I saw him again, Lenin, his face above mine. I hated my legs for opening. I hated spring for making my legs open; it didn't matter to spring who it was. The worst part was my laugh.

It was supposed to have been Marek (I said to my stupid cells). And I was supposed to spend the day inside his smell. And not have to do this. Have to wash Marek off to get Lenin off me.

By the time I had returned from Stockbridge, said an awkward good-bye to Marek, and begun my desperate showering, it was late in the afternoon. As I turned off the shower, I heard someone or something banging on the glass door. I jumped out of the shower, nothing but a towel wrapped around me. It was my friend.

She grabbed my arm and squeezed it so hard, while her eyes locked onto mine. She could barely speak, and when she tried, tried to tell me what had happened, what—she gulped for air. She held her hand over her heart, at her breast. "He has . . . he says . . . he found . . . He was waiting for me, last night, on my doorstep. Benjamin alone in his house. Only me, Meem, only me, right? This would only happen to me. You were right. It was dangerous, I didn't know, there I am preaching to you about art being dangerous and—Meem?"

As her voice made its usual glissando upward into the high notes of her natural hilarity, it seemed to rise up, crest, and then rise up higher into that further descant where terror also lives, and in those few words which claimed her story as hers alone, "Only me," she went past hilarity into hysteria. She wept; beat her hands gently against me as I held her, like a child, until she had quieted enough to get the story of the pictures and the diary out.

When she was through, she asked for a cigarette. She didn't smoke; a childhood of asthma had scared her away from it. But it turned out that she had started smoking since she found out that some of the pictures— Did I remember? The pictures, that morning, when I had dreamt about the lizard? She didn't want me to see? They had been missing for a while. And her diary. He had asked for a key. Practical, he said. So that he wouldn't have to bother her at work all the time when Benjamin forgot something. It seemed a good idea to give him one. "I thought that the key was insurance against a custody suit. A sign. A symbol that we didn't need to do that." I lit her cigarette for her, and one for myself. My friend, holding the cigarette awkwardly as a novice smoker does, looked at me, her usually vibrant eyes dulled. Tears began to stream down her face again, this time quiet ones. She held her head with a kind of dignity I had not seen before. It was almost aloof, a quality that my extroverted friend with her democratic heart had never displayed. "I just came from a lawyer," she said. "He says it's not good."

"So get another lawyer."

She coughed as she inhaled. She said, "He's had experience in this area before."

"He's dealt with cardboard Lenin cutouts who read *Playboy?*"

My friend cracked a smile which disappeared almost as quickly as it came. "He says all the judges in family court here are pretty conservative."

"So they just pretend they don't read *Playboy,*" I said.

"Meem."

"Sorry."

She smoked, waited. My mind produced chatter, argument, stupidity, denial. "A conservative judge is even less likely to take a child away from its mother," I said. "The least likely to do that."

"Depends on the mother."

"You're an incredible mother," I said.

This comment brought tears, but she shook them away, forcing herself to keep steady in order to accomplish some task, I didn't know what.

"You don't know what the pictures were of," she said in a soft voice, one I had not heard before. "Sort of weird, don't you think? For me not to let you see them."

"I don't let you see my writing."

"Me, Meem. Me who tells everybody everything."

"Women?" I said, stalling.

"A woman," she said.

My belly flipped.

"When I started the pastels, the ones he, those, those ones he *took* when I began, you know? Meem? I was thinking of her. I didn't know you knew her. She's so beautiful, you know? But then, then when I was inside it, I was inside it and I didn't really think, my hands were thinking for me and I was drawing that long scar you have, you know the one, like a crescent moon that curves above your hip . . . Meem? Meem, I think it's beautiful, that scar. It just found its way into the picture, and the next thing I knew it wasn't her, it was . . . I was . . . loving, this way, with chalk, loving with chalk, and her body turned into yours, and then my body was there, with yours, which was hers, and . . ."

"All it was was chalk," I interrupted.

My friend lifted her face to me. "It's very graphic chalk."

I said, "He came here. Lenin came here and accused me of being your lover. I told him I wasn't. I told him we never did anything. And we never did."

"When? When did he come here?"

"Weeks, months . . . the day of the funeral."

"What funeral?"

"Gwen's sister . . ."

She asked for another cigarette. "This lawyer," she said, exhaling the smoke. "He knows what to do. He's had experience with lesbians."

The word hung in the air between us.

She went on, "He says . . ." She choked back the tears, took a huge gulp of air. "He says that I'm probably going to lose Benjamin. It doesn't matter that I was room mother in preschool. It doesn't matter that I make chocolate cupcakes with orange frosting and squeezed spiderwebs on them from those stupid tubes every year for his school Halloween party, and it doesn't matter, really doesn't matter, that I drove him back and forth across the river for karate, and down to Poughkeepsie for tutoring, and I was the one who set it up with the neighbor Mr. Tumey for him to build a record player from scratch last summer, which was the one thing in the whole world he most wanted to do, or that I'm the one who . . ." Her voice cracked, "I'm the one who entered him into the Dutchess County Fair talent show, and he won, remember, Meem? Remember when he dressed up as a garbage can and did that song? 'Feed Me'? 'Feed me what you don't want, I love it'?" she sang in a halting voice.

She smoked. She looked out at the trees. "It was his idea. To have Benjamin. He tells me this now. That Benjamin was his *idea*. Like he thought him, so he belongs to him." She shook her head, the tears abated.

"One time, after I went to Del's with Benjamin, we came home, and I threw away our cups. And then . . . I reached into the garbage can and I got them out and I took them outside to the big garbage can, where I knew he wouldn't find them. . . . that's when I knew I had to leave him. Because I couldn't eat soft vanilla ice cream with my son without thinking about how my husband wouldn't touch me." She laughed. "My mother, she keeps asking me, why am I doing this? And I can't tell her. I can't tell her that it's about being ashamed and scared to eat vanilla ice cream. About walking along the side of the road with Benjamin and collecting all the junk he loves and then going to celebrate at Del's. And how I can't live with someone who punishes me for celebrating." She shook her head. "Stretch marks. I had this idea of these little wrinkles like when you lose some weight, you know? Not the road map of the Nile I got."

She lifted her shirt. Her belly was mottled and cracked like the surface of a cauliflower. I had seen her belly many times before, at the Y, but I had never studied it as she was inviting me to study it now. She looked up at me. "We're both scarred. Badly," she said. "We're pretty scratched up, you and me. But we're beautiful to each other. Scars and all. Aren't we, Meem? Aren't we beautiful to each other?"

She sat there, looking at me, biting her lip as tears threatened her again, her belly exposed. She had lost her husband from the birth of her child; she was losing her child in the rebirth of her soul; would she lose me too, in the rebirth of her art? "I imagined . . . I wrote . . . in my diary, I wrote that you touched me. It was a fantasy. You touched me. Here. Kissed me where he wouldn't. Where the most beautiful boy in the world left me ugly to his father. Because I wasn't carrying an idea, more like a watermelon. You should have seen me, pregnant. I wish you had. . . . I wrote in my diary that you loved me here, right here, where that wonderful boy was made. And it's true, isn't it, Meem? You would touch me, wouldn't you?"

I saw my hand reaching out toward her. This impulse to touch the scars of life on another, and feel the warmth flowing between you, it is prayer. The prayer of the beautiful in peril of ashes burning the beautiful away when it is too cold with grief, too hot with rage. I could see my fingers follow on her belly every track life had made in her when she carried life for life's sake as I looked at my friend's belly, corrugated as a cauliflower. You will wonder at how I could envy such a beaten, battered, marred thing. Yet I did. I would have given anything for the smooth surface of my belly to be stretched and broken open by life as hers was. For it would never happen to me, scarred by the force of life growing in her, the evidence on her skin that she had been the one who carried life. All I could do was trace the map of the scars on another woman and feel the warmth. I had lost hope, what the virgin poet in Massachusetts called that thing with feathers, when my Nebraskan lover had tried with me and tried, until he could try no longer to keep me warm, for there was no warm to warm me anymore.

I even lifted my hand to initiate this prayer of one daughter among the Children of Ashes and bring my fingers to touch the map life had etched on her. But my hand stopped, midprayer, refusing to touch where life had loved another woman with the hand of madness.

Dream blasted a friendship apart; art—a marriage; fantasy—a child.

And a Panther who had invaded the wombs of my mothers effortlessly entered mine through the sluice of a springtime dream of making ecstatic love with a tyrant.

In summer in the mid–Hudson Valley the air is cloyingly sweet, settling along the banks of the river, which runs dark and blue and strong as it flows toward the ocean. Summer was its season, the time for which this region of the cosmos was created in its forms and shapes to realize itself most fully, unrolling in a perfect complement of sky, field, hill, river.

I lost myself in the winding maze of unmarked roads woven through the valley. I would get into my car in the early evenings, when the sound of the insects was a great, global hum, no destination, not even the alluring destination called "away," "escape," for I felt I had nothing to escape from. I passed from nothingness into the winding green of summer, over and over again, swimming in trees. But I was lost now in the infinite currents of the impersonal blunt green magic of life, beyond the reach of even my own story. It is one thing to write about swimming in trees, quite another to *be* there. I was lost in a way I had never known, before or since, so lost that I was not even lost *to* myself, there was no longer that anchor of self, that steadiness of my being in history, to be lost to. If I could be made inside art into a woman I was not; yet if that woman I was not could cause a mother to lose her child for real—existence of any kind was perilous to too many souls I loved. And I wanted out. For me to *be* was too dangerous: Murder of some form was the result, no matter what my placement, within, inside, beyond, dream, art, fantasy, history, every form of story there is. Every Rhinebeck now held murder inside it, and I, its Hamlet, bringing the Panther with me wherever I went—especially toward those I loved. For Manda was winning, if not already the victor: The Murder Mystery *was* a love story, and after all the killing was finished, she and my soul would live happily ever after, the Woman Who Means What She Moves teaching the Nazi-Panther to dance for eternity.

The only place that seemed safe was swimming in trees, where life and death move in and out of each other, and the dead are never named, or the living either. And it is safe there for Children of Ashes, baby boomers like me who carry the weight of the funerals of the living wherever we go. In Gaia's channel you are beyond history, out of reach of language and self. You are no longer held together by the strokes of the smallest words, the "beside" of friendship, the "with" of love, the "for" of the champion, the "to" of longing, the "against" of evil, the "below" of desire, not even the "up" that takes you out of the underworld into the Ark is a point on the compass of life before it falls into the fatal accident of selfhood, and the human story of love and loss. All is anonymous inside the trees, for earth magic broaches no authorship; it is that old religion of place without the anchoring ego of monotheism. I was not writing the plot of this story. I was not its source, its creator, but, inextricably, a murderer inside it. Only in the trees could I escape the form my being was taking in Manda's plot.

I passed the back sides of farms where cow's tails swished in the limpid air; rose and fell over gentle rollicking roads as the mists of evening leaked from the masked stars and coolness made its downward pilgrimage to earth. Not one of the farms or roads had a name I knew. The cows were nameless too, and instead of the distinct sound of a bird, the anonymous buzz of all the wings and antennae of unseeable creatures filled the air, itself a sheath in which all the aromas of life were contained. I drove through them sucking in the spilling green perfume of summer to inhale what I was losing—the way life loves me, knows me alive to it. Finds itself, in me. Recognizes itself in me.

A round pond of great green velvet opened before me, like the eye of Gaia herself. It seems to me now that I went there many times, guided on the same route to it not by the names of the roads but by their shapes and lights, before I finally stopped. The low sun behind the shields of the leaves and the green of the water glinted the same yellowing green hues. I sat in the twilight, my feet dangling in the water, looking down into its depths in search of a different face to call by my name.

I saw in Her open green eye a young woman whose own hand had betrayed her. My hand frozen in midair, I had watched as my friend slowly let her shirt drop. I watched her stand; I stood. I watched her looking at me; I looked at her. And I saw, in my friend's eyes, a wrinkle of terror like a child first discovering a parent's cruelty. My friend had finally met Manda, and she was wearing my face in our story.

After she left, I could not move for a long time from the spot. When I finally heard the phone ringing, and picked it up, Marek said, "Were you outside?"

There is an outside so far in that when you touch it you are turned inside out. It is there that the cells find their way to pump the nightmare into you, and if the man on the other end of the phone, with the voice like rippled honey which has made both your tongues fluent in languages they never knew existed, speaks in your native tongue and you cannot understand a word.

"Strange," Marek was saying. "Everyone here is upset, they are worried, about a patient. Mine, unfortunately. The one I was telling you about."

"What happened?"

"He stole a car so he could drive back to Rhinebeck. He was driving very fast. Much too fast."

I swallowed. "Was there . . . an accident?"

"I'm afraid so."

"Is he all right? Your patient?"

"If you mean is he alive, yah. All right—no." Marek sighed. "I wish this did not happen last night, of all nights."

"Maybe it's a sign."

There was silence on the other end of the phone. "Please don't say this. It is just life, that is all."

It is the Panther, Marek, who is taking over life wherever I am living it. I may yet survive, though I doubt it. But if you change from a man whose body is my only harbor into the authority who must put me inside, then I will lose what infinitesimal courage I have left, even if it is only the courage to take the fatal plunge I have been delaying all this time. So I must ask you, silently, to leave me to face my fate alone, where you cannot see me or touch me, my rhinoceros husband, escort down Main Street, kind, sad man who walked into a woman's life at a time when she was better off dead than alive with the Panther inside her.

One of these summer days, I will dive into the green eye of Gaia and stay there forever, and I do not want you to shout to Noah to wait because there's a missing half of one of the pairs of all creation yet to board. Go into the Ark where you will be safe, Marek, and let me remain swimming in trees while the world ends.

It was freakishly cold that day in August when I left the cottage in the woods for the pond. The weather reports declared there was a bizarre Arctic airstream passing through the region, and there was a chance of frost forming overnight. I was certain no one would be there on such a cold, cold day, yet I waited until late in the afternoon to remove all possibility of a stray visitor to see me dive in.

The beach was empty, but the sand was rumpled with the signs of life. I sat on the sand, gently tracing with my fingers the indentations left by children who had played here some warm day before. I dug my fingers into the sand. The deeper my hand went through the skin of the earth, the colder it was within. It was a good day to merge my cold with Hers, Gaia and I together inside the breath of the Panther blowing through the valley in the medium of the murder of inspiration. I had no more story left in me to live, no version of The Murder Mystery I desired to create, except to surrender to its end, which was its beginning, and kill Her who was already dead and be done with inspiration forever.

The green waters of Gaia's eye were almost black. It was time. I stripped naked and dove in.

I was shocked, not by the cold but by the warmth on the surface where the sun had penetrated through the Panther's breath and the algae had absorbed its sky-food, taking the warmth into itself. I swam for a while, feeling the silken strands filled with sun move over my body, just to let myself know that I had, once upon a time, been alive. It made crossing over to the side of the dead a clear, definite action, and I wanted clarity more than all else. The clarity of bringing an end to my swimming in trees. I was tired of swimming back and forth, back and forth, between the land of the living and the realm of the dead. It was time to choose one side or the other, and I had made up my mind. When the mother of the wise boy who brought me special twigs to keep me warm saw Manda inside my eyes, I knew which side I had to cross to reach, the only asylum into which a Stokes Sister whose womb has been impregnated by the seed of madness should lock herself. I had lost the only pair of eyes that saw magic in the sister my brother made me into, and without them, the magnets that had the power to make life stick to me with love turned against each other. Air itself buckled, refusing to let life love me, as all I inspired was the pantherine atmosphere of fatal sisterhood. It was time to complete the spelling test of my soul and answer the Chief's question in the affirmative: "Yes, Sister is on the side of the dead."

I left the warm surface and went down (down).

Summacious! Can you hear me?

No talking during spelling tests, Manda. Those are the rules.

I just came here to tell you how it went with Lexy. I didn't want you to die without knowing how the only story that matters—Hers—ends.

It ends where it began: You killed Her.

Actually, Summacious, there was a big surprise waiting for me in the apple orchard.

Let me surface.

Hold on, Summacious, I've got rules too. You only get to hear this story when you are where you are, right now, at the center of Her maze, about to enter into Her dark pupil and die.

I'm running out of breath, Manda.

You don't even know what a breath is, Summacious. That's how come you can't count them in your dream. And what does the holy figure inside that tree in your dream tell you to do?

Keep breathing even if I don't know what a breath is.

Because why?

It's my destiny.

So. Isn't it time you followed your instructions for your destiny?

Please. Tell me. What happened.

I've been waiting a long time for you to ask me that question, Summacious.

I get to the apple orchard at Riggs, pretty much on schedule despite your soul trek down Main Street and the time spent persuading you into getting into the Ark—for which I have yet to receive any thanks, by the way. I have every expectation of things going pretty much the way they have for twenty-seven thousand years, with this petal and perfume variation on asylum for the big moment we've all been looking forward to from the very beginning. When I finally get to the setting for the murder scene, this Hamlet-orchard play within a play you've got going—your grandmother was right; there's no such thing as too much Shakespeare—and I see Lexy sleeping under the apple tree, I confess I was momentarily seized with unexpected sentimentality. Spring got to me, Summacious, and I have to say, I liked the little taste of it I got. I've never tasted spring before. I confess I was thinking about Moms and her anxiety about getting the colander to the moon. It wasn't fair to Moms to have to go through all she'd gone through with me and King Pain and my sister when all she ever wanted was to get to the moon with her leaky variation on your grandmother's sacred amphora, that urn with holes she bought when, for once in her life, she happened to be in the right aisle when they announced a blue-light special. As I am thinking about Moms's Kmart rhapsody in aisle three, I think it was, Lexy opens Her eyes. For the record, She is over-joyed to see me.

I am telling you the truth. Imagine, Summacious, if you can, the torture it is for Lexy to have to sustain for so long the knowledge that I will, eventually, find Her and kill Her, again. It is always a relief when I do. The waiting for the inevitable is over. But even more inconceivable is that every time, every time I find Her and She awakens to my face, the True Inconceivable for Children of Ashes like you is that Lexy hopes that this time I am going to tell Her I love Her and She will not be murdered.

I will tell you, Summacious. Nobody else. Ever. Not in twenty-seven thousand years have I admitted this to anyone. But I have this incomprehensible affection for you. That moment, the one when Lexy opens Her eyes and I see the hope in them that I will tell Her I love Her this time— that's what keeps me going. That's the moment I live for. The instant of hope after all the times I have proven to Her that there is no reason for Her to hope—it is more delicious than you can know. It is the kind of moment, Summacious, which helps a god bear the burden of being immortal.

And it is, of course, why I kill Her. So that I can have that moment of hope again and give my immortality some punch, theatre, sensation, vivacity, nerve, pulse—that's the word: pulse. Hope when there is none is the pulse of immortality. Because it's pointless to satisfy hope—then it isn't hope anymore. So I do what I am here to do; it is why I am necessary, and why I am the most important teacher you will ever have in your lifetime and more real than you can even imagine, Summacious: I kill Lexy so that hope is born where there is none and pulse happens inside eternity.

I always strangle Her, by the way.

But what happens this time? What happens this time that has never happened in twenty-seven thousand years? Aside from doing the usual strangulation with rainbow chiffon.

I look into those green eyes of Lexy's that I have looked into countless times before—no hope. No hope in Her bright green eyes that I will tell Her I love Her. Maybe I should make this situation clearer: no hope that *I* will tell Her I love Her. And do you know why, Summacious? Do you know why Lexy doesn't care after twenty-seven thousand years whether *I* love Her or not?

Because someone else does. Some baby boomer who actually *wants* to be a Child of Ashes has done something that never happened before. Instead of the usual reaction to seeing the ashes on both sides and making sure that you hoard your creation to yourself, someone has let Lexy carry creation for her. Someone who doesn't trust herself to create anything alive or even like life on this side because she is a Sister, and in her ancestral clan, Sisters who are creative wind up on the wrong side of Main Street.

What usually happens at this point in the only story that matters is we both go into the nearest tree and start breathing again (I always hold my breath when She loses Hers). Then we start running to the next place where we can find asylum on your side. But you, Madame Rhino, Deaf to Noah's call to Creation, Sister Meem Determined to Be Barren in All Ways, Interrupter of the Dance, Nice Girl who turns the Woman Who Means What She Moves into History, Summacious who is the Sum of Ashes, have taken *my* hope out of Lexy's eyes. *My* hope that She wants me to tell Her I love Her—again. And my hands, they refuse to move toward Her throat.

Lexy and I, we're looking at each other under that apple tree in Stockbridge and neither one of us knows what to do without the usual skulls in the scene. It was weird, being new and forced to improvise after twenty-seven thousand years. Let me just say for the record, I hate your goddamned destiny dream about not counting the breaths the usual way. I should have known better than to answer when you called. I thought I'd covered all the destinies there were, but improvisation—it's a stumper. How can improvisation be the thing that's *foretold?*

It was my idea to go to your ancestral summer home. I thought it was an elegant, literary touch, going to the same place where your wingless Elizabeth watched her mother walk into the sea. Which is why your mother sold her share of the property to Sister. Didn't want to be where Mommy had, you know, let her mother die. I think you call it psychology? I believe the last time you were in this seashore house where your Great Whatever Mother spent her summers was when you were four, and your brother showed you a trick with magnets—? Thought so.

There were some very weird books in that ancestral property; I don't blame your mother for getting rid of it. Bug books. Weird ethnographies from the 1930s, with strange etchings of indigenous ritual objects, and Audubon, lots and lots of Audubon. Every book you opened up, you found bizarre drawings of animals with names you never heard of, and I don't know how many languages. It was more like a zoo than a library, a fantastic zoo. Oh, yeah—all over the walls were maps, historical maps, of what explorers thought it all looked like. Continents in shapes they aren't. Places they aren't. And more animals. Animals on all these maps of the world the way it isn't, strange animals like hippopotamus-headed lions and more variations on whales than even your eccentric Stokes Sister mind can conceive. One map was Spanish. California. 1600s. Weird Amazons with giraffe necks in that one. Sea serpents too. And there were these drawers and drawers of these bugs. Pinned. Bonus allusion to Nabokov; I'd go for it if I were you, Meem. Butterflies, beetles, spiders, pinned under glass. Lexy used to sit and look at them. I was the one who found the old man's journal. Your great-uncle's journal. In a nifty secret box that was fitted into the seventh stair, like the stair was a drawer.

Your great-uncle, Summacious, he loved bugs. Deeply. Even slugs. I am reading this journal, and Lexy, She's poring over some of the other papers and books we find in the seventh stair. It turns out that this great-uncle, he was Kinsey's mentor-type person—Kinsey the sex guy. I tell you, improvisation is weird, but a bug man hired to catalog human sex— that's weirder than weird. What's weird to your great-uncle, though, is the feelings he is having about his young male student, which he has put into his journal and hidden in the seventh stair along with the sex books. It is killing him that his former protégé who went searching all around the swampy saltwater marshes for some creepy crawler that was sacred to them both had gone off to ask these '50s housewives who all want to be Queen for a Day about orgasm. Your great-uncle feels betrayed. He thought what mattered was their mutual quest for a rare type of slug, okay, I will admit it was a sea slug. When the first books start arriving from his former protégé, your great-uncle records in his journal that he has decided to build a secret drawer in the seventh stair (counting from the top down). So in addition to monsters, unfinished continents in the wrong place, alphabets I can't decipher—did I mention this Russian book about tundra? I think it was Cyrillic—and crucified butterflies, we've now got anatomy bug books, anatomy animal books, and anatomy human books. Anatomy is new territory to me, especially a fiction about female ecstasy by a bug guy who doesn't like making love to women in the first place. Your ancestors are very strange and delusional people, Summacious; they think this stuff is the authoritative map of Her maze.

Anyway, Lexy takes a book out of the seventh stair, and She curls up on a chair and She does not move for days, it seems. It starts raining. I swear to god, it starts raining and raining and raining, like it's last spring, not this one. Like when you have to improvise after twenty-seven thousand years, the first test is to go backward and do all that make-up work I've been warning you about. Remedial—remedy. Lexy is curled up by the fire, hidden under all those blankets. From somewhere in that catacomb by the suicidal sea She's hauled out an old beaver coat. She's wrapped in '40s fur and looking like a great fuzzy cocoon. Her improvisation, it's turning out, is hibernating in the rain.

Out of nowhere, She speaks. This is an event. She's said nothing to me since you took your walk down Main Street, because—in the usual version of this story—I always make sure I kill Her before I hear Her voice. I'm no idiot; I know what would happen to me if my cells ever heard the voice of hope speaking to them. I'd lose my big part in the story of creation. So I make sure I never hear Her speak to me. But, as I said earlier, a certain Sister I know has messed up the usual cosmic pattern, in spite of all the pains I took to make sure she did the story right.

Anyway, Lexy starts talking about this stuff She's reading in this book. It's about this woman, she was from England, she was forty-three. Forty-three and a virgin. There was this forty-three-year-old virgin who was sitting in her London flat knitting when the Blitz happened. The bombing. And when it was all over, this woman, she went back to her life, kind of shattered and freaked out, but she went back to her life, such as it was. Only one thing. She was pregnant. No, two—she never knit again.

Lexy is reading this to me, right? She's reading to me from this book, under the beaver cocoon. She's reading about how this is the only recorded case of immaculate conception for real. There was no explaining it. The woman sort of went into a kind of time-lapse fallopian ballet during the bombing, hymen intact, no sexual experience she swore to god and the doctors, but it was her sister's testimony which really counted, and nine months later, she has a child. Normal, healthy. The only explanation these Kinsey types give is that the trauma of the bombing produced some sort of eruption of testosterone inside a virgin womb, and a mushroom cloud turning all the Children to Ashes outside is a blooming blastophere inside a woman who didn't feel the hands of the god of death when he made her explode.

Lexy, She says to me—I remember the exact words, Summacious. She says, "Do you know what this means, Manda?"

I don't know what to say, now that I've lost the plot.

Lexy says, "Hitler made a Dring."

I love Rhinebeck, Summacious. I love your Hudson Valley and your bridge and your river and your presidential grounds and your Kingston Y and most of all, Summacious, I love the steam room where a woman made out of cardboard turned on the lights. And I love Lexy for choosing your valley in the first place. I think maybe I love Lexy more now than ever before. Killing Her this time is going to be like no other time before, I can feel it, you know what I mean? And all because of your beloved valley and that carbuncle on the other side of the river called the Y, Lexy's eponymous local shrine, the law of The Murder Mystery—the murder mystery of your soul in your phosphorescent valley of life.

See, Lexy had a message to deliver too. She had to get to the asylum where Freddie was locked up to give him the news that his Moongirl was going to give him his dead sister back, alive for real, after all this time. A miracle had happened. Baubo got through and Hitler couldn't stop her dancing anymore, because of your beloved valley. We have a cardboard woman and a barren sister and a schizophrenic transvestite and a lackadaisical police chief and last but not least, Main Street, America, to thank for the miracle of Lexy carrying the creation of a Child of Ashes for the first time in history.

Lexy, being the eternal optimist She is, hoped for a wooden rainbow god to come out of the ashes this time. But it started to wobble, even for sure-footed, graceful, able-to-dance-on-the-rocks-in-bare-feet Lexy Herself. Poor Freddie. When he gets the news from Lexy, he freaks. He starts calling up all these women his mother's age and giving them instructions in how to have ecstatic sex without—I repeat, *without* the risk of any more Freddies running around splintering into madness. Because that's all there is left for Adonis to make love to, Summacious, no matter what his leading lady's name, Venus, Moongirl, Lexy, and countless more names than you blood bags on your side even know. The names for Her have been inscribed on the wooden figurines, buried in the earth where they rotted, hidden deep inside the bins of grain where Her name is slowly but surely eroded by the seeds of the harvest, year after year, can you still hear me? I said, the seeds of the harvest. The assurance that life will continue. There will be enough food from Her love—the seeds of life itself are what began destroying her twenty-seven thousand years ago, in the Fertile Crescent. All She is Summacious, *all* She is now, is a splinter.

But Lexy, She's holding out for the rainbow god anyway. Because Lexy hopes when there is none, She can't help it, it's how She means what She moves no matter what. Which is how come the story of how I kill Her is the saddest story on earth and the only one that matters. Right now, Lexy believes that Baubo is warming up for her cosmic belly-dancing routine to dance when Freddie's kid is ready to pop out of Hitler's Dring. She doesn't know about how you are at the bottom of this pond in Elizabethville—what, you didn't know that? Didn't you read the sign? This pond is in Elizabethville, Summacious, and guess what? In the spelling test? Elizabethville is paired up with Eleusis. Lexy always closes Her eyes in Elizabethville, Meem, so She can dream the dream where She hopes, anyway. So She can't see you right now. She's thinking She's going to give you cocoon-unfurling lessons after the birth. She doesn't know what's happened to the dance studio since you had a dream about the soldiers.

But I do.

You forgot a crucial part of the plot, Summacious, *our* plot, you and me and the Woman Who Means What She Moves. You forgot the critical lesson she was trying to teach you when you were her apprentice in Vermont. But I remember everything for you that you don't want to remember. It was in the hallway as you were going into the multipurpose activity room, they called it, with the old geezers and the Queen for the big dance. I was there, hiding behind a garbage can, catching my breath, hoping nobody would hear me breathing so hard and lock me back inside my solitary cell. When I saw you and the Woman Who Means What She Moves coming down the hall, I stopped breathing. It wasn't fear,

Meem; it was love. I loved the Woman Who Means What She Moves, and I never got a chance to tell her either. As you passed by me on your way to the Queen's ball, I heard what she told you, Summacious, the instructions she gave you so that you could learn to be like her, the one thing in the whole world you wanted to be and still want to be. "Don't worry about the steps," said the Woman Who Means What She Moves. Especially the waltz, which is a lot more difficult than you realize until you start trying to do it with someone who doesn't know how. What you want to do is move with them, however they move. And the most important thing of all—*follow their lead, wherever it takes you.*"

You know, before I got put in Queen Isabel's linoleum asylum for paranoid phosphorescence, I was a messed-up smart kid with a definitely bad moment in my childhood which could have gone either way. Thinking I killed my sister. Thinking I'd given her a gift with my stories, so maybe I wasn't all bad. Told her about the Drings. Wondering if there was some way to change the story so that the Eaners didn't come next time. And even when I was going through the d.t.'s and getting off the shit I'd been shooting into my veins ever since Moms went loony when King Pain made his entrance by exiting, in my own humble self-diagnostic opinion here, I think I had a chance. Slim, you say. But I say it just takes a slit, that's all it takes, life doesn't need any more than that, it can force its way through and it does so every time. Just a crack and—presto change-o! Shazzam! Form happens. Form always happens in between, Summacious, that's the trick of evolution. And I had that little in between where I might have formed the sister in me differently if you hadn't come along, Miss Interrupter of the Dance.

Again.

Before I say good-bye and you swim through Her pupil and die, I just came to remind you of the cue that you were—let me make myself perfectly clear—you *were* supposed to follow, if you were to become a woman who means what she moves and pass the spelling test for your destiny. *My* cue, Summacious, for your murderous dance with the Panther that you should have been following from the very beginning. It isn't a mad grandmother afraid to open a kiln, or a soul stroll arm in arm with a rhino down Main Street. The cue for murder in this story isn't even your own hand in midair unable to touch where life loved your friend before Lenin seized art for his propaganda. *My* cue, for when it's time to murder Her in *my* story so that I get to live happily ever after dancing with the Woman Who Means What She Moves, is when Baubo starts warming up for her cosmic belly-dancing routine to dance the life out of a woman giving birth. Like I told you in the beginning—Baubo went down with Her. But you didn't follow that cue like you should have, if you were following your soul's instructions wherever they took you, even if it was to the Eleusis on the other side of the pair with Elizabethville.

You, Meem, have given me Gaia Herself, the Dringing song of life itself, making it sing again in Hitler's century. And for that, my humble, heartfelt thanks to you and all your Stokes Sisters who made it possible. You've given this Panther a greater role in the story of creation than ever before. This time, it isn't a life I get to destroy—it's life itself. And all because of you, Summacious.

We made a hell of a team, you and me. I'm actually sorry we have to part ways now. But don't worry: I'll be there inside Gaia's pupil with you before too long. I just have to finish what I came here to do for you.

Thanks for calling.

I lay on the shore, gasping for air, naked and numb. The frigid air hurt my lungs, each gulp a cramp, each gasp another wound. My eyes flitted in and out of blindness until, after I do not know how long, I realized that the trees above me and the stars beginning to show themselves inside their branches were dry. I had the sensation of an immense dream having moved through my cells, a dream in which I died.

I stood up. I wrapped a towel around me and slowly made my way to my car. There I put a sweatshirt and sweatpants on over my frozen, damp body. I turned on the heat full blast and began driving. In my rearview mirror, the sign for Elizabethville retreated behind me.

Which way to Eleusis? I asked myself.

It was at that moment that I caught sight of Manda slipping into the trees and starting to run. And where numb and death had been, I had but one feeling surging through my entire being: to get to Baubo before the Panther did.

I raced down Route 9, passing through a small town called Red Hook with the familiar sensation that Manda was running in the same groove with me, both of us inside Gaia's channel. *Follow their cues,* I heard the Woman Who Means What She Moves telling me, and I surrendered to the only guide who had the power to lead me to Lexy: Manda. I drove with no other sense of purpose than to follow the path I sensed the Panther was taking inside the trees, letting her lead me in the dance and to practice this Nazi waltz step of having hope in my eyes when there was none.

I was not surprised to find myself driving on River Road, toward the bridge. I made the turn to cross over, feeling Manda crossing with me. By the time I arrived at the Y and pulled into the parking lot, I was dizzy with weakness and cold. I was not good at improvising this part of the plot; hoping when I had none was a new, difficult art, and my mind and my cells rebelled. My mind was saying, None of this is happening, go back to the cottage and go to sleep and forget this all ever happened. My cells were saying, After all this time of teaching us how to be cold, why do we have to practice being warm now? We need a script.

There is no script.

Then how do we know how to do this?

You don't. That's the whole point: We don't know how to be warm. We wanted to be a barren sister. But we've changed our mind.

Who, we?

I'm not sure myself, but I have a hunch that it's we Sisters. We Stokes Sisters and we Rulla-Baubo Sisters, all stuck inside asylums up and down the Main Street of this green valley in America. Which is how come we're here. To try to find Baubo before Manda does. The Queen of the Y—she matters. She matters to the story of creation.

Betty raised her eyebrows when she saw me. "Now, how'd you do that neat trick?"

"What trick?"

"Being all wet on your way in, instead of on the way out."

I drowned.

"So, how about this weather, huh? Weird. Hey—where's your friend? She hasn't been here in ages. Her stuff's still here. There's this rule. I gotta watch my you-know-what. I have to give up a basket, owner doesn't come three months consecutive. You take her stuff off my hands?"

"Sure," I said.

Betty went to fetch my basket. She returned with it and my friend's workout clothes in a plastic Kmart bag, folded neatly, her shoes turned

upside down on top. "Normally, I'd keep her basket for her. But I got myself into sort of some trouble. I think you should know. That woman, she
went and told them about Rulla living here. Reported her to the authorities. I don't like her, I don't mind telling you. Not on account of what she
did to me, you understand. I'm okay."

"Where'd Rulla go?" My voice quivered.

Betty shrugged her huge, bony shoulders. "Who knows? I told her,
that woman, I told her she was throwing Rulla out on the street. What
did she care? Between you and me," Betty leaned in close, "there's
Christians and there's Christians, you get my meaning? I tell that
woman, where's her sense of charity? Fssshhhhht," Betty snorted. "I figured, summer, Rulla'd be fine. But this weather . . . I don't know."

"You're a good woman, Betty," I said.

"I'm a sucker is the truth. I didn't have an easy time, you know. I'm
not complaining. I'm not saying anything except, I know. I know what it
is to have nothing, you know what I mean? She got nothing, Rulla. She
got less than nothing."

I looked at the door of the senior women's locker room. "Anybody in
there?"

"It's the six o'clock prenatal water aerobics. Steam room's open, but
the whirlpool is closed for repairs."

How slowly and gracefully they moved in the water, the pregnant
women, the weight of their huge bellies lifted as they bounced, elegant in
their easy, gravid lumbering, moving in one great mass of feminine flesh,
their feet bouncing them off, lifting their bellies upward, and then,
slowly, coming down as they moved through water to the music, elegant
hippopotami. Floating in fluid as life floated in fluid within, they danced
to a gently pulsating tune, lifted their arms up and over, then back, liquid
dancers. The waters swirled around their huge bellies in soft, tidal swells
in rhythm to the music as they turned around, moving through densities
of waters. On either side of their circle in the shallow end of the pool,
swimmers did laps, moving in rapid lines back and forth while the mothers continued their gentle tidal dancing.

I returned to the locker room and waited until they flowed in, bellies
first, the sounds of their voices filling up the silence. I pretended to be get-

ting ready for a workout as I posted myself at my locker, giving myself a full view of the mirror. The secretaries from the aerobics class flocked in, their chirruping, lively voices adding to the softer melodies of the mothers exchanging confidences. The mothers clung to each other, moving through the locker room as a solid mass, touching each other in the way pregnant women do, comfortable with the merging of flesh, boundaries enfolding themselves back into the seamless web of life, skin within skin, as the secretaries whirred around them in a frantic motion of schedules, each one a separate entity moving in time to industry. They went one by one to the mirror, fixing mascara, rubbing in foundation, as the mothers completed the day's migratory route, den to watering hole to den. The secretaries brushed dyed and permed hair into place and raised themselves on tiptoe to examine the fit of their clothes, then flitted away, one by one.

I went through the labyrinth of tiled halls past the whirlpool, drained, the concrete cracks darkly veined with new mortar and sealant, till I reached the steam room. Outside, a bright new sign had been posted, red plastic etched in white letters: LIGHT SHOULD REMAIN ON AT ALL TIMES TO AVOID INJURY. I looked through the portal at the billowing white vapors, my body filling up with the fog of despair at history repeating itself in our blind eyes.

Hope where there is none, I said to myself, is what hope *is*.

As I passed by Betty, she said, "You just watched, didn't you? I do that sometimes. Watch those mothers-to-be in the water."

I stared at Betty. There are things you can say, when you're dead, that you wouldn't dare say if you were alive. "You know that beautiful redhead?"

"The really beautiful one?" Betty grinned ruefully. "Not like the rest of us pretenders."

"She had the baby yet?"

"It's time. Ol' Betty can tell. They get kind of soft all around the edges, especially their eyes."

I drove home, my heart pierced. As I was crossing the bridge to my side of the river, I almost continued on straight, past my turnoff down River Road. Straight ahead of me lay Stockbridge, the Ark and Marek, who could touch me and change my story from murder to a love story. Thinking only of his touch, I passed the turnoff for River Road, heading for the brilliantly lit intersection where the hoods of the cars glowed in the light perpetual of this world of Eaners. All I had to do was stay on the road, straight through the intersection, and reach the man who had carried me into the Ark.

I would have gone to him but for the knowledge that she was loose, somewhere in the trees, in this unseasonable cold. I couldn't escape to my own Ark of love on the other side of Eaner territory with the Panther loose, risking another twenty-seven-thousand-year murder spree of all the sisters on earth who want to mean what they move inside the dance of life. I turned at Route 9G, south toward Rhinebeck. Manda, show up, damn it, I said silently to myself. Show yourself so I can follow your lead.

I passed Del's Soft Ice Cream Stand, usually busy in August—empty, owing to the freak chill. Benjamin's face filled my eyes and heart as I saw him licking vanilla with glee as he was last summer. I slowed down for the light at Mr. Bert's smoke shop, Freddie's wooden rainbow god keeping vigil as he has silently done throughout this entire story. Was it my desperate imagination? Or was the rainbow god pointing south, in the direction I was driving? I moved through the intersection, passing The Beekman Arms, stately and indifferent as Riggs to the fate of its visitors. I kept on the road, heading south to my cottage, cursing Manda for being invisible inside the trees, challenging her to come forward and show herself for our long delayed battle.

The abandoned stone house with the sign, Zoned for Antiques, came into view on my right. At sight of it, I recalled, as if freshly hatched, my determination to construct blood-proof walls to keep the other Rhinebeck from emerging in the space in between fiction and life. I slowed down, my heart pounding. I was in the gap, the slit, the space, where the other Rhinebeck emerges and the trick of evolution happens— if Manda had been telling me the truth when I was drowning. Was this Eleusis? Is that the name of the region between life and fiction where evolution is possible?

On the hill to my right, away from the river, stood the church where Freddie Van Heusen had wailed and wailed in unabashed rage against the death of his sister in madness, his friend in prison, Moongirl, Sister. Freddie, incarnated not as Melina Mercuri playing Medea, the bright blonde hair, black-kohl-rimmed eyes. The strains of the tune the actress carries with her wherever she goes, the *plinka-plinka-plinka-plinka* of the Greek lyre plucking out the theme song, "Never on Sunday," began to sound in my mind. With the plaintive melody came the inevitable vision of Mercuri dancing, her long legs, her striped top, dancing with free sensuality, in celebration of her erotic being, on the craggy streets of a harbor with the Greek sailors gathered around her. And then, where her long legs were dancing on Greek ground, I saw my mother's long legs on American ground, dancing in our living room in Washington, D.C., to the same tune, while a war in a foreign Asian jungle exploded inside our house. My father, in his high government post, sits night after night and day after day at long tables with dark-suited men around the president, trying to stop the bombs that have the power to kill his own son.

My mother dances, in spontaneous celebration of her feminine beauty, tracing out the steps of the Greek folk dance with her elegant, narrow feet, bare, on the living-room rug.

My father grits his mouth at dinner, mumbles something about, "He can't hear, Johnson, he's got these enormous ears and they can't hear a damn thing." I tremble, looking across the dinner table at my brother.

My mother dances, nothing will stop her from dancing in celebration of her radiant vitality, a woman in her prime, voluptuous, willowy, sensual, as the deaf tyrant continues dropping the bombs no matter how much my father tries to reason with him.

And my mother dances, dances until the seed is planted inside her vigilant rhinoceros girl, watching her mother's unquenchable vitality and beauty, the seed of hope that someday she will shed her rhinoceros skin and her nearsighted rhinoceros eyes and her stupid turned-up snouty nose and her clunky hooves and her big rump, and she will become this amazing creature before her, this curvaceous, soft, radiant being who can dance in pure exaltation (as the bombs continue, strange syllables erupting inside the familiar words of my native English, My Lai, Tet, Hanoi). Nothing stops my mother from loving life with her body, alive to the music, not even a war that could turn her beloved husband into their own son's murderer and did turn her daughter into a grieving, guilty, tormented young woman who could not bring herself even to try to dance with Her—

Dance, Sister, dance, and all the vital beauty a woman is will be yours.

Crash, car. Crash, and all the magic my brother sees in me will stay here.

I pulled over to the side of the road and stopped. I was benumbed by memory, dizzy and spent from swimming in trees all my adult life. I should have wept; I did not. The ordeal in the pond in Elizabethville, the horror of Manda, the eruption of the war that had destroyed my brother's beautitude and beaten, fully, my hope of dancing with Her and believing in my own beautitude, till all I had left of Her was an impenetrable barrenness of spirit and body alike, had wearied me beyond grief. I was the one who felt she had been swimming in trees twenty-seven thousand years, chasing, chasing, chasing after the beautitude of an American brother and sister who had been murdered in our story of war, our time in history.

Night deepened around me as I sat in my car, feeling nothing. As lost as I had been to myself before diving into the pond, I now knew that I yet had a destination. The desire to die had moved me through the back roads to Elizabethville, a place on the actual map of the Hudson Valley I had never seen or even knew existed. I had been conducted there by forces for which I do not have a name. "It," the patient had said to me in the asylum in Vermont, "it" comes to those who mean what they move. And I had meant to move toward death.

What had made me surface? I asked myself, sitting in the in-between, off the side of the road. In my beaten, numb state, I believed it was a mistake. For I had surfaced on the same side, the side of the beaten, fully, no alchemy having taken place, no soul journey through death to beautitude on the other side. After twenty-seven thousand years of swimming in trees, beautitude was as elusive to my soul as ever, and I still unable to master the art of evolution to find hope where there is none. I glanced up the hill at the stone church, the memory of Freddie Van Heusen wailing about Moongirl mingling with the story Manda had revealed to me while I was dying underwater. Freddie's Moongirl, Gwen's niece, Lexy—each one a sister born in the Rhinebeck of a young boy's schizophrenia, a frail woman's dream, a broken sister's guilt, and an ugly daughter's despair. She, this Rhinebeck Sister Freddie and Gwen and I had in common, was the being Manda was stalking to kill. Had Manda been telling me the truth when she said this Rhinebeck Sister of madness, dream, grievous guilt, and dispossessed hope was at this very moment giving birth? And was I responsible? The part of me that was grateful I was cold, the part of me that meant to be cold, sought barrenness, craved sterility, refused to let life love me again, the part of me that would not stop swimming in trees beside my brother, holding close to his eyes which could see the way life loved me and called it by its real name, magic. I was the Stokes Sister who had poured her guilt and despair into Her cells, and they had responded to Her toxic medicine by creating the coldness in me I desired, I had refused to live the life I am here, alive, living—and given the power to create life itself over into the Panther's murder plot.

My heart pounded furiously, as though it were trying to get me to hear the sound of the pulse inside me, to make me believe in that ancient drumming of the oldest human song, and the newest. Manda said that I had given her the power of life itself because I didn't want it. This was the improvisation, the new script, the bonus that Manda had not enjoyed for twenty-seven thousand years—to have the power to destroy the power to create life—not the creation, the already made, but the urge toward life, the movement of the cells to dance inside life. I had given that to her. Everyone else just gave her *a* life. But I gave her the making of it.

But if I could give the making of life, the dancing toward it, over to Manda, then I must still have the power inside me to make life. I must still have in me whatever "it" is that makes us dance into life, even when every other part of us seeks to move toward death. The moving into the dance of life was a dance still within me that yet could happen and—if Manda was telling the truth—was happening, in spite of my body moving me to the pond in Elizabethville to die. "It" had made me surface; not I. Even if I would not dance, life was still dancing, anyway, toward me. *She* was still dancing through the grief, through the horror, through the murder, through the wars, through the bombs, through the guilt, through the anguish—and through my own absolute cold. It took surrendering my willful ego to death before It could break through and propel me to the surface.

Energy swept through me. It was as though my spirit, which had been drenched in the desire to die, were ignited by a spark that I did not know I had. Somewhere in the Rhinebeck in between, where madness, murder, and despair lived, there was a Sister about to give birth to what I, myself, had killed—the way life loved me.

But where? I looked all around, and then, directly ahead of me, I saw the driveway to Gwen's house. Gwen. She lived in the in-between where form happens.

I still did not know how her dream, on the bridge, ended.

Gwen opened the door to her strange little upstairs house. When she saw me, her face lit up. "I knew you'd come to see me today," she said.

"A dream?" I offered, a cue to my objective.

"I went to the dry cleaner and they asked me if these were mine? They were about to donate them to charity," she said, turning around. She picked up my pants from the funeral, covered in thin plastic skin from the dry cleaner. "And now you're here! Life," she said. Then she took in my appearance, which I frankly cannot imagine. "I was just about to eat dinner. I have plenty," she said. "I made a big soup—weird, to be making soup in August. But it's so cold."

The walls sparkled with fresh new paint. The dingy curtains had been replaced with new ones. And Gwen's voice had found the one resonance inside that mistral of shame, the single note on which she could fasten her body. She babbled on as we ate the soup, explaining the cheer within (and the cold without) as the consequence of the shifting of planets. She said the word "trine" many times, her new damp voice alighting on the word whose meaning I did not understand except through the music she was making that she could not make before. Pluto, she said, had been trining some house of hers, but that was over, thank god, and now the planets were lining up with Gemini, which was good news for her.

I said, "With all due respect to the stars, Gwen, my own theory is a certain good-looking chief of police."

I had not heard Gwen laugh before. Her laugh reminded me of the bells of the Washington National Cathedral, where I had first been kissed by my rhinoceros husband, which would sound, suddenly, when you least expected them, issuing over the roofs of the houses and spilling into our neighborhood—a sudden, spontaneous, cascading melody.

"He can't believe he's in love with an astrologer. But it's in his chart. It's absolutely there. You can see it. It's the Taurus in him, making him into the police chief. Taurus and Virgo. But he has all this Pisces all over the place; it drives him nuts! And," Gwen's eyes sparkled with delight, "his moon is in Scorpio! It makes him an incredible lover."

She made tea, which we had in her living room, where a fire glowed in a fireplace I didn't recall seeing before. She sat down on the couch and nestled in, curling her long legs under her. She waited. I didn't know how to introduce the subject with grace or courtesy. With this new joyousness in Gwen, it felt awkward to ask her for the rest of her dream and take her back to the time of her grief, in the middle of this surprise trick of joy from her mischievous stars. Cruel and unfair.

Gwen said, "Did you find your teacher?" I was startled. She went on, "In your palm it said that a teacher would show up."

Manda had been telling the truth about that, then, too? "What did the teacher bring me?"

"Your life line breaks in two," Gwen said.

This was Manda's gift?

"And then, when it joins up again, all the other lines flow into it." Gwen shook her head. "Nuts, isn't it? All this astrology. Palmistry. That's what you're thinking, isn't it?"

"I have a hard time with systems," I said. And then, amazed at my own words, I said, "I only trust improvisation."

Gwen nodded. "The stars, they hold it all still for me. They contain the messages, the strange visions. I just use them to sort out what comes at me from all over, inside and out. What I told you, when was it? A year ago? Not quite. This weather, it's so confusing. Could have been all wrong. I think the most I do is plant a seed in someone, about what their destiny might be. A foundation for their own improvisation. It's hit or miss, really. All of it."

"I didn't come here for the stars," I said, finding my opening, wondering if she had known I needed it and deftly supplied it for me to slide through.

"Well, no, you wouldn't. Your eyes, they're earth eyes."

"They're my grandmother's eyes," I said. "She was a poet and a potter. She went mad." I sighed. "I don't want to upset your new life," I said. "But I need to know how that dream ended. At the risk of sounding quite nuts myself," I said, "I think I'm stuck in the middle of your dream. The one about—"

"My sister." Gwen nodded, slowly, thoughtfully. She dropped her head and studied her hands in her lap. Then she raised her blue crescent eyes to me and said, "What made you call her my sister?"

"I come from this strange family where all the women call themselves Sister." I said. "It isn't political, and most of the actual sisters don't even like each other. In fact, they hate each other. But if you are a Stokes woman, you are a sister, regardless of whether you are loved or hated. Even mothers and daughters, they call themselves Sister in my mother's family."

Gwen seemed to drift away for a while. Then she said, "There's no way of knowing, then, is there?"

"Knowing what?"

"If any of the sisters in your family are sisters who shouldn't be. It could be a lie, hiding a terrible secret. Or it could be protecting yourself. It works both ways."

"I think my dream was trying to tell me that if I had been more like a sister in spirit, my niece would never have fallen and died."

Gwen did not recognize the bridge in her dream. It was just a bridge. Suddenly, she said, it began to move. "It sort of wiggled and turned into this sea serpent, this horrible monster, ocean snake," and the Sister (as she called her) was trying to hold on as it began to rise and fall, in ripples. It seemed as though the snake were trying to throw her off, as if it were deliberate. Gwen saw herself watching this horrible battle between the serpent and the Sister, and then, suddenly, there were two serpents, coiling around, the Sister between them as the two-headed beast carried the Sister and the bridge upward.

Gwen was running to catch the Sister, she said, because she knew she was going to fall. Gwen watched in horror as the two mouths of the beast opened on either side of the Sister to devour her. Gwen yelled at the top of her lungs, "Jump! I'll catch you! Jump!"

"And she jumped," Gwen said, tears forming at the shores of her blue eyes. "I ran toward her falling body to catch her. But the bridge disappeared beneath me. I yelled at her not to jump, there was no bridge, I couldn't catch her. But she had already jumped. I reached out for her, just to hold her with me as we both fell. But I had no arms," she whispered inside the husk of her despair. "I had no arms. I must have made myself wake up before the bridge totally disappeared out from under me."

We sat in silence, the only sound the fire. After a while, Gwen rose and tended it, expertly turning the log. The flames caught, and Gwen replaced the fire screen. She returned to the couch and looked at me. "I still believe that it was a message telling me that her healing would not be complete, she would not be made whole, until I held her in my arms. Her official diagnosis was multiple personality," Gwen said. "The dream was telling me that I was the medicine she needed. But I didn't have a bridge to her to get me to her so I could hold her and heal her."

I stared at her.

"You can't see it? It's the symbol for medicine. The two serpents— it's the medical symbol. Ascepalus, Apollo's son, ruled over a sacred temple with snakes. Snakes appear wherever healing's required," she said. "Trans-formation, true healing. The shedding of the skin that snakes do is the symbol for dying to the illness, not to death. The healer's art." Gwen looked back to the fire. "But I didn't have the arms or a bridge to become the medicine a sister needed," she said. She raised her eyes and looked at me. "Is that any help to you?"

It was late. I was spent, yet restless, as I stood outside Gwen's small house. I knew how the dream ended now: a failed healing. An incomplete medicine, death the consequence, no bridge. But all my bridges so far have disappeared out from under me, I thought.

I stood under the vaulted canopy of encroaching dark, my mind bending itself around and inside out to bring my murder mystery to an end. But if I had learned anything in the nine months of dancing with the Panther, it was that I was lousy at murder mysteries. Whenever I went into the plot of The Murder Mystery, instead of adding another clue to a line leading to the inevitable end, my plot went in circles, contradicted itself, spun out in different directions, radiating, shrinking, until it finally came to a stop. I needed to grow a bridge out of nothing if I were ever to reach beautitude on the side of Eleusis, and escape being beaten, fully, in Elizabethville. And I needed arms I did not have to catch my soul as it fell down, for Eleusis was happening in Rhinebeck now, and Manda was trying to get there before me to bring the plot of The Murder Mystery to end her way.

It was cold. The weather report had said something about an Arctic stream blowing directly through the valley in a freak warp off the Canadian tundra. Tundra, I said again to myself, feeling something stir inside me. Tundra . . . freak. What sort of a pair was this? Freak . . . monster . . . *monsters, unfinished continents in the wrong place, alphabets I can't decipher . . . this Russian book about tundra . . . anatomy is new territory to me.* Manda's words floated to me on the Arctic air, cataloging the books in the ancestral home where my Great Whatever Mother had walked to her death. It struck me now as a bizarre thing to be talking about at such a moment—books in my great-uncle's library as I was dying? What had made Manda even bother? And she had even sounded urgent, I now recalled. "Did I mention," she had said, "this Russian book about tundra? I think it was Cyrillic—anatomy is new territory to me." Russian anatomy, a foreign territory, an alphabet Manda did not know how to read. *You say my name like a Hungarian woman, this is wonderful!* Marek and his mother and father, and Mihalyi, who is the King of the Land of the Drings, their native language was on the same branch of the tree of language as Russian. Another tree, I thought. If I can get into a different branch on the universal tree of language, then I can get into a territory Manda cannot penetrate, decipher, understand, an anatomy beyond her. A different story. What was the Russian book about tundra my great-uncle had?

My body went electric as I saw the book inside my eyes. The book about the tundra had been removed from the ancestral home a long time ago. Manda had been lying to me, but it was a Cretan sort of a lie, for the book had been there, that place was its source. After my grandmother's death, the book had come into my mother's hands, and now it lay on a table beside my parents' bed. There was a family story, designed to confirm my mother's eccentricity inherited from her mother, about how my mother had traded the valuable first-edition Audubon in order to have in her possession this slim blue volume in Cyrillic, an alphabet she could not even read. But at the time of my grandmother's death, when her notebook of poetry was bequeathed to me, I was studying Russian, and I could read the book.

What I was remembering that was sending spasms of energy through my despondent self was when my mother had asked me to read the title of the book to her. We went to her bedroom, where she handed me the well-worn book, frayed at the edges, the spine battered, the seams loose. I read the title out loud. I was hard pressed to translate it until I read the name of the author, and then I knew immediately what the book was.

"It's a famous book," I said. "The author was the Russian Darwin. It's his theory about how evolution depends on mutual aid—that's the way the title is usually translated. It completely contradicts Darwin's theory. The species that depend on each other, support each other across their differences, are the ones that survive."

Tears welled up in my mother's eyes, and she slowly shook her head back and forth, her face wearing an expression of poignancy I could never forget. "It was your grandmother's most beloved book, and I never knew why until now. It was given to her by a woman your grandmother always described as the most beautiful woman she knew. She gave it to her when your grandmother went mad."

"Mad?" I said, shocked. "Grandmother went mad?"

Tears were streaming down my mother's face, and it was a long time before the story of my grandmother's madness came out. The entire time she spoke of her mother's illness and institutionalization, she held this book against her, embracing it, and without any awareness at all, she rocked back and forth, as though the book were an infant she was cradling. When she finished her tale, she closed her eyes, holding the book against her body. Then she said, "What was it called again?"

On Mutual Aid. I was about to tell her about the fate of the scientist who wrote it when my mother lifted the book from her breast and said, "This is what she said gave her hope. This book. And she couldn't read a word of it. But a beautiful woman, the most beautiful woman, she always said—long red hair, bright green eyes, I met her when I was a very little girl, and I've never forgotten her either. This light about her. This life. This energy. Passion. She told Sister this book had hope inside it. And it must have. Because she did come back, my mother. She survived her demons. And she wrote beautiful poetry," my mother said. "Which she asked me to give to you."

I remained silent, stunned by the knowledge that a book by a man who was assassinated by Lenin had given my grandmother hope that she would survive psychosis. And not a word of it could she read. Then my mother handed me my grandmother's notebook of poetry.

The tundra breath blew over me, and I had the strangest sensation that it was Manda. *You, Summacious, you are the magnet turned the wrong way. Your destiny's so not happy it's almost communism in disguise,* I could almost hear her whispering again to me as she had what seemed to be many lifetimes ago. I had to turn myself around, the sister-magnet which locked me to my brother inside a tyrant's war, and cross over to the other tree of my ancestry, where an unreadable book had taken my grandmother to Eleusis, out of the death of the soul we call madness into a writer of poetry. I had to do something like make an unreadable story out of The Murder Mystery if I were finally to leave the tree where I was swimming beside a death that had more names than I knew death could have, and swim in the tree where my destiny lay.

And no bridge would take me there that would not crumble on me halfway. I had to leap across the Great Pass.

I shivered. I walked to the car, with no other thought than to get out of the cold and into someplace warm. No foreign theories of evolution, no unreadable alphabets, no disintegrating bridges—basic, bodily warmth. As I got in the car, I saw my friend's things in the back seat. I'll go to town, I told myself, and return them to her. Her upstairs apartment was always overheated by the widow who lived below turning up the thermostats. The widow was always cold; my friend always hot. I turned on my headlights as I pulled out onto Route 9, heading toward town. The sign Zoned for Antiques jumped into view, the abandoned stone house behind it. My headlights illumined the stone sides of the house, revealing their color, a reddish hue. I had seen a similar red stone as decoration on an elaborate gatehouse on River Road. The association spawned another, as I realized that this same warm reddish stone had been used to build the Carmelite Retreat on River Road, where nuns kept a silent order. Sisters, I thought. Where the Sisters live, who are not. Women gathered together inside stone as they were at the Y. Whether this sturdy, simple building here, in the emergent space of dreamtime Rhinebeck, between fiction and life where evolution may happen, had ever been part of the Carmelite Sisters' original property, I don't know. My friend would, I could not help but think. She knew all the old maps of this region.

I was seeking warmth, that is all; but instead of going to town, halfway there I was called to move toward the ruinous stone of a house that had, perhaps, once belonged to silent Sisters beside a river, conjoined in passionate prayer. Whatever roads might have led there had long since grown over, past the point of being able to see them with my own eyes. I would have to traverse the ravine and go through the underbrush, no path to guide me as the light fell behind the riverbank. I thought for a moment about leaving my headlights on, when the same force that was calling me to go to the house seemed to instruct me to move toward it in utter darkness. I turned off my headlights and got out of the car.

The ravine fell sharply down. I tripped, barely caught my balance. The brambles stuck to me, and the roots and rutted ground wreaked havoc on my ankles and knees. Thorns caught and tore at skin and clothes. I put my foot out, and I felt nothing. I looked up, the craggy shadows of the stone house barely readable against the night sky. I jumped, grabbing onto black air before landing on the other side of the ravine, sliding on loose dry earth as my fingers grabbed at invisible threads of roots and vines to haul my body up. I closed my hand around a nettle and yelped in pain.

Inside, I took out my ever-present smoker's matches and struck a light.

Nests take their shape from the mothers who build them, holding in their architecture the imperatives of survival as a mother has imagined need. A mother knows she must survive for her young to survive. There is no difference; life is mutual for herself and her offspring. For Rulla, little was required other than a worn Persian carpet, so threadbare that the pattern was but a shadow in the warp and woof of the loom, the residue of the vegetable dyes leaving the barest outline and hint of color on the sinew of its threads. The best and thickest part of the carpet, the section that still had some nap and fur, she had cut up and stitched into a muumuu, the same one she had worn the night she danced with Santa Claus. In a corner, on a makeshift rack, I saw white towels with the Kingston Y insignia on them, and beside those the same plastic baskets that held my and my friend's gear in the lockers. I walked over to them.

They were all broken somewhere; Betty's excuse, I thought, for charity. Inside the baskets were scarves, the ones she wore around her head when she danced, the golden thread frayed, mixed up with cuttings from newspapers in an alphabet I could not read. A dress lay in shreds, the dress my friend had bought Rulla for the opening.

Her body was curled up, in fetal position, in a corner on an old mattress, caught in a wedge of shadow between windows. She was naked. All the roseate pink had drained from her skin. I touched a strand of her hair. It broke off.

I sat beside her for a few eternities, through many eclipses of the moon in midday frightening the inhabitants of the earth foretelling the end of the world.

Baubo went down with her. It was a sad, sad time.

Manda was sitting on my couch when I returned. Smoke twisted up from her curled lips. "I didn't really want it to get this far. I mean, killing Baubo, I never intended to do that. But when you didn't do what you were supposed to do in the pond in Elizabethville, I had no choice." Manda stomped out her cigarette butt. "You're supposed to be dead, Summacious."

"I am, Manda."

I went outside and retrieved Benjamin's twigs from the woodpile. Special fire, Benjamin had said. To keep you warm and stop the sky from having to do your crying for you. I held Benjamin's twigs and stood for a moment in the night, gathering courage for the task ahead. A sickle moon, pelvic shore of my own battered womb, hung in the sky. I was relieved to see the crescent shape of woman, not the full round one, for it gave me the courage to believe that the cosmos approved of what I was about to do. The moon was a rhyme with the story I was living, and the language etched on the skin of the cosmos, I now believe, indecipherable as that ancient earth alphabet is to the modern mind. Yet it remains the sign that we are living our story truthfully, in synchrony with the way life wants us to live it.

I returned to the cottage, avoiding Manda's glare. I put the twigs beside the fireplace and began to lay Benjamin's special fire. My lips were shaking, and I watched my hands as though they belonged to someone else. I kept telling myself that it was the only way, the crescent moon my only assurance. Manda watched, smoking, silent, as I took Benjamin's twigs and laid them over the others in the fireplace. I had no plan, no strategy, no understanding. All I was doing with Benjamin's special fire was praying. I had nothing left but a prayer that there is warmth and I could find it in the medicine a child had brought me.

I struck the match and threw it in. The fire blazed high and bright and powerful. I stared at it, and then, without thinking or understanding, I crossed the room to my desk. I began gathering up the yellow pages of the manuscript of The Murder Mystery.

"Summacious? What are you doing?"

"Making an unreadable book out of our story," I said.

"I don't get it."

"You didn't walk down Main Street, Manda. But I did." As I carried the stack of newsprint over to the fire, I said, "Only a book you cannot read is hope, if you're a Stokes Sister. And I am a Stokes Sister, and I don't have any hope, Manda. Not after finding Rulla dead. And I've got to figure out some way to make hope where there is none. And this is the only way that fits, that fits the story I'm stuck in with you."

I knelt before the fire, stalling, my heart pounding. Make the book unreadable, I told myself. Do it. It is the only shape hope takes in this story.

I heard Manda's voice behind me saying, "Summacious, how many times do I have to tell you? *I* got stuck in *your* murder mystery."

I spun around in fury. "You were out there waiting for me to call," I spat out at her. "And when I did, you ran here so fast, you were so excited, because you had heard someone on my side calling you into a story." I beat on the manuscript of The Murder Mystery in rage as my voice blasted at her. "It is *you,* Manda, *you* who wanted this story to become a murder mystery," I said, pounding on my fiction. "*You* who needed me to give you a thrill ride inside *my* mortality, *my* power to die, my human fate to become ashes, my love story with barrenness. Because you can't resist torture and war and murder and death and disease and the cessation of life in any and all forms. Only when you immortal freaks of dreamtime can get yourselves inside a human plot do you get the vicarious experience of hope. Burial plot, Manda, graveyard plot and narrative plot, asylum asylum, your trick pairs on the spelling test, the ones that are spelled identically but are the opposite. Your bonus Main Street trick spelling pairs. Your Main Street, Manda, your Main Street in eternity doesn't have those pairs. It's all the same on your Main Street. So you cross over the Great Pass to get to Main Street on our side. We are your asylum, Manda, we alive, suffering, hurting, sick, out-of-our-minds, loving, losing human beings you call 'blood bags.' Our human, mortal, story-making ancestral blood is your sanctuary from the interminable boredom of pulseless eternity. Bloodless eternity doesn't have any stories in it, and you can't stand it. You use us and use us and use us, driving us mad when you do, creating story plots from the plot of our inevitable burial in the earth. You are the one who lusted for a human tale of death for me to write and live and dance and perform for you, here in my green valley of Sisters with my Main Street running through it all the way from Elizabethville to Stockbridge. You ran here as fast as you did because I was in the middle of a good story, Manda, a really good story—a *love* story about Sisters in a secret realm of Eternal Dew and mystical steam—and it was you who wanted it to be a murder story, Manda. You who wanted to kill Lexy, the Law of the Y. Because only if there is death in the story do you get your taste of spring."

Manda had not moved the entire time I screamed at her. She said, "You throw The Murder Mystery into the fire, Summacious, and you turn Lexy to ashes."

I stared at the fire, the manuscript beside me on the floor. But no heat came into me or from me. As hot as I had been before, that was how cold I was, spent by my outburst. A chill seized me, and it was a deadly stillness all about me as I said to Manda, "This is an American story you ran into, Manda, complete with its very own Main Street. And in America, murder is the medium."

I gathered a sheaf of papers into my hands and held them against my breasts as my mother had held the unreadable book of hope against hers. "Your teacher is waiting, Meem."

Tears streamed down my face as I saw Rulla again, dead, in the abandoned stone house. Sitting beside her as the world came to an end, all I could think of was the Y, Rulla's realm. The senior women's locker room of the Y filled my eyes, that locked chamber where the real bodies of women gather together to dance, swim, jiggle, shimmy, soak, steam, flirt, kick, slide, lift, stretch, do whatever movement it is that makes them feel the life loving them when their bodies love life, all those stretched, scarred, loose bellies which have given birth, the firm, taut ones that have bounced back from giving birth, and the vision of the pregnant women in the water I had feasted my eyes on this very evening—the bellies of women involved in the living and loving and making of life were my Sister medicine, which had the power to make me whole again. The Y was Eleusis; I was already there when Manda showed up, and I didn't know it. And now the Queen of that amazing realm of belly-wise Sisters and the nurturant Dew was dead.

It had taken what little will was left in me not to return to Elizabethville and finish the murder of my own soul which had been interrupted by hope, the hope that It had come to me, that life had loved me anyway, and that I would become a woman who means what she moves on the side of the living again. I sat in the dark beside the dead Queen, in her ruinous tomb where the Selectric had been guiding me all this time inside my story with Manda, and I hated the hope that had made me surface from the pond. I hated hope for finding me when there was none. I hated life itself for being stronger than I was, and dancing in me when I could not. And I hated Manda—not for killing but because she had stalled for so long, torturing me with life all this time, moving into the heart of a rapturous friendship, holding off on the death until that magic Dew of Rulla's steam room took hold inside me and I did feel life loving me again. Enough, just enough, so that Lexy would be created, the Law of the Y embodied, and Manda could kill the mystery of Eleusis itself as it was awakening in a green river valley I called home. I hated the Panther for sending me into the Ark to make love with Marek and experience meaning what I moved with a man and wanting to live, again, and dance, again, inside a man's embrace. Most of all, I hated her for showing up when a boy was cataloging slugs in order to predict how many rainbows he could hope for in the future, and asked me to join him in his world.

I looked over at Manda, who remained on the far side of the room.

I said, "If I hadn't been so convinced that Elizabethville was the only destiny a Stokes Sister had, if I had realized I was in Eleusis already, Rulla would be dancing right now."

"But that's not the story, Summacious, is it?" Manda asked.

I shook my head, holding The Murder Mystery against my body. "No," I said, my voice its own husk, "that's not the story." I almost keeled over as revelation surged through me. The pattern is never obvious until you see your own place in it. For every Sister, there was a tyrant: Medea's Jason, Rulla's shah, Gwen's father, Phosphorescence's Stalin, my friend's Lenin, Lexy's Hitler, and my mother's American president. And so long as I wanted to keep my brother's magic gaze only on me so that I could believe I would, someday, grow up into a beautiful, dancing woman, then *I* was the Nazi in this story. If I had never believed, in my soul, that I had killed the beautitude in my brother, Manda would never have gotten into my story, the living story of my soul's sojourn on earth. Swimming in trees was The Murder Mystery Manda got stuck inside, that mysterious death by another name, when we lose the spirit of an Other, and our spirit goes with them.

I pulled the manuscript of The Murder Mystery away from me and looked at the yellow pages, seeing the yellow BMW before me. The pages were riddled with X's and crossouts and typographical errors and red circles around paragraphs. I studied my unreadable book, and suddenly I laughed. "There are no page numbers," I said.

"What do you expect from somebody who doesn't know how to count her own breaths?" Manda said. "You think such a person has any idea what the sequence is for the story she gets to live on earth? What you call your destiny?"

I shook my head. "This time it's you who are wrong, Manda. My story doesn't go in a straight line. It goes backward into memory, and leaps forward into imagination, and circles back through real life."

"Don't you mean our story, Summacious?"

317

I nodded. "Yes. Our story, Manda. Of who gets to be the one to dance with Her. It's a waltz, Manda. A circling, three-step waltz, our story. The page numbers wouldn't go in a straight line to tell it, even if I had put them in."

I threw one page on the fire.

"Summacious! Lexy's in there! *She* is in there."

I held my breath and threw a few more pages on the fire. They instantly curled in on themselves, forming charred nests inside their own dying. "It's because Lexy is in The Murder Mystery that I have to burn it. It's the only way I can kill the tyrant in me. The murderous tyrant in me who wants Her all to myself. Just like you do."

I threw the rest of the handful on the fire and watched the flames rise into the chimney. The heat from the very walls themselves was making me sweat all over. I took another stack from beside me and said, "I won't fight you anymore for who gets Lexy. Neither one of us will, Manda. The Law of the Y just is. It is, and it is beautiful, and nobody gets to have it for herself to dance with it after all the killing is done and live happily ever after with Her." I threw more of the book on the fire.

"Summacious? You're a liar."

I whirled around to face Manda, pages sliding off my lap, hatred sputtering all over me. "I'm speaking the truth!"

"Cretan liars do that," Manda said.

"I don't understand."

Manda shook her head slowly back and forth. "We both told you—we can't take the test for you."

"Okay, Manda, okay," I spat out at her, furious. "You think I don't know Crete? I know Crete. I've been to Crete. I've been to the cave where Zeus . . ." I stopped.

"Where Zeus what, Summacious?"

"Where Zeus was hidden away," I said, slowly, "by Gaia."

"Go on," Manda said. "Hidden away by Gaia . . ."

"Who was plotting . . ."

"Plotting?"

"Revenge," I said, swallowing hard. "Revenge against Uranus, the star god, for throwing away their children he thought ugly. And Gaia hid

Zeus away, on Crete, until he grew up. Then she sent him after his own father to kill the part of him that could make life."

"And after the killing was all done?" Manda said. "After the killing of the part that can make life, then what happened?"

I looked again at the fire burning my pages. "Venus . . ." I fumbled. "The goddess of love. Venus was born from the foam of death in the sea. Love was born from revenge. Hatred. Murder. By life," I said.

"Good story," Manda said. "Don't you think so, Summacious? I don't know why your kind keeps calling it a lie."

"We don't want to believe it's true, Manda."

"Explain, Meem."

"We want to believe that *we* make beauty. That we are the creators of it. The creatures on earth who make art," I said, looking down at my sterile fiction, my novel about a murder in Rhinebeck which was supposed to have brought me literary recognition. A pang went through me. I could not help it; I thought the book had promise. I closed my eyes, this time, as I forced myself to throw away some beautiful prose, some inventive plot twists, some interesting story making.

"The patient in Queen Isabel's Land of Linoleum had it right all along, didn't she, Summacious? About the Woman Who Means What She Moves."

I nodded, moving away from the increasing heat of the fire, the burnt pages of art flaking away, their ashes flitting about like the skeletons of ancient moths in search of a tomb.

"Finish the spelling test, Summacious."

"It comes to you," I said to Manda, though my eyes were fixed on the fire turning my creation to ashes. "But it can't come until life has beaten you fully. Give up the power to create life your way, decide for yourself what is beautiful. And that is why I have to burn this book. I have to let go of the part of me that makes life, whether it is the life inside a womb, inside a heart, inside a mind, a soul, an imagination. I have to kill my claim to authority over life, to let beautitude, love, and beauty be born in the story of my life. If it ever does.

"I don't know what will happen after I burn this," I went on. "I only know I have to burn the story with Lexy inside it, for She is the part of me that makes life, the making dancing part of me. Her. But—Sister Stokes opened the kiln. She opened the kiln a lot of times, and found only ashes. She hoped for the oxblood in between every time."

Manda was absolutely still. She stood at attention. Her expression was blank. She held my eyes in hers—hidden—yet I let her hold me in her obscure gaze until it seemed she had held me long enough to know that I had, at last, come to the end of our story. Then I said what must be said, if I were to escape swimming in trees forever. "Thank you, Manda, for coming when I called."

She nodded, and a hint of a smile came to her mouth. But I could feel her ebbing away from me, her spirit departing now that she had done her job.

Manda then did what I only now realize she never did, ever, while we were in hock to a song of murder in a fairy-tale cottage in the woods: She turned her back to me. I stared at her back for a long time, until I could no longer remember the face on the other side.

I looked down at the page I was about to throw into the fire. It was the unfinished scene with Moms and Manda in jail. The colander rested between them. Moms's hands were in her purse, on Mihalyi's scissors. I kept the incomplete scene in my lap as I stared at the fire, as if to draw into my own eyes from its warmth the courage to survive what I was about to see.

"I'm ready now," Manda said.

I turned slowly.

Manda's hair was cropped short. I made myself look into her eyes. Manda's eyes carried inside them the murderous rage of Gaia, her mica-flecked anger at the star god for rejecting her creations as not beautiful enough. I made myself look at Her furious eyes in Manda's face, the shorn hair giving Manda the aspect of martyr, prisoner, nun, concentration-camp victim, witch about to fail the test of drowning, terminal cancer patient. Yet more than all these aspects, the shorn head was the near naked head of the child when it first slips from Her channel into the peril of history. I was looking at the face and head of the novice, the initiate.

"It's time I joined Moms and her prairie moon."

I looked out the window. The sickle moon hung in the trees.

320

Manda followed my gaze. "That moon is your moon. But Moms's moon is double that size. And it's always over Chicago."

"I have to let you go west, then," I said.

Manda nodded. "West," she repeated.

I took the pages of the scene with Moms and threw them one by one onto the fire. As I watched the fire gather its raging lips around the paper and open its jaws to consume my words, I began to whisper.

Out.

Out of me.

I mouthed the words slowly and quietly at first, but as the flames leapt up the small chimney, and I threw the hundreds and hundreds of pages onto the fire in larger and larger piles, the roar of the fire merged with my own voice, and I roared with it, *Out! Get out of me!* And as the fire ignited the debris in the chimney and the whole chimney caught fire and I saw the sparks falling onto the old wooden porch outside, great huge fireballs of murdered art, I was screaming at the top of my lungs, OUT! GET OUT OF ME! I DON'T NEED YOU! My body heaved and stiffened; I threw myself against the chair and my back arched and I screamed, and my belly rolled in great tidal heaves as I pushed her down from my throat where she lived, the voice of the Nazi artist inside me, down through my breasts, I felt her moving as the fire and I roared together and the fireballs exploded into the night sky, I pushed Manda down into my pelvis which had been crushed when I dove into the trees between grace and murder, beauty and war, dancing and bombs.

She took hold of me in the ossified hammock of my pelvis where the loss of the soul of my brother and me to our time in history grieved in me, and would not die. I felt the Panther's hand grab my hips, woman's portal to life, and all sound ceased. No dring—dring—dring. No Ace, Ace, Ace. I opened my mouth, wanting to call that song back, the song of my brother's beautitude—but the Panther wrapped her entire being around me, and locked my throat into her lethal power.

The roar of the fire alone filled me, for it was my own voice I had to push out through the damaged, brittle, white bones of the hammock of life inside me, it was my own voice I had to push down and out through that archway, sweat from the heat of the fire slick all over my body through the sheer effort of pushing out the hurt one, the Hitler in me, the rasping Nazi who had been born inside my terror of giving birth to madness, the barren sister whose wish to keep her brother all to herself had murdered his beauty. I felt the heat of the fire opening my vagina as I pushed Manda out of me, my Nazi artist, my pelvis ached with the agony of releasing the stranglehold on my womb which had been locked into their anatomy of guilt and grief all these years, exiled and cursed with sorrow as Medea. I heard a great crack, and I will never know whether it was my bones or the wood of the fire, for we are the same, the wood and I, we are both Her.

Aristotle looked up as I walked into the police station. "Can I do something for you?"

"I saw this woman," I said. Pause. "Running through the trees. Running hard. Out of breath. Like she was escaping something. She stopped, and she came to my door. She said she was thirsty and would I give her something to drink. So I gave her a diet cola and she said something about how she always imagined she was an aborigine when she drank diet colas and that a white man had given it to her because he wanted to kill her and she'd killed someone and it was important always to think aboriginal—"

"Stop. Could you go back. . . ."

"She said that whenever she drank diet cola—"

"Not that part. The other part."

"She had killed someone."

"Can you describe her?"

"Black hair, about this length," I said, hitting the middle of my neck. "Thick, very thick, shining. She was wearing a new black leather jacket."

"How do you know it was new?"

"It squeaked when she moved."

"Yeah, go on."

"Black jeans, big boots. Lots of silver on the jacket. Studs. She looked like a Panther."

"What were her words exactly?"

"She's dead," I said, seeing Rulla inside my eyes as I had known her at the Y, her beautiful rose flesh threaded with the coppery sheen of the fossils of her torture. "She killed Her," I said through my tears.

"Killed . . . who?"

I cleared my throat, wiped my eyes. "The Dancer," I finally said out loud, "is dead."

Aristotle said, "Is there somebody I can call for you?"

"My best friend," I said.

"Shall I call her for you?"

I nodded. "Yes," I said, my voice cracking. "Would you?" I gave him the number. "Tell her that her short-armed sister is here with her stuff from Betty's basket and she doesn't want to drop what's in it as she goes through the door."

"Hello? Yes. This is the chief of police. There's a woman here at the station with me. A friend of yours. She said to tell you she's a short-armed sister . . . that's what she said, yeah. . . ." He hung up. "She's on her way."

I nodded.

"Ummm, so . . . this woman," Aristotle said. "What happened, exactly, between the time she arrived and when she left?"

A year of swimming in trees. A dance with the Panther.

"Did she hurt you in any way?"

Every way I could hurt, she hurt me.

"She's out there now?"

Free. They both are. Free to continue the dance of life with death for eternity, without me interrupting anymore.

"I'm going to call my deputy, Daryl. Put out a bulletin. He's on his way home."

"Wait. It's not going to make Daryl late, is it? He's going to get home on time?"

Just then my friend appeared at the door. "Meem?"

"I wasn't sure you would come," I said.

"But you're my short-armed sister," she said.

In a world where we all mean what we move inside the dance of life and bring each other mutual aid, the arms you grow to save yourself are not your own.

It was time for the child to be born.

That's what Betty had said. Guardian to the gateway to Rulla's paradise, gatekeeper and sentinel of the senior women's locker room, sanctuary of women, she had told me it was time. Betty, who had probably never heard of Baubo in her life, and if you said the word "goddess" would think Marilyn Monroe, and for "myth" would think somebody exaggerating the truth who should get in trouble for it too; Betty, literalist, pragmatist, ineluctably down to earth, homegrown philosopher about the nature of charity. Soft around the edges, Betty had said. Especially the eyes.

I opened my car door. "Follow me," I said to my friend.

"What? Meem? Where . . . ?"

"We're going to Rulla."

"Meem! It's almost midnight. The Y's closed."

"She's not at the Y."

We drove in separate cars. She followed close behind, dangerously close, afraid she would lose me unless we were almost touching. We glided down the hill out of Rhinebeck, heading south toward the abandoned stone house. I pulled over to the side onto the gravel plain, my friend right behind me. She was out of her car before me, standing in the freakish chill summer night, her eyes huge and afraid.

"Do you have a flashlight?"

My friend ran back to her car and rummaged through Benjamin's collection of treasured junk. She came back, holding out a key chain with a small flashlight attached to it. She said, "Benjamin found this on the sidewalk. It's all I've got." She pressed a switch, and a faint light came on.

We made our way through the brambles and loose dirt. I warned her too late about the thorns; she yelped. She missed a vine and began sliding. I held out my hand, and she grabbed it. We said nothing as we struggled, the significance of these small acts not lost on us; but we did not refer to them out loud. The crescent moon shed little light.

All this time my friend had obeyed me as if surrendering to the imperatives of rescuing our friendship as I was creating them. But as we reached the outside of the house, almost at the threshold, she grabbed me and held me back. "I have to touch you," she said. "I have to hold on to you if I'm going in there." We heard a noise. We jumped; my friend threw her body against mine. She grabbed my hand, which held the tiny key-chain flashlight and waved the light in all directions at the overgrowth around us. The stone house loomed like a huge rough wart, hideous in the shadows cast by the beam. The flashlight blinked, and the stone house seemed to shudder. Then the flashlight died, and we were standing in the dark, only the craggy shadow of the house visible. Wings flapped. We watched as the black holes of the glassless windows seemed to bend against their own dark, folding inward.

Within, a faint light began to glow. It glowed a coppery rose color, the color of Rulla's skin. We squeezed each other's hands at the sight. We were like two little girls trespassing on forbidden territory as we stood staring at the light filling up the tomb, the light of the Dring turned stone to protect itself from the Eaners, swelling inside. And with its increase of issue came the sweet hum of a woman's voice. "That's what Rulla sings all the time," my friend said. She looked at me. "Meem? What is this place?"

"I think," I said, "this is Eleusis."

Many years earlier, the man who had first made love to me had shown me Leonardo da Vinci's study for Saint Anne at the birth of the Christ child, attending to Mary. As I stepped into the stone house, the light around our Sisters we found within was rose and coppery like

Leonardo's ancient crayon cartoon. It could have been this study, which Leonardo had left incomplete. I had wept at Leonardo's drawing when I was a young woman; I never did know why. And now I laughed at the same vision, this time inside life. I couldn't help it. Rulla was jiggling her hips, shimmying her shoulders, trying to get Lexy to laugh the child out of Her. Lexy was in the final stages of labor, Her red hair moist with Her sweat at Her brow, as Rulla winked at her and shook her enormous, pendulous bells of breasts. I looked at Lexy. She held up her hand to me as She breathed: One finger went down. Another breath, the next finger went down. Another, another, and then the thumb, which makes our hands human ones, crossed in a diagonal across the lines of the four fingers, and I knew how to count breaths: not line by line, but hand by hand.

Lexy gripped the edges of the mattress, a sudden pain on Her. I rushed to Her side. "I'll count for you," I said. "Just keep breathing." One finger, one breath, one finger, one breath . . . cross the thumb, begin again. Hand by hand, in concert, Lexy and I breathed new life out of the small surround of woman into the great surround of life, while my friend joined Rulla in her dance, both of them being natural clowns. When my friend tried to teach Rulla a tap routine to the tune of "Singin' in the Rain" and Rulla, naked, breasts swinging, turned into Gene Kelly, Lexy burst out laughing and the child popped out.

"A boy!" Rulla shouted. "A boy has come to us!" She held him up and kissed his penis and said, "Make beautiful babies, my beautiful baby!"

As Rulla and my friend caught the boy in their arms my heart leapt up and crashed, breaking into a thousand pieces. Together they wrapped the infant in one of Betty's charitable towels and handed him to Lexy. Lexy's gaze was fixed upon the boy as She rocked back and forth in time to Rulla humming the tune of that one moment of pure exuberance in American art when a man sings and dances in the rain for no reason but the joy of dancing.

"Meem," my friend said, standing near us. "You have to look at the baby. You have to see his face."

I have never known, nor ever will know, joy and awe as I knew them when I first looked down at his newborn face. I burst out laughing. My

328

friend laughed with me. "You see? Why you had to see him? Those funny eyes so close together and all wrinkly—you see?"

He looked just like a rhinoceros. "I think he's beautiful."

"That's what all mothers feel," she said.

I looked down at his wrinkly rhino face, falling in love. Then I raised my heart and my eyes from his face to his mother's. Lexy sat quietly, Her face radiant, as She held him. Then She looked up at me. I returned the look and entered into Her green eyes. I let myself be suspended inside Her gaze, the mystery of life holding me inside its green glimmering as She offered the boy to me to hold. I took him in my arms, this life born inside a murder mystery, and rocked the beautiful rhinoceros boy to the rhythm of my friend's gentle music as she played at her grandmother's levitating piano, which had, as you know, a remarkable history of being found, perfectly intact, inside a bombed-out home after the Holocaust, no one ever knowing how it had survived.

The fire finally died down. I stirred the ashes to see if there was any glow left. Nothing. I put the grate over the fireplace and looked at the ashes of my writing. A strange feeling of peace filled me. I would take those ashes and put them in the compost bin tomorrow morning.

As I turned around to take myself to bed, I caught sight of a page on the floor. It was slightly singed, some of the words burnt away. I picked it up.

This is exactly how the fragment reads:

beautiful, Manda said, rocking the boy in her arms, dancing with

Listen, Child of Air That Kicks. Listen. Once upon a time there was a woman. Wooo-maaan. Beautiful word, woo-man. Sweet. Sounds like the swoosh and lap of the placental juice that you still remember when you were inside her, don't you, that's right, of course you do. You began inside woman, a woman, awoman most beautiful awoman— world, awomanworld was your mother. Mother, has a muffled sound, muuu-tthhh-r, flesh baffle, skin over her stomach stretched tight like a buffalo drum, how we sounded, us out here on this side . . . muuuther, won't be soft like that again, ever, now that you're out. So you're going to have to remember," she says as she rocks the boy in her arms in a room with concrete walls all around her, somewhere in the Four Corners area of the Southwest, crooning and rocking a lullaby with the power to dislodge the moon, now, while there is still time before the authorities find her and put her away, she sings to the boy, Remember woman. Remember mother. Beautiful beautiful awomanworldmother remember Her